ReFocus: The Films of Yim Soon-rye

ReFocus: The International Directors Series

Series Editors: Robert Singer, Gary D. Rhodes and Stefanie Van de Peer

Board of advisors:
Lizelle Bisschoff (Glasgow University)
Stephanie Hemelryck Donald (University of Lincoln)
Anna Misiak (Falmouth University)
Des O'Rawe (Queen's University Belfast)

ReFocus is a series of contemporary methodological and theoretical approaches to the interdisciplinary analyses and interpretations of international film directors, from the celebrated to the ignored, in direct relationship to their respective culture – its myths, values and historical precepts – and the broader parameters of international film history and theory.

Titles in the series include:

ReFocus: The Films of Susanne Bier Edited by Missy Molloy, Mimi Nielsen and Meryl Shriver-Rice

ReFocus: The Films of Francis Veber Keith Corson

ReFocus: The Films of Jia Zhangke Maureen Turim

ReFocus: The Films of Xavier Dolan Edited by Andrée Lafontaine

ReFocus: The Films of Pedro Costa: Producing and Consuming Contemporary Art Cinema Nuno Barradas Jorge

ReFocus: The Films of Sohrab Shahid Saless: Exile, Displacement and the Stateless Moving Image Edited by Azadeh Fatehrad

ReFocus: The Films of Pablo Larraín Edited by Laura Hatry

ReFocus: The Films of Michel Gondry Edited by Marcelline Block and Jennifer Kirby

ReFocus: The Films of Rachid Bouchareb Edited by Michael Gott and Leslie Kealhofer-Kemp

ReFocus: The Films of Andrei Tarkovsky Edited by Sergey Toymentsev

ReFocus: The Films of Paul Leni Edited by Erica Tortolani and Martin F. Norden

ReFocus: The Films of Rakhshan Banietemad Edited by Maryam Ghorbankarimi

ReFocus: The Films of Jocelyn Saab: Films, Artworks and Cultural Events for the Arab World Edited by Mathilde Rouxel and Stefanie Van de Peer

ReFocus: The Films of François Ozon Edited by Loïc Bourdeau

ReFocus: The Films of Teuvo Tulio Henry Bacon, Kimmo Laine and Jaakko Seppälä

ReFocus: The Films of João Pedro Rodrigues and João Rui Guerra da Mata Edited by José Duarte and Filipa Rosário

ReFocus: The Films of Lucrecia Martel Edited by Natalia Christofoletti Barrenha, Julia Kratje and Paul Merchant

ReFocus: The Films of Shyam Benegal Edited by Sneha Kar Chaudhuri and Ramit Samaddar

ReFocus: The Films of Denis Villeneuve Edited by Jeri English and Marie Pascal

ReFocus: The Films of Antoinetta Angelidi Edited by Penny Bouska and Sotiris Petridis

ReFocus: The Films of Ken Russell Edited by Matthew Melia

ReFocus: The Films of Kim Ki-young Edited by Chung-kang Kim

ReFocus: The Films of Jane Campion Edited by Alexia L. Bowler and Adele Jones

ReFocus: The Films of Alejandro Jodorowsky Edited by Michael Newell Witte

ReFocus: The Films of Nuri Bilge Ceylan Edited by Gönül Dönmez-Colin

ReFocus: The Films of Claire Denis Edited by Peter Sloane

ReFocus: The Films of Yim Soon-rye Edited by Molly Kim

edinburghuniversitypress.com/series/refocint

ReFocus:
The Films of Yim Soon-rye

Molly Kim

University Press

Edinburgh University Press is one of the leading university presses in the UK. We publish academic books and journals in our selected subject areas across the humanities and social sciences, combining cutting-edge scholarship with high editorial and production values to produce academic works of lasting importance. For more information visit our website: edinburghuniversitypress.com

© editorial matter and organization Molly Kim, 2023, 2025
© the chapters their several authors 2023, 2025

Grateful acknowledgment is made to the sources listed in the List of Illustrations for permission to reproduce material previously published elsewhere. Every effort has been made to trace the copyright holders, but if any have been inadvertently overlooked, the publisher will be pleased to make the necessary arrangements at the first opportunity.

Edinburgh University Press Ltd
13 Infirmary Street
Edinburgh EH1 1LT

First published in hardback by Edinburgh University Press 2023

Typeset in 11/13 Ehrhardt MT by
IDSUK (DataConnection) Ltd

A CIP record for this book is available from the British Library

ISBN 978 1 3995 1306 7 (hardback)
ISBN 978 1 3995 1307 4 (paperback)
ISBN 978 1 3995 1308 1 (webready PDF)
ISBN 978 1 3995 1309 8 (epub)

The right of Molly Kim to be identified as the editor of this work has been asserted in accordance with the Copyright, Designs and Patents Act 1988, and the Copyright and Related Rights Regulations 2003 (SI No. 2498).

Contents

List of Figures vii
Notes on Contributors viii
Acknowledgments xi

    Introduction: The Korean New Wave and The Single Woman 1
    Molly Kim

1 "Ugly Men Shall Prevail": Representations of Masculinity in the Films of Yim Soon-rye 12
  Hwang Kyun-min
2 Politics of Slow: Yim Soon-rye's *Promenade in the Rain* (1994) and *Waikiki Brothers* (2001) 30
  Kim Chung-kang
3 The Cinematic *Naturecultural Turn* in South Korea: Ecofeminist Pastoralism in the works of Yim Soon-rye 46
  Lee Yun-jong
4 The Woman with a Movie Camera: Dismantling the Male Gaze in Yim Soon-rye's *The Whistleblower* and *The Weight of Her* 64
  Margaret Rhee
5 Dropping-Out and Truth-Telling (Both Acts Rather Unpopular): Sovereignty, Biopolitics and Critique of the Nation-State in Yim Soon-rye's *South Bound* (2013) and *The Whistleblower* (2014) 81
  Kim Kyu-hyun
6 Sensory Connections Between Food and Femininity in Yim Soon-rye's *Little Forest* and Lee Seo-gun's *The Recipe* 96
  Bonnie Tilland

7 "I Want to Live a Life that I Choose": Romanticized Queer Family
   and Nature in *Little Forest* (2018)   113
   Kwon Jungmin
8 Korean Cinema and Me: An Interview with Yim Soon-rye   130
   Molly Kim

Index   143

List of Figures

1.1	*Three Friends*: watching a cheap adult film after the graduation ceremony	17
1.2	*Waikiki Brothers*: Sung-woo on the stage with his first love	23
1.3	*Rolling Home with a Bull*: Hyun-su and the cow coming home together	24
4.1	Sun-kyung gazing at examples of eyelid surgery on a digital monitor in *The Weight of Her*	69
4.2	*The Whistleblower*: Yi-seul pictured in the background holding a camera	73
5.1	*The Whistleblower*: the characters find Molly the Dog	90
5.2	*South Bound*: the aftermath	93
6.1	Hye-won hangs persimmons outside her countryside home to dry (*Little Forest*)	97
6.2	Hye-jin hangs *meju* (fermented soybean cakes) on the rafters of her countryside house to dry (*The Recipe*)	97
6.3	Hye-jin (*The Recipe*) waits for the *doenjang* to ferment while she waits for her lover to return	107

Notes on Contributors

Hwang Kyun-min is a film scholar specializing in post-war Japanese films. She received her Ph.D. from the Department of Art Studies at Meiji Gakuin University. Her research area lies in history, gender and genre of Japanese cinema. She has taught Japanese film history and avant-garde/experimental film at Meiji Gakuin University and Tokyo Zokei University in Japan. Her academic publications include, "The Spatial Representation of Desire in Imamura Shohei's *Intentions of Murder*" (2017), "The Embodiment of Gaze and Female Oppression in The Pornographers" (2017) and "Locating Iwai Shunji's *Love Letter* in the Context of Korean Melodramas of the 1990s and 2000s" (2020).

Kim Chung-kang is an associate professor in the Department of Theater and Film at Hanyang University, Seoul, Korea. Her research considers the realms of Korean and East Asian cinema, cultural studies, gender, race, and sexuality studies, and (trans)national visual culture. She is currently working on a book manuscript, *Entertaining the Nation: Politics of Popular Culture in Trans-War Korea (1937–1965)*. Her articles appear in various Korean journals including *Journal of the History of Sexuality*, *The Journal of Korean Studies* and *The Journal of Literature and Film*.

Kim Kyu-hyun is an associate professor of Japanese and Korean History at University of California, Davis. He is the author of *The Age of Visions and Arguments: Parliamentarianism and National Public Sphere in Early Meiji Japan* (2007), and is currently working on a new book on late colonial-period Korea. He has written numerous articles and book chapters on Japanese and Korean histories, Japanese and Korean popular culture and cinema (including essays on Park Chan-wook in the edited volumes *Korean Horror Cinema* (2013) and *Rediscovering Korean Cinema* (2019)), and on the comic book representations of the Pacific War and colonial experiences by Japanese and Koreans (in *Divided Lenses* (2016) and *Korean Popular Culture Reader* (2014)). He also regularly contributes film reviews and essays to <www.koreanfilm.org>.

Molly Kim is a film critic and film scholar specializing in the history of 1970s Korean cinema, film censorship, and genre. Her doctoral research focused on the representation of women and sex labor in the 1970s Korean hostess films. She is an adjunct professor of the College of Humanities at Hanyang University. Her publications include "The Idealization of Prostitutes: Aesthetics and Discourse of South Korean Hostess Films," in *Prostitution and Sex Work in Global Visual Media: New Takes on Fallen Women* (2018), "1970s Korean Cinema and Ha Gil-chong" (*International Journal of Korean History*, 2019), "Women-made Horror in South Korean Cinema," in *Women Make Horror: Feminism, Filmmaking, Genre* (2020) and "Revolutionization of the Erotic Screen: The Films of Doris Wishman and Wakamatsu Koji," in *ReFocus: The Films of Doris Wishman* (Edinburgh University Press, 2021).

Kwon Jungmin is an associate professor of Digital Cultures and Film Studies in the School of Film at Portland State University. She earned her Ph.D. from the Institute of Communications Research at the University of Illinois at Urbana-Champaign. Her research interests include digital culture, film and media, gender and sexuality studies, media industry and fan/audience studies, and Korean/East Asian popular culture. She is the author of a book entitled *Straight Korean Female Fans and Their Gay Fantasies* (2019). Her work has been published in academic journals including *Television & New Media*, *International Journal of Communication* and *Journal of Fandom*.

Lee Yun-jong is a research fellow at the Asian Center for Women's Studies, Ehwa Woman's University, Seoul, Korea. She has published the articles "Mun Ye-bong, a Partisan Maiden in a 'Partisan State'" (*Korea Journal*, 2020) and "Woman in Ethnocultural Peril: South Korean Nationalist Erotic Films of the 1980s" (*Journal of Korean Studies*, 2016) as well as a book chapter, "Between Progression and Regression: Ero Film as Cinema of Retreat" (*Revisiting Minjung*, 2019).

Margaret Rhee is a poet, scholar, and new media artist. Her debut poetry collection, *Love, Robot*, was awarded a 2018 Elgin Award by the Science Fiction Poetry Association and 2019 Best Book Award in Poetry by the Asian American Studies Association. She has taught at the University of Oregon, Harvard University, UCLA and SUNY Buffalo. She received her Ph.D. in ethnic studies and new media studies from UC Berkeley. Currently, she is an assistant professor in the School of Media Studies at the New School.

Bonnie Tilland is University Lecturer of Korean Studies, Leiden University. Her research thus far has focused on South Korean women's negotiations of care labor in the family, the senses and the affective afterlives of television dramas. She received a Ph.D. in Sociocultural Anthropology from the University of Washington, where she also completed a graduate certificate in Feminist Studies and an M.A. in Korea Studies. She has recently published in the *Journal of Korean Studies*, *Acta Koreana*, and edited *Transgression in Korea* and *Korean Families Yesterday and Today* (2020).

Acknowledgments

During the writing of this book over the last few years, numerous Korean female filmmakers have successfully debuted to great critical attention, especially within the festival and independent/art cinema circuits. Nonetheless, very few major/commercial films directed by women have been released in movie theaters. Despite the expanding scale of Korean cinema, women filmmakers in Korea are still struggling when it comes to making the transition to the mainstream film industry. This book is dedicated not just to women filmmakers in Korea, but all women filmmakers and female cinematic artists and workers across the world who nonetheless persist in creating the works that are so meaningful to many of us. I would like to thank Edinburgh University Press for giving me the valuable chance to pay tribute to one of the most important women filmmakers in Korea. I am also grateful to Luke Houston and Max Balhorn for their invaluable work in helping with the translation and editing of this book. Lastly, many thanks to those who directly contributed to the writing of this book. The intellectual brilliance and generosity they have shown throughout the process of publication has continuously motivated me to successfully finish this project. I optimistically and sincerely hope the words and ideas presented in the pages that follow might serve to further motivate many more scholars and Korean film fans around the globe toward further critical and creative action.

Introduction: The Korean New Wave and The Single Woman

Molly Kim

WOMEN FILMMAKERS OF KOREA

Korean cinema has never offered a level playing field for women filmmakers. Only five females had managed to leave their names on the credits as directors before Yim Soon-rye started to make her own films (after completing her apprenticeship under Yeo Kyun-dong) in the late 1990s.[1] While this number is confined to the commercial cinema sector, the total sum of women filmmakers in Korea is still near to non-existent, especially in comparison with the larger and annually increasing number of male counterparts. Yet despite their limited number, the history of Korean female filmmakers is not a short one. The first Korean female director was Park Nam-ok and her first feature was released in 1955, only two years after the Korean war ended. The only woman director at the time, Park's debut, *The Widow* (*Mi Mang-in*), tells the story of a war widow in post-war Korea. It addresses sensitive but critical women's issues such as sexual desire and remarriage. Perhaps this cinematic depiction of a woman was too intimidating or progressive for the era, as the film did so poorly at the box office it was taken down from theaters just three days after its release. No investors and producers approached her to support a second feature, and unfortunately, *The Widow* became Park's first and last film.

Hong Eun-won came on the scene slightly after Park produced her major work in the 1960s. Hong started out as a scriptwriter for Choi In-gyu in 1948, and after fourteen years in the industry, she finally made her first feature debut. This film, *A Woman Judge* (*Yeo Pansa*, 1962), is widely considered to be her best work, and it received substantial attention as it was inspired by real-life events; namely the unsolved mystery of the death of the first female judge in Korea, Hwang Yoon-seok. The film traces the story of a parallel fictional female judge, Jin-sook, and her struggle between work and family. In this film, Hong portrays Jin-sook as a "superwoman" who holds a high-status job and somehow still manages to fulfill her traditional familial responsibilities. As Joo Jin-sook points out, Hong's films conceptualized the potential of a new woman in the new post-war generation, but with clear limitations.[2]

The 1960s witnessed two working female directors during the same period for the first time in the history of Korean cinema. Choi Eun-hee, one of the leading actresses of the 1960s, directed three feature films, including *The Girl Raised as a Future Daughter-in-law* (*Min Myuneuri*, 1965) and *One-Sided Love of Princess* (*Gongjunimui Jjaksarang*, 1967) at SHIN film, run by the director Shin Sang-ok, her husband.[3] Her debut feature, *Min Myuneuri*, as with the prior examples of Park and Hong, highlights the lives and suffering of women. In this case, the film was inspired by the tradition of "min myuneuri," the child marriage system during the pre-modern Joseon dynasty period, through which young girls were bought and taken by the groom's family. The heroine in this film doesn't problematize the social norms (such as in *The Widow*) and doesn't represent the unconventional social position (as with *A Woman Judge*) but is rather depicted as submissive and compliant in relation to what life has given her. Nevertheless, the film is one of the rare cinematic productions that dares to account for the cruelty of the pre-modern marriage system from a woman's point of view.

Despite their short careers as filmmakers, Park, Hong, and Choi's films enunciate the ideals and struggles of women through female-driven narratives mixed with powerful storylines and informed by their own reality as film directors. In subsequent decades, Hwang Hye-mi (*First Experience, Cheot gyungheom*, 1970) in the 1970s and Lee Mi-rye (*My Daughter Rescued from the Swamp, Sooreong aeseo gunjin nae ddal*, 1984) in the 1980s assumed the mantle of this first wave of female filmmakers in Korea, but they continued to lead a lonely march as virtual "sole woman directors." Their films were often primarily marketed as novelties, or "rare films made by female directors," a label which served only to emphasize the scarcity of women directors within the industry.[4] Moving into the 1990s, the industry finally witnessed the emergence of more female directors, starting with Yim Soon-rye and Byun Young-joo, who was working in documentary film. They were soon followed by several others from a more diversified range of genres, including: Lee Seo-gun (sci-fi/*Rub Love, Leobuleobu*, 1997); Lee Jeong-hyang (melodrama/*Art Museum by the Zoo, Misulgwan-yeob dongmul-won*, 1998); and Park Chan-ok (romance/*Jealousy is My Middle Name, Jiltuneun naui him*, 2002).

THE EMERGENCE OF THE KOREAN NEW WAVE OR NEW KOREAN CINEMA

This period coincides with the peak of the Korean New Wave or, as others have put it, the "New Korean Cinema." As Kim So-yeon has claimed, the Korean New Wave is a "messy concept,"[5] not least as it is hard to define exactly how and when it started. Certainly, it did not begin as a movement, but was more of a tendency, provoked by the political and social changes that emerged at the end of three decades of military dictatorship (1960–1988).[6] With the termination of this prolonged political tyranny and its attendant censorship of culture and film, many of the films produced around the 1990s contained a substantive focus on social and political commentary, a characteristic which scholars considered as broadly representative of the "new wave" of Korean cinema. Films commonly included in this category include: *A Petal* (*Kkot-nip*, Jang Sun-woo, 1996); *A Single Spark* (*Areumdaun Cheong Nyun Jeon-teil*, Park Kwang-soo, 1995); and *Rosy Life* (*Jangmibit Inseng*, Kim Hong-joon, 1994), all of which accentuated the pain and suffering of people during the dark days of authoritarian rule. The emergence and success of this group of films instigated another phase of new wave productions, characterized by even more severe social critique, and a more extreme mode of visual representation. The new directorial talents behind these works and the films themselves attracted global attention "both from mainstream audiences in Asia, and from festival attendees and film enthusiasts further afield."[7] One such critic, Darcy Paquet, has noted that this so-called New Korean Cinema, that evolved from the Korean New Wave, is founded upon "an appreciation for the demons South Korean society has wrestled [with over] the last three decades, and how much has changed in that time." This foundation is exemplified by films including Yim's *Three Friends* (*Sae Chingoo*, 1996); Lee Chang-dong's *Peppermint Candy* (*Bakasatang*, 1999); Park Chan-wook's *Joint Security Area* (*Gongdonggyeongbi-guyeok* JSA, 2000); and Bong Joon-ho's *Memories of Murder* (*Sarinui chueok*, 2003), in which the protagonists tend to be seen as the victims of political trauma or social problems.

As noted, Yim Soon-rye entered into the industry at this tumultuous time, as South Korean cinema was inundated by the shifts occurring both in and outside of the film industry. After completing her studies in France, Yim came back to Korea and started her film career as an assistant director on Yeo Kyun-dong's black comedy, *Out to the World* (*Sesang Bakeuro*, 1994). It is significant that Yim's very first industry work was with Yeo, because Yeo was a prominent auteur/activist who created numerous socially conscious films defined by satire and critique, productions which helped to form the basis for the Korean New Wave. Yim's first short film, *Promenade in the Rain* (*Woojoong Sanchek*,

1994), was very much created under the influence of contemporary political and industrial changes, and her active involvement with Yeo's productions. Yim's short film portrayed one special day in the life of a ticket salesgirl at a run-down movie theater, and it received enormous critical acclaim, enough to elevate her as one of the emergent directors of the 1990s. *Promenade in the Rain* received the Grand Prix at the 1st Seoul Short Film Awards (1994), and with this recognition Yim was able to secure enough funds for her first feature, *Three Friends*.[8]

Three Friends centers on three young misfits who didn't get admitted to college and are desperately searching for the chance to do something meaningful with their lives. Tae-moo is a comic-book writer, but with no prospects. Se-in, a victim of domestic violence, is gay and wants to be a hairdresser. The overweight Seung-ho lives only to eat and watch movies. He goes to interviews for part-time positions, but no one wants him because of his "heavy" figure. Unlike most coming-of-age films which tend to be cheery and hopeful, *Three Friends* is characterized by its grimness and dark humor. The characters' lives don't improve in any way and/or they don't achieve anything that they had wished for. When mandatory military duty beckons, Tae-moo and Seung-ho will seemingly do anything to avoid it, such as eating all day to ensure they are above the healthy weight limit or injuring themselves to be exempted. Only Se-in wants to go into the military to "cure" his unmanliness. *Three Friends* is a realist drama that focuses on how these men with not enough education ('go jol'[9]), from a low-status familial background, and of questionable masculinity, are situated and treated in Korean society. Nevertheless, the film is sympathetic to the characters, as the ending sequence shows them happily reunited when Tae-moo is discharged from his military service. Yim has jokingly mentioned that this film was made to "celebrate all lazy people in Korea," because the Korean people are too hard-working and Korean society is not generous with its "failures." *Three Friends* garnered critical acclaim, winning the NETPAC Award (1996) at the 6th Busan International Film Festival. Additionally, given the film's presentation of socially conscious issues surrounding school violence and military abuse, as well as its novel approach to visual representation, Yim was quickly identified as a prominent member of the newly emergent Korean New Wave.

Perhaps most importantly, Yim was the only woman in the Korean New Wave. Because of her "singular" status, her achievements were inevitably labeled as multiple "firsts." She was the first woman to be awarded with the highest prize from any film awards ever held in Korea.[10] She was also the first female director to secure an entire production budget from a major studio. Of course, these labels didn't come easily. In addition to exceptional technical and professional skills, women filmmakers were required to possess some kind of unique "flair" in order to fit into the Chungmuro (a Korean equivalent of Hollywood) system, as Yim Soon-rye reveals:

> I started working in Chungmuro from 1993. Old Chungmuro was in transition to New Chungmuro. The whole system was changing. Lee Mi-rye, another woman filmmaker who worked right before me told me that her male staff tossed dirty jokes at her and forced her to drink [alcohol], so she talked "dirtier" and drank more to overpower them. I went through the same thing. While shooting *Waikiki Brothers*, we all went drinking after shooting. I knew it was a test. I didn't hold back on drinking for a full week, and no one looked down on me [afterwards]. We, women filmmakers used to say to each other, we must "castrate" our femininity to survive here. Lee Jeong-hyang (the director of *Art Museum by the Zoo*) once told me she had to cut her hair short and played "tough" to survive. The moment your feminine side leaks, you lose. All this "look" thing disappeared gradually when we had [a greater] female force in the film industry after 2000s.[11]

Apart from these "firsts" that Yim garnered as a woman director, her most singular and notable element was her films. Yim's films are easily distinguishable from those of her male contemporaries in the Korean New Wave, as well as those produced by earlier female directors. Many of Yim's films, especially the ones produced in the 1990s and the 2000s, deal with the theme of failure from a male perspective, a thematic interest which I label "the rhapsody of failure." As with the three young men in *Three Friends* I discussed earlier, Seong-woo, the bandleader protagonist from Yim's second feature film *Waikiki Brothers* (2001) is also an unfortunate character. Seong-woo strives to stay afloat and not to dismiss his band, the "Waikiki Brothers," but he can't find gigs anymore, as the country's IMF crisis sends him on a constant downhill trajectory. This tragic situation does not just affect Seong-woo, as all his Waikiki brothers and his mentor are caught up in the same recession. None of them have their own place to stay or something better to do. Similarly, Seon-ho, the struggling poet in *Rolling Home with a Bull* (*So-wa-ham-kke-yeo-haeng-ha-neun-beop*, 2010), has never even published a single poem, and now finds himself living with his parents. Because he never accomplished anything, he remains single (the same as all the Waikiki band members). This is one of the recurring character set-ups throughout Yim's films. The man suffering low achievement or no achievement at all remains single; the marital status of male characters symbolizes their (social) functionality.

Basically, in these films, all the male protagonists are portrayed as unsuitable to be either a member of society or a patriarch, a role still considered pivotal in Korean society. However, Yim doesn't derogate or degrade these characters for their failures, or for "not making it." Rather, these characters help pinpoint the idea that it is the society that makes them fail. From the three friends who have suffered deeply-rooted violence from school to military service, through Seong-woo's struggles with the financial crisis relative to the IMF, and on to Seon-ho's battle with hierarchical corporate culture, Yim's films are determined to expose the injustice of the social system, especially that specific to patriarchal Korean culture. In this sense, Yim's thematic focus differs from that of her female antecedents who focused explicitly on feminine issues from a female perspective. This doesn't make her films distant from such issues or perspectives; in fact, Yim's films are the only feminist films within the arena of the Korean New Wave. This is particularly demonstrated by the fact that her works disavow one of the most defining elements of Korean New Wave film—violence against women.

(Sexual) violence is the most salient tendency of the Korean New Wave cinema. As Kim Kyung-hyun explains, the (New Wave) films frequently deployed such violence both to literalize and metaphorize historical trauma and post-traumatic recoveries from historical catastrophes such as the Kwangju Massacre (*A Petal, Kkotnip*, 1996), the military dictatorship (*Declaration of Fools, Baboseon-eon*, 1983), and the IMF crisis (*Happy End, Haepi-end*, 1998). Within these films, the female characters tend to become the victims of male violence provoked by their trauma. In this regard, the Korean New Wave typically employed rape or any extension of sexual violence as a metaphor for political and social suppression. For example, Jang Sun-woo's *A Petal* (1996), one of the most representative Korean New Wave films, centers around a socially marginalized male construction worker Mr. Chang and the little girl whom he encounters one day. In portraying the historical trauma of the Kwangju Massacre, Jang foregrounds the outrageous sexual relationship that develops between this man and the girl who is actually herself a victim of the Massacre. In short, the man takes her home and continuously rapes her throughout the film, and the sexual violence he exercises on the girl is portrayed as a somewhat nuanced lesser form of trauma than what she went through in Kwangju. Here the rape becomes a perverse mnemonic to remind the girl of the Kwangju Massacre (as at other times she can't recall the incident).

Apart from the explicitness of visual representation used for the rape scenes, the film utilizes rape as an inevitable, necessary device for the girl to regain her memories of tragedy. However, while Jang portrays historical trauma or violence by focusing on and exaggerating "his historical subject's sadistic impulses: cruelty, brutality and anxiety" taken out on females,[12] Yim explicates the issue of violence by contemplating the subject's own, lived experience of violence in Korean society. Violence is neither transferred to other human beings nor justified as a cinematic device. For instance, in *Three Friends*, Se-in has been abused by his alcoholic father for many years and

Tae-moo was beaten by his high-school teacher because he didn't pay attention to class. Later in the film, Se-in gets beaten and supposedly raped (it is not shown in the film but implied from his hospitalization) by his male neighbors because he is gay. Tae-moo goes into military service but soon gets discharged because of an injury he receives from a beating at the hands of his superiors. In this respect, the film portrays social violence through a personal trajectory that showcases the level of violence that needs to be tolerated in order to survive as a man in Korean society; *Three Friends* doesn't spectacularize violence and the action of violence doesn't feed back onto other people in the plot.

Yim's emergence during the 1990s was, therefore, significant not just because she marked herself out as the solitary female filmmaker in the male-dominated field of New Wave cinema, but because her films contradicted the exploitative, misogynistic tradition of the Korean New Wave and the larger context of Korean cinema, arguably for the first time. In this sense, both Yim's status as a director, and her films themselves signify an important turning point in the history of Korean cinema. And, while it is laudable that she consistently produces films that stand strong in the film industry, it is perhaps lamentable that most of her "first" labels have not yet been rendered obsolete by the parallel achievement of other female directors. Just last year one additional "first" got attached to Yim, as she was the first female filmmaker to direct a blockbuster project, *The Point Men* (*Gyoseop*, 2023), budgeted at over 15 billion won (equivalent to over 13 million US dollars). Up until this point, no female filmmaker in Korea had ever been awarded any big-budget, blockbuster film commission because undertaking such a film was considered to be "men's work." As another Korean woman filmmaker, Lee Su-yeon, has mentioned in interview, the (film) investors and producers have a strong prejudice that women filmmakers can't handle such pressure, which has resulted in a dichotomy between female directors overseeing mid- to low-budget drama productions and males directing big-budget epic films.[13]

In this regard, I would further offer that the deep-rooted industrial biases toward female filmmakers such as Yim have also affected the lack of academic research on their work, both inside and outside of Korea. For instance, *The Korean Film Directors*, one of the most significant book series, targeted at global audiences and created and supported by the Korean Film Council, has produced a total of twenty-five volumes on the key directors of Korea: including Lee Chang-dong, Kim Ji-woon, Lee Man-hee, etc. The series has produced only one volume dedicated to a female director, Yim Soon-rye (2008). Considering this remarkable lack of academic and archival work, the current volume is significant in that it will be the very first full-length book on Yim Soo-rye, or indeed any Korean woman filmmaker. It premises to highlight her notable "first" achievements, alongside many others which have not been properly accounted for or addressed. Working within the male-dominated Korean film industry, Yim has consistently produced critically and commercially influential productions and has been recognized at numerous festivals/awards both inside and outside of Korea. And over the last twenty-five years, she has produced/directed over a dozen films including shorts—the highest number of any female director in Korea. The chapters that follow offer in-depth analyses of the cinematic works created by Yim from 1994 to the present day, including her shorts and omnibus projects. These chapters are organized in chronological order relative to their corresponding film(s) so that the book as a whole sketches out how Yim's cinematic vision has transformed and developed in accordance with the changing dynamics of Korean society and culture.

In Chapter 1, Hwang Kyun-min explores the representation of masculinity throughout Yim's work. While Yim is an active feminist director known for her extra-cinematic activities and advocacy for women in the film industry, her films do not tend to be explicitly identified with feminism or gender issues. They rather maintain a subtle, nuanced voice and focus on strategic depictions of how gender and sexuality are supposed to be perceived and portrayed. Hwang focuses on this aspect of Yim's films, to see how this subtlety otherwise functions to address gender politics, specifically by examining *Three Friends* alongside other subsequent works. She details how the dysfunctionality of male characters or their failing to fulfill the social expectations of their masculinity is not undermined but utilized to symbolize the ideals of gender equality.

Kim Chung-kang's Chapter 2 illuminates the notion of "slow cinema" relative to *Promenade in the Rain* and *Waikiki Brothers*. She argues that Yim's slow cinema constitutes a specific attempt to move away from the banality and boredom created through our increasingly digitized world. By focusing on two of Yim Soon-rye's early works, Kim highlights the cinematic slowness of her films and the ways in which Yim has created her own unique form of cinematic temporality. Kim uses the term "aesthetics of slow cinema" to refer to Yim's filmic style and the pacing of her screenplays and narrative structure. This particular "aesthetics," however, is not merely a reference to a set of stylistic characteristics. It also represents a critical approach to understanding Yim's portrayal of contemporary life. Yim once mentioned that the films identified with her own auteuristic approaches have always been failures at the box office. In this regard, her cinematic slow pace certainly could not be considered as belonging to the 1990s mainstream South Korea filmmaking, which had just begun to go toward the profit-oriented global standard, and overt technological development.

Within this context, Kim traces how Yim's films thus offer a significant attempt to provide an alternative aesthetics, one that privileges its characters' "slow" existence, in deliberate opposition to the speed-obsessed nature of Korean society.

Lee Yun-jong, in Chapter 3, describes how Yim's frequent theme of "pastoralism" as an intervention in neoliberal Korea is symbolized and visualized in films. She particularly examines Yim's depiction of human companionship with plants and nonhuman animals in relation to ideas of ecofeminism, as presented in *Rolling Home with a Bull* and *Little Forest* (*Li-teul Po-le-seu-teu*, 2018). Lee delves into how the framework of ecofeminist pastoralism has grown relative to Yim's career and how these films resonate with the parallel contemporary South Korean pursuit for "healing" in nature. Finally, she argues that Yim's vision of pastoralism is not only linked to the idea that a routine of hard work is needed to support a life of co-habitation with plants and nonhuman animals, but is also a recognition of the difficulty of productively achieving the tightrope walk between the anthropocentric binarism of nature and culture, and a Buddhist–Daoist pursuit of unity between human beings and the natural order.

In the fourth chapter, Margaret Rhee discusses how female labor is portrayed through the female gaze in *The Weight of Her* (*Geunyeoui Muge*, 2003) and *The Whistleblower* (*Je-bo-ja*, 2014). While not explicitly focused on gender-based themes, the film subtly negotiates the politics of women's labor, bodies, and the male gaze through the inclusion of the camera in the film. *The Weight of Her* tells the story of the struggles of South Korean women high-schoolers and the pressures of a patriarchal society on their body and appearance. These pressures relative to the ideals of having a "normative" body result in a devastating impact on the professional opportunities and psyches of young women which leaves male dominance intact. Labor and the body are a key theme in both of Yim's films mentioned here, and closely examined in this chapter is how Yim dismantles the "male gaze" specifically through the incorporation of the camera as a feminist metaphor and object in her films. Rhee investigates how the female body is portrayed in Yim's films and relates it to the notion of women's labor as cinematically represented in the setting of the workplace.

Chapter 5, Kim Kyu-hyun's "Dropping-Out and Truth-Telling (Both Acts Rather Unpopular)," looks at the representation of politics in Yim Soon-rye's work. Kim focuses on two films, *South Bound* (2013) and *The Whistleblower*, problematizing the way in which "politics" is reflected in the cinematic text as a concern, a problem, or a message. This chapter premises to serve as an act of critical intervention that challenges or at the very least questions the conventional understanding of the sphere of politics (the usual Korean term for politics is *jeongchi*, composed of the two Chinese characters used for "governance" or "rule") as understood in South Korean popular culture. In this realm, the sphere of the political tends to be construed as an exclusive discursive domain of the hypermasculine educated elite, media opinion-makers, "keyboard warriors" and other anonymous "angry citizens." This domain is then all too easily conflated with the national public sphere that determines in substance who gets to be included or excluded as a political agent. Against this context, Kim illustrates how Yim critiques the patriarchal imposition of the political in Korean society by presenting the protagonists who escape the power of the state apparatus.

In Chapter 6, Bonnie Tilland comparatively analyzes *Little Forest* by Yim and *The Recipe* (Doenjang, 2010) by Lee Seo-gun, another Korean female filmmaker who debuted around the same time as Yim. These two films are distinctive from one another in terms of the genre and overall style, and the fact that both were directed by female filmmakers should not by itself justify their comparison. Nonetheless, according to Tilland, the films commonly display a sensory focus on food and its connection to female identity, which is further complexified by the gender identity of the filmmakers. Tilland begins the chapter with a discussion of the thematic foci of female filmmakers in South Korea, and how the expectations placed on them have shaped their career trajectories. She then highlights the sensory focus of Yim's *Little Forest* alongside other films in her career path, before analyzing food and femininity in the greater South Korean media landscape, including within Lee Seo-gun's *The Recipe*. While Little Forest is a rich film through which to explore multiple aspects of South Korea, including the urban–rural divide as well as Yim's own activism around these issues, in this chapter Tilland primarily analyzes the relationship between the sensory experiences of preparing and eating food and women's identity in the film.

Kwon Jungmin in Chapter 7 situates *Little Forest* in conjunction with the discipline of queer studies. She particularly examines the rendering of family and space in *Little Forest*, dynamics through which Yim's feminist, queer, and ecological approaches are interwoven. Kwon discusses how Yim fleshes out a new model of kinship, which she calls a queer family, as it does not require the heterosexual man emblematic of a conventional family unit. Then she examines the diegetic space of the film in relation to the idea of a queer family to see how nature operates in the narrative to characterize the protagonists and their relationships. She offers a critical analysis of Yim's romanticizing and dichotomizing perspectives about gender, queerness, and space, and ultimately argues in support of the need for wider cinematic explorations of the diversity of queer communities that embody a fluidity beyond the traditional modernist binaries.

In the final chapter, Molly Kim offers an interview with Yim. This in-depth dialogue provides a detailed account of the production of Yim's films and her inspirations. Furthermore, Yim gives a personal historical account of women working in Korean cinema by sharing her experience as a woman filmmaker in the male-dominated Korean film industry. Simultaneously, then, in addition to offering an autobiographical chronical of Yim's work, this chapter offers a previously untold history of Korean contemporary cinema addressed from the perspective of a woman.

NOTES

1. When Yim Soon-rye debuted with *Three Friends* in 1996, only five other female filmmakers' films had been theatrically released. See Purplay's special column on Korean women filmmakers, <https://m.post.naver.com/viewer/postView.nhn?volumeNo=28246180&memberNo=37085286> (last accessed 20 October 2021).
2. Ju Jin-sook, "Hankook Gamdok Yeoseong Yeongu: Sinario Yoojeong Moojeong eul Joongshimeuro bon Yeoseongdeul" [A Study on Women Directors in Korea: The Representation of Women in the Film Script, *Affection and Apathy* by Hong Eun-won], *Youngsang Yesul Yeongu* [The Journal of Visual Arts] Vol. 7, no. 7 (2005): 80–5.
3. Choi directed a total of three films including *Bachelor Teacher*, which she made in North Korea after she was kidnapped.
4. Molly Kim, "Women Made Horror in South Korean Cinema," in *Women Make Horror Filmmaking, Feminism, Genre*, ed. Alison Peirse (New Brunswick: Rutgers University Press, 2020), 137.
5. Kim So-yeon, "Hankook Younghwasa aeseo Modeonism eui Taljoniraneun Moonje: 1990 nyeondae Korean New Wave younghwa eui dandokseong eul haemyung hajiwinhan notu" [On the Problematics of Modernism in the History of Korean Cinema: Notes on the Singularity of Korean New Wave Cinema During the 1990s], *Younghwa Yeongu* [The Study of Films] Vol. 85 (2020): 399.
6. Ibid.
7. Darcy Paquet, *New Korean Cinema: Breaking the Waves* (New York: Wallflower Press, 2012), 3.
8. Yim received the entire production funds for her first feature from the Samsung Entertainment Group (SEG), which was the main sponsor of the Seoul Short Film Awards.
9. *Go jol* is an abbreviated word for high-school graduates. It is used as a derogatory term for the people who do not have a college degree.
10. Yim was a recipient of the Best Director award for *Waikiki Brothers* at the 21st Korean Association of Film Critics' Awards, 2001.
11. Park Sun-hee, "Yim Soon-rye's interview: Younghwa Baegeup Gujo Bagguieoya Yeoseong Gamdok Neuleonanda" [Distribution system needs to change in order for an increase of women filmmakers], <http://www.womennews.co.kr/news/articleView.html?idxno=215032> (last accessed 29 October 2021).
12. Kim Kyung-hyun, *The Remasculinization of Korean Cinema* (Durham, NC: Duke University Press, 2004), 111.
13. Kang Pu-reum, "Dayangseong, Yeoseong Moksorireul ileoganeun Hankook Younghwage" [Korean Film Industry Losing Its Diversity], 26 October 2017, South <http://www.womennews.co.kr/news/articleView.html?idxno=117699> (last accessed 20 October 2021).

CHAPTER I

"Ugly Men Shall Prevail": Representations of Masculinity in the Films of Yim Soon-rye

Hwang Kyun-min

> Korean society is an extremely violent society. And when I consider where all this violence comes from, for me the answer is the Korean education system and military. In this regard, Korean society is extremely uniform, rigid, and violent, and I have thought a lot about the role of the education system and society.[1]
>
> Yim Soon-rye

INTRODUCTION

This chapter examines three films by South Korean female filmmaker Yim Soon-rye that place men at the center of their narratives: *Three Friends* (1996), *Waikiki Brothers* (2001), and *Rolling Home with a Bull* (2010). I examine the shifting representations of men as "losers" across these films to clarify how representations of masculinity are intertwined with the larger thematic concerns present across director Yim's film career. She is one of the few female directors in South Korea to have consistently produced films over several decades. Between the emergence of South Korea's first female film director, Park Nam-ok, in 1955 and the debut of Yim in 1996, there have only been five female directors in South Korea. Put differently, Yim is just the sixth female director in the South Korean film industry, which has long persisted as an apprentice system dominated by men. This system fundamentally changed in the 1990s around the time Yim began making films. Beginning with the release of *Marriage Story* (dir. Kim Ui-seok, 1992), so called "high-concept films" (*gihoek yeonghwa*) and diverse kinds of genre films targeting younger audiences began to appear. However, these changes did not open the doors of the film industry to women, nor did they alleviate restrictions on creative expression. Producers continued to exert overwhelming power over directors' artistic visions, and in this environment, prevented the rise in numbers of female directors, which was already far below that of men.

Considering these circumstances, it is miraculous that in 1994 director Yim not only worked on the 1994 commercial film *Out to the World* (dir. Yeo Kyun-dong) as a scripter, but also made her debut in Chungmuro, the Korean equivalent of Hollywood, with her own short film about the melancholy lives of youths. In *Three Friends*, Yim's first feature-length film, she used non-professional actors to tell the stories of three alienated and marginalized young men, a choice which reflects Yim's equally brazen and obstinate artistic vision.

South Korean female directors before Yim told stories about women from a female perspective—an approach that at the time was seen as both inevitable and natural. In their films, female directors of the 1950s and 1960s critiqued the social expectations placed on women and the stifling of their sexual desires and social ambitions. For example, *The Widow* (Mimang-in, Park Nam-ok, 1955) is a film about a female protagonist who, after losing her husband and the father of her child in the Korean War, falls in love with a young man. *A Woman Judge* (Yeo Pansa, Hong Eun-won, 1962) recounts a female judge's solitary struggle as both a housewife and career woman and her subsequent suicide. *The Girl Raised as a Future Daughter-in-Law* (Min Myuneuri, Choe Eun-hui, 1965) deals with the patriarchal marriage system through the representation of a woman who, due to poverty, must perform grueling housework at another man's house before she officially marries him. Hwang Hye-mi and Lee Mi-rye, the sole female directors of the 1970s and 1980s, respectively, expressed the tedium and discomfort of life under the system of monogamy through the theme of women's sexuality[2] and revealed women's exposure to various forms of sexual violence.[3] As women, they each adopted unique approaches to interrogate the repressive social structures surrounding them. These directors, who were put in the spotlight and subjected to scorn just for being women, saw it as their duty to discuss women's issues. In this context, Yim's choice to cast a woman as the protagonist in her first work, *Promenade in the Rain* (1994), appears natural.

The short film *Promenade in the Rain* tells the story of Gang Jeong-ja, an older, unmarried woman who works as a box office clerk. Commentary on the film has largely understood it as a "women's film," with one reviewer writing, "Although the film offers an objective look at the feeling of emptiness of the old, single female ticket clerk Jeong-ja, one gets a sense of the warmth with which the director views the female protagonist."[4] I mostly agree with these assessments, however, the film cannot simply be reduced to a conventional female-centered narrative. Besides Jeong-ja, most of the characters are unremarkable men who frequent the shabby theater, and similar such men reappear consistently throughout Yim's subsequent films. Yim's characters are mostly pitiable men and she does not approach these characters through a critical, gendered lens that would be expected from a female director; rather, Yim's films reveal a spirit of fellowship and empathy with these men.

After her first feature film, *Three Friends*, Yim directed four more films with male leads: *Waikiki Brothers* (2001), *Rolling Home with a Bull* (2010), *South Bound* (2013), and *The Whistleblower* (2014). Excluding *The Whistleblower*, the male protagonists of these films are alienated and incompetent failures. Failures—or "losers"—have appeared regularly in Korean films. In 1990s Korean gangster films, men are depicted as losers or social misfits who have been expelled from society. In these films, however, the lack of patriarchal masculinity is compensated by the protagonists' imposing physical stature and intimate male comradery. These tragic narratives, which often end in death, glorify the tragedy of the men's lives, which are defined by violence and crime.

In the male-centric war, action, and gangster-comedy films which predominated Korean movie theaters in the 1990s, powerless men continued to be summoned to the screen. The more defeat and misery these on-screen men experienced, the more excessive and high-powered their representations became. As men on the screen grew stronger, women "were robbed of their own narratives, and always appeared naked next to men."[5] Women served either as sacrifices for male desire or passive objects to be abused. Amid such intensifying gender inequality, Yim, as a female director, deliberately chose not to tell stories about women. Although Korean men depicted from this perspective [of Yim Soon-rye] are shabby, cowardly, and worn-down characters,[6] they are not represented as completely pathetic beings.

It is within this context that I became curious about how one should understand the films of female director Yim with her male characters. How do we explain the perspective of a female director who focuses on stories about men to deal with contemporary issues? This chapter begins from this simple question, from which I will discuss three main concerns. First, I analyze Yim's initial representations of men in *Three Friends*. Then, I examine how these representations of masculinity both persist and transform in *Waikiki Brothers* and *Rolling Home with a Bull*. Finally, I offer conclusions regarding the relevance of these representations in the context of Yim's overall understanding of contemporary South Korea and address how these representations of men relate to larger structural problems of South Korean society.

MISFORTUNE WILL SET THEM FREE: YIM SOON-RYE'S FIRST FILMIC REPRESENTATIONS OF MEN IN *THREE FRIENDS*

By winning the Grand Prize at the Seoul Short Film Awards in 1994 for *Promenade in the Rain*, Yim caught the attention of the Korean film world as an emerging filmmaker. As one reviewer stated,

> There is no doubt that she is "this year's director to pay attention to." She appeared like a comet and literally swept away all the new directors in Chungmuro as if they were the "old wave," and through this festival she has been anointed the reigning queen.[7]

At a time when female directors were scarce, Yim, who had just one feature film to her name, burst onto the scene as a filmmaker with the power to destroy the entrenched practices of the South Korean film industry. At this film festival, she netted both the Grand Prize and the Young Critics' Award and secured funding for *Three Friends* from the Samsung Entertainment Group.[8] Unlike the raucous praise that had greeted her first film, *Three Friends* met considerable obstacles before it was produced. As a new award-winning filmmaker, she was approached by multiple producers with film proposals. Yim replied to these proposals by giving them the script for *Three Friends*. However, no producer came forward to make the film: not only was the film's genre unlikely to appeal to audiences, but the story itself was depressing and populated by loser characters. Eventually, Yim contacted the Samsung Entertainment Group and convinced them to give her 430 million won, telling them that "for any event, the very first award recipient has to do well for the event to continue in the future."[9]

Three Friends features Tae-moo, who dreams of becoming a comic-book artist, Se-in, who wants to be a hairstylist, and Seung-ho, a movie buff. Having recently graduated high school, the three friends are taking their first steps in the world as adults. However, unable to attend college, their prospects are depressing. Their families—particularly their fathers—do not try to understand them, and the adults in their lives ignore them. In this environment, the three friends each struggle independently to reach their goals. The film's sequences are only loosely connected, and the story is simple; nevertheless, the problems faced by these three friends are a microcosm for the larger social structure of South Korean society.

More specifically, their struggles are inseparable from the patriarchal and authoritarian structures represented by school, family, and the military, and the failures of these three young men are depicted as inevitable outcomes of such a society.

The opening scene is of a boisterous high-school graduation ceremony. Tae-moo, Se-in, and Seung-ho stand around awkwardly, and only one of them is holding a diploma. With no families to take pictures with, the three friends roam the school grounds before sharing a simple meal at a neighborhood restaurant. Afterwards, they head out to a dark video shop and watch a banal movie. As new graduates, the only congratulations they hear come from the employee at the video shop, who lets Seung-ho, a regular, watch a "brand new film" free of charge. The three friends, who are now adults, watch the film—which is punctuated by periodic female moaning—with blank expressions.

This opening sequence contains several important implications. First, a typical graduation day in South Korea involves parents congratulating their kids, taking photos, and eating a meal at a fancy restaurant. However, not one family member comes to congratulate the three friends, intimating that they have strained relationships with their families. Second, the sequence establishes the personalities of each character and foreshadows the development of their narratives. Seung-ho is overweight, loves eating, and enjoys movies, and among the three friends, he is the most optimistic. Although he has no nickname in the film, Yim refers to him as "Fatso (Samgyeop)" in several interviews. Se-in, on the other hand, has a petite figure and a sensitive personality, which has earned him the nickname "Petal (Seomse)". In one scene, he refuses to eat after seeing a cockroach in his food. In response, Seung-ho tells him off, saying, "Huh? Is that how a man acts?" This dialogue, which repeats later in the film in a conversation with Se-in's father and Tae-moo, reinforces Se-in's introverted personality, ambiguous sexuality, and feminine disposition. Se-in is consumed with anxiety over the fact that he is an "unmanly" man, and Seung-ho's belittlement of his sensitivity clearly demonstrates the types of emotional expression that are prohibited by normative masculinity. In this sense, Se-in is the least masculine of the three friends. Later in the film, the shock that results from being subjected to physical violence by two other men leads him to be hospitalized at a mental hospital. In the end, he receives a medical exemption from compulsory military conscription. Conversely, "Independent (Musosok)" Tae-moo has a rebellious personality: he smokes cigarettes at graduation and in Chinese restaurants and talks back to older men who tell him not to smoke. Early in the opening sequence, dialogue from Seung-ho intimates that he was physically abused by teachers in high school (this is also hinted at in other sequences, including in his flashback and in the ending scene). Indeed, the hardships that Tae-moo has experienced and is still going through have shaped his personality.

In this way, the personalities of the three friends—which are revealed through their actions and dialogue—are connected to their troubled masculinities, and the final shot of the opening sequence is a frank representation of the three friends as social failures. Like most of the shots in the film, the camera in

Figure I.1 *Three Friends*: watching a cheap adult film after the graduation ceremony

the opening sequence is fixed and captures the three friends sitting down in a straight-on shot. The room is dark, and spot lighting illuminates the faces of the friends. Their faces reveal no hint of happiness or sense of liberation regarding graduation. Enveloped in darkness, the three friends appear as if caught in a swamp from which they cannot escape. This shot, which appears twice in the opening sequence, is a lucid representation of the three friends' listlessness, isolation, and bleak prospects, and the episodes that follow can be seen as an extension of the frustration and failure.

In most societies, entering university is seen as one of many prerequisites for achieving success. In particular, the prestige of one's alma mater has a significant impact on one's life possibilities in South Korea. Only by graduating from a prestigious university can one get into a good company. Even for those with a high-school degree who, with some luck, get a job, it will be a while before they are promoted, and they will always earn less than their colleagues who graduated from university. High-school graduates will always be behind their college graduate peers. In 1990s South Korea, parents who did not receive an education themselves were desperate to send their children to college and rescue them from the cycle of poverty and failure. This tendency intensified in post-1997 South Korea following the Asian financial crisis, referred to as the "IMF crisis" in South Korea. *Three Friends* was released just before the crisis struck, and it clearly reflects these social anxieties. In 1996, the year the film was released, the college enrollment rate reached 54.9 percent, reflecting the growing power of a university degree in South Korean society.[10] In this context, the melancholy scene in the cramped, dark, stuffy video room is a symbolic representation of Tae-moo, Seung-ho, and Se-in's failure to enter university and take their first steps into adulthood.

Nevertheless, their alienation and frustration can be traced back to a more fundamental cause: their relationships with their families, particularly their fathers. Within the context of South Korean films, representations of fathers have varied across historical periods. In 1960s films, household patriarchs were caricatured as financially destitute and behind the times; however, these representations were motivated "not by contempt or cynicism, but rather compassion."[11] In the 1970s and 1980s, under the military regime, sons were either tormented by their patriarchal fathers or rejected and resisted them. However, by ultimately replacing their fathers as the family patriarch, they ascended to the position of "guardians" of the patriarchal system. In addition, the financial crisis that hit Korea destroyed the prevailing model that combined industrialization with a patriarchal, Confucian social structure. In the aftermath, the collapse of South Korean masculinity was often represented on screen.[12] In *Three Friends*, the father–son relationships are inseparable from the three friends' narratives of frustration and failure. Although these male narratives forefront the loss of patriarchal authority, they do not conclude with the restoration of masculinity. Instead, *Three Friends* offers an interpretation which differs from those of other films produced around the IMF crisis.

According to Han Kyeong-hye's study of father–son relationships in South Korean society, sons who grew up the 1990s remember their fathers as "strict 'symbols of authority'" who acted "like seasoned soldiers" and were "averse to conversation with their children."[13] This period also witnessed the collapse of fathers as family breadwinners. Indeed, 1996 was a year of suffering for Korean men, particularly fathers. Numerous newspaper articles around this time described fathers as objects of pity: "The Era of the Disappearance of Strong Men," "An Era When Fathers and Breadwinners Have Become the Objects of Pity,"[14] "Fathers with Bowed Heads – Expansion of the Salaryman 'Early Retirement Syndrome'."[15] Many fathers were forced out of what they assumed were "lifetime jobs," and the time when economic power served to guarantee a father's patriarchal authority came to an end. Amid these seismic changes, fathers had no choice but to hang their heads.[16] The fathers that appear in *Three Friends* are of a similar type. These fathers, who mindlessly nag their sons or ignore them altogether, have no relationships with their sons. Seung-ho's father regards his son as pitiable; Tae-moo's father shows no interest in him whatsoever; Se-in's father presses him about not going to university and shows no interest in Se-in's passions. Se-in's father is unique, however, in that he has failed as a family patriarch and expresses his feelings of inferiority through violence—a situation that is intimately tied to Se-in's deep-seated anxieties regarding his own "unmanly" masculinity.

Se-in's father is a jobless alcoholic who served in the Vietnam War. When he drinks, he inevitably talks about how "being in Vietnam was the best time of my life." Yet, Se-in's father's drunk outbursts carry a significance beyond his own personal memories and sense of pride. Soldiers who served in Vietnam "were flag bearers for the modernization of the homeland from the perspective of the nation, bread winners from the perspective of the family, and males that had transformed into 'real men' through their war-time experiences."[17] This narrative represents both Se-in's father's proud past as well as the standard of masculinity that his father desperately demands from his son. However, Se-in's physical stature and mental state are far too weak and sensitive for him to become a "real" Korean man. In a scene in which Se-in is walking with his fellow female students from the beauty school, a group of men accost them without differentiating between Se-in and the women. In another scene, Se-in nearly gets mobbed by a group of high-schoolers. These scenes construct Se-in as non-masculine and girl-like. In the scenes where his meek physical stature is attacked by other men, his masculinity is clearly defined as "unmanly."

At the start of the sequence described above, Se-in, who had been cleaning his mother's beauty parlor, puts on a woman's wig and examines his reflection in the mirror. Two men burst into the beauty parlor demanding Se-in tell them if he has seen his cheating girlfriend. Still wearing the wig, Se-in starts crying in fear. One of the men smacks him on the head, "Is it a man or woman? This is the kind of thing I hate most in the world. What the hell are people like you after? You wanna do it with me? Do ya?" Faced with these violent words, Se-in puts up no resistance and drops to the floor. The men's sleeveless shirts reveal their muscles, demonstrating their physical superiority. In comparison, Se-in's body is weak and insignificant. In the shot that follows, Se-in is sitting in a daze on a bed at the mental hospital, and even after being discharged, he is not able to snap out of his stupor. Seeing him in this state, his father states, "A man doesn't react this way just because he caught a couple punches." Even his best friend Tae-moo condemns him, softly saying, "Yeah, if you were a man. . ." These scenes imply that Se-in's delicate constitution is rooted in his sexuality, which is exemplified through the visual contrast between his weak physical stature and the robust physical frames of the two men.

Se-in is belittled and attacked by other men for his unmanly figure and sensitivity. Out of a desire to overcome this lack of masculinity, he is desperate to enlist in the army (unlike Seung-ho and Tae-moo, who avoid going into the army). His eagerness to join the army is not rooted in a desire to "save his father's reputation." Rather, his eagerness comes from a desperate need to rescue himself from his own wimpish nature. However, Se-in's hopes are dashed by his mental health records.[18] This also results in the collapse of his father's wish for his son to leave a stable life, graduating from university and fulfilling his compulsory military service before becoming a salaryman. In South

Korean society, "becoming a soldier is equivalent to obtaining state-sanctioned masculinity."[19] Likewise, the compulsory military service system functions to manage masculinity through the sorting of which bodies are qualified for military duty.[20] In this context, Seung-ho lacks a sanctioned form of masculinity. When his father states, "a man has to go to the army to become an adult," Seung-ho replies, "No matter what anybody says, I'm not going to the military." Soon after, he starts purposefully gaining weight. His bulky frame, which is a result of his unparalleled appetite and laziness, does not meet the standards of "state-sanctioned masculinity."[21] For this reason, Seung-ho is discriminated against and ignored. Firm in his resolve, Seung-ho achieves his goal of avoiding military conscription by eating, gaining weight, and embracing his disqualified status. For Se-in, his inability to enlist causes him despair, for Seung-ho, however, it becomes his first memory of achievement. Seung-ho and Se-in are both men that are unable to attain the status of "normal" Korean men.

If these episodes with Se-in and Seung-ho reveal how the army functions to establish norms of masculinity,[22] then the episode with Tae-moo in the second half of the film reveals that this system in fundamentally based on a male-centric, authoritative hierarchy and verbal and physical violence. Tae-moo, who is as equally unenthusiastic as Seung-ho about the military, asks his friends to hit him over the shoulders with a piece of wood and drinks ink in an attempt to fail the army physical; however, his pitiful attempts are in vain. After being unwillingly dragged into military service, Tae-moo is physically abused by those above him in rank. The scene of Tae-woo being physically abused in the military is crosscut with images of him silently enduring a teacher's physical abuse in high school, which is shown via the film's only flashback. This high-school beating injured one of his ears; the second beating in the military causes him to lose his hearing completely. Now hearing-impaired, Tae-moo is "released" from the military. Despite being robbed of the ability to hear his friends call his own name, Tae-moo, who before showed no emotion, smiles for the first time in the film. The image of Tae-moo looking calm and peaceful despite having lost his hearing may appear rather odd; yet contrary to expectation, this moment of true despair ironically transforms into a moment of hope. Although his loss of hearing was caused by irrational violence, his smile is an expression of relief, as he can now ignore the calls from outsiders who wish to harm him. In this sense, it is highly symbolic how the fixed camera in the first and last shots of the film traps the characters in place before delicately ascending into the air.

Returning to the first sequence of the film, the camera first scans left over the schoolyard where the graduation ceremony is taking place before ascending upward. This camera movement represents the exit of the three friends from the formal space of the school system and their entrance into society. The fixed shot that appears later depicts their suffocating reality. Excluding one or two shots, Yim permits almost no camera movement. Consequently, the final sequence gives the impression of relieving the stiffness that has persisted throughout the film. In a scene in which Tae-moo bumps into pedestrians on his way to the center of the market, the camera movement mimics that of the first sequence, indicating that the friends have begun a new chapter of their lives. The characters now stand before a multitude of new starting points, yet none of them are likely to lead to success. Here, Yim's simple and clear camera work and directing give the viewer the impression of stepping back from the narrative, delivering the message that it is precisely because of the likelihood of failure that the characters must continue to press on and live in the present.

Ultimately, Seung-ho, Se-in, and Tae-moo are all rejected from military service. None of them conform to the "standards" demanded by South Korean society, meaning they have all failed at living up to the standards of normative masculinity. However, Tae-moo's smile demonstrates that that these men's unresolved misfortune and inability to conform to state-sanctioned masculinity cannot simply be read as the narratives of losers whose lives are defined by frustration and failure. The camera, as if matching their unsteady gaits, begins to move carefully. In this moment, Yim's camera work expresses sympathy for these three friends, who, as their nicknames express, must keep living their lives despite being lazy, sensitive, and having no place to belong, and whose lives, upon meeting a multitude of new starting points, must inevitably diverge.

LIVING WITH DESPAIR: REPEATING AND CHANGING REPRESENTATIONS OF MEN IN *WAIKIKI BROTHERS* AND *ROLLING HOME WITH A BULL*

As a result of the 1997 financial crisis, families that had lost their patriarch collapsed. However, in short time, these discarded men returned to movie screens armed with powerful bodies and a thirst for violence. Beginning with *Swiri* (dir. Kang Je-gyu, 1998), male characters in gangster, action, war, and history films such as *Friend* (dir. Kwak Kyung-taek, 2001), *Silmido* (dir. Kang Woo-suk, 2003), *Taegukgi: Brotherhood of War* (dir. Kang Je-gyu, 2004), *R-Point* (dir. Kong Su-chang, 2004), *Antarctic Journal* (dir. Yim Pil-sung, 2005), *The Chaser* (dir. Na Hong-jin, 2008), and *The Man from Nowhere* (dir. Lee Jeong-beom, 2010) either "returned to the past in search of a lost masculinity" or reconstructed a "new patriarchal order" as new fathers.[23]

After 2010, male protagonists in Korean blockbusters and hit films like *Punch* (dir. Lee Han, 2011), *Miracle in Cell No. 7* (dir. Lee Hwan-kyung, 2013), *The Attorney* (dir. Yang Woo-suk, 2013), *Ode to My Father* (dir. Yoon Je-kyun, 2014), and *Roaring Currents* (dir. Kim Han-min, 2014) were depicted as heroes from history or sub-standard family patriarchies. However, as men who have lived through the loss of male authority, they safeguarded the fraternity of men and the status of the patriarch by making noble and tragic sacrifices.[24] Around this time, Korean movie theaters were dominated by films populated by men in both major and minor rolls, including *The Unjust* (dir. Ryoo Seung-wan, 2010), *The Man from Nowhere* (dir. Lee Jeong-beom, 2010), *New World* (dir. Park Hoon-jung, 2013), *Veteran* (dir. Ryoo Seung-wan, 2015), *Inside Men* (dir. Woo Min-ho, 2015), and *Asura: The City of Madness* (dir. Kim Sung-su, 2016). Moreover, by implicating power struggles between men and their failures and victories with the rise and fall of nations, all of public space is made into something that is only for men in these films, in turn "confirming that men are at the center of society."[25] According to the Korean film critic Song A-reum, these films

> look familiar because the main characters tend to be limited to a particular class of people, such as policemen, detectives and gangsters. [. . .] Because these films are set against a backdrop where class superiority is taken to be embedded at the very center of society, the hard bodies of young men are actually debased as unsophisticated and dimwitted.[26]

In this way, while the men on screen search for a lost masculinity, Yim Soon-rye's men experience unending frustration within their chaotic daily lives and exhausting realities. Despite seeming to wander pointlessly, their lives are not completely stagnant. The ending of *Three Friends* affirms that a contemptible existence is still an existence after all; this message takes on a multilayered meaning through the identical camera work that appears in the first and last scenes of the movie. Similarly, in the first scene of *Waikiki Brothers* Yim uses this same camera movement to show Seong-woo's band performing their last concert at a hotel nightclub. This camera work appears again in the last scene showing Seong-woo performing at a new venue with his first love, In-hee. This simple and plain directing creates an unsuspecting moment where Seong-woo feels a glimmer of hope despite the deplorable situation he has been thrown into.

Sung-woo, who is now thirty, was formerly the guitarist and vocalist for a "promising" high-school band. Now Sung-woo performs with his other troublemaker bandmates at a dying nightclub, barely making ends meet. Despite having no following, he is determined to keep the band going; however, problems with alcohol, marijuana, and girls cause the band members to disappear one by one until only Seong-woo remains. His wretched state reaches its peak in a scene in which he plays the guitar naked in a private karaoke room. Captured in a bust shot, the image of Seong-woo singing and playing guitar "stripped completely naked" is followed by a shot of Seong-woo and friends stark naked charging into the ocean. This old memory, which bubbles up in this moment of shame and humiliation, plays back as grainy footage on the TV in the karaoke room, creating a clear contrast between his inaccessible, innocent past and the tragic present. This scene, which is the emotional climax of the film, is filled with a sense of despair—not only over his childhood dreams having been dashed, but also over the inevitability of failure despite him putting his all into his music and band.

It is at precisely at this moment, when the difficulties of Seong-woo's circumstances have prompted him to give up music, that he reveals a melancholic and indecipherable smile. In the ending sequence, Seong-woo is on stage with Jung-seok, the former keyboardist who has rejoined the band, and his first love, In-hee. In-hee is now a tough, middle-aged woman. Although she is singing sad trot music, Seong-woo gazes at her with an expression of happiness on his face. After several cuts, the camera slowly backs up as in the first scene of the film, revealing their shabby stage and the audience: this moment fills the frame with a strange energy and sense of relief.

Figure I.2 *Waikiki Brothers:* Sung-woo on the stage with his first love

The final scene of *Three Friends* depicts Tae-moo simply living his life, bumping into pedestrians while walking through a crowd. Similarly, in the final sequence of *Waikiki Brothers*, Yim's camera work makes the musicians appear to slowly dissolve into anonymity within the crowd, underscoring Seong-woo's hopeful acceptance of his dreary life. On the level of composition and camera work, this scene formally resembles the initial sequence, and Seong-woo and the band members find themselves facing a similarly uncompromising reality. However, after a long and bitter battle, Seong-woo's smile is a sign that he accepts himself on this little stage. This moment offers a glimpse of what can be called a "Yim Soon-rye-style fantasy."

In the above films, Yim displays an attitude that respects all lifestyles and modes of living, an approach that she explores further in her 2010 film *Rolling Home with a Bull*. The film is based on a Buddhist worldview, and its protagonist, Sun-ho, is an old bachelor who is days away from his fortieth birthday. Although he is a university graduate who once lived in the capital Seoul, he was unable to give up on his dream of becoming a poet and now helps his parents on their farm and lives a vagrant-like lifestyle. His patriarchal father constantly grumbles that he is less useful than the family cow. Feeling pity for her son, Sun-ho's mother pushes him to get a foreign wife from Vietnam. Sick of his parents nagging, Sun-ho leaves with the family cow in a fit of frustration. However, he has trouble selling the cow. Having been kept for too long on the back of his truck, the cow gets sick, halting Sun-ho's travel plans. Then he hears news that Min-gyu, a friend and the husband of his ex-girlfriend, has died. Caught between feelings of betrayal and a desire to see his ex-girlfriend, Hyun-su, Sun-ho attends the funeral. However, seeing Hyun-su brings up past trauma, and Sun-ho ends up leaving the funeral without a word. Hyun-su continues to try to get in touch with Sun-ho, but every time she shows up, Sun-ho reacts hysterically.

Sun-ho's journey never had a destination. Selling the cow was his initial excuse to leave, but his true motivation was to escape his parents' nagging and his squalid existence. In one scene, the cow runs off and Sun-ho is forced to chase after it. The cow, which is a constant pain and source of anxiety for Sun-ho, represents the problems dogging him in the present while Hyun-su, who digs up his painful past, reminds of the lingering trauma; while Sun-ho's vagabond meanderings are a clear reflection of the very state of his life itself.

Figure 1.3 *Rolling Home with a Bull:* Hyun-su and the cow coming home together

In this sense, the final frame of the film, which depicts Sun-ho's return to his parents' countryside home now working in the fields—is meaningful. This image differs both from the original artwork that provides the motif for the film, the Buddhist painting *Ten Ox Herding Paintings*, and the ending of the same-titled original novel by Kim Do-yeon. The *Ten Ox Herding Paintings* depicts a boy searching for a cow as a metaphor for human nature. The young boy, who rides the cow, eventually returns to his village alone after reaching complete enlightenment. In the novel, Hyun-su and Sun-ho, accompanied by the cow, witness a Buddhist temple engulfed in flames. Seeing this, Sun-ho says, "Let's stop fighting and go home now."[27] Contrastingly, in Yim's film, Sun-ho returns to his parents' home with Hyun-su and the cow, and a shot of them sitting together in a field implies that Sun-ho's present reality and past problems remain unchanged. The meaning of this shot is clear. Living as a farmer and working like a cow is not the lifestyle that Sun-ho wanted, and Hyun-su, who has already hurt him once, will continue to remind him of his past pain. However, Yim's narrative suggests that living with unresolved trauma and torment is a fact of life. Indeed, she intimates that coexisting with such disappointment and trauma is simply another form of living.

This Zen Buddhist ending seems to deliver a different message from the two films discussed earlier. *Three Friends* dispassionately represents the structural problems of Korean Society and the resulting fractured masculinities of men. Likewise, *Waikiki Brothers* offers a blunt and honest portrayal of pitiable men who have nothing to show for their efforts. By comparison, *Rolling Home with a Bull*, which drifts between reality and unreality, considers the situation of the thirty-year-old protagonist while exploring his internal life. Nevertheless, Yim has employed the same approach to the lives of all her male protagonists. In *Three Friends* and *Waikiki Brothers*, Yim's perspective is conveyed through the particular camera work that repeats throughout the film. *Rolling Home with a Bull* employs this same narrative structure and develops it further to connect the opening and ending sequences of the film. This circular structure is a metaphor for a social structure that has stymied the masculinity of the three friends as well as Seong-woo and Sun-ho. Moreover, the cyclical structures of these narratives, which resemble the laws of nature, reflect Yim's own perspective on life. Therefore, compared to *Three Friends* and *Waikiki Brothers*, the theme of loser men accepting and coexisting with failure and despair is further developed in *Rolling Home with a Bull*, and the film can be understood as a transitional moment in Yim's development. I will now return to the question presented at the beginning of the chapter. Why did Yim choose to tell these stories about men?

In a 1998 interview, Yim stated that during her third year of high school, when Korean students usually double down on their college entrance exam prep, she suddenly dropped out of school. "I slept when I wanted to, ate when I wanted to, read when I felt like it, and just lived an idle life for a while." During this time, her small frame ballooned up like "Fatso" in *Three Friends*. Moreover, quitting school was not a protest against the irrationality of the public school system, but rather an action rooted in "a passive, defensive personality seeking to protect one's 'slow' inner world which is starkly at odds with the speed of the outside world." She also stated that quitting school was a "defensive act related to a temperament that has a tendency to enjoy being lazy without limit or regard for any future plans." Yim was careful not to assign any particular meaning to her actions. However, she implies that one's innate nature cannot be easily changed by the judgments of others, and that it is not valid to denounce others just because their choices and actions differ from the norms of society.[28] Yim's admission of enjoying a layabout's life overlaps in a peculiar way with the lives of the protagonists in these three films. Although it may appear that the men in Yim's films align with the typical image of the loser, it may in fact be more accurate to consider these characters not as men at the margins of society, but rather as people living according to their own pace.

Yim represents a South Korean social system in which it is impossible for these stigmatized losers to succeed. However, by focusing not on oppressed women but instead on failed men, these films suggest that criticizing the current system in terms of the gender binary alone is not sufficient. In some respects, taking up the theme of the unequal treatment of women as a female director can be seen as an easy method for questioning the status quo. At the same time, there are already a multitude of films that deal with the existential problems of humans through the experiences and frustrations of men, who already hold a privileged place in society over women. In this context, the criticism that such films deal in a self-satisfied form of humanism is not unwarranted. Despite this, Yim's films hold a special meaning: Yim does not forefront her own identity as a woman; rather, she approaches the Other on an equal footing, transcends the oppositional relationship between genders, and presents an alternative perspective on masculinity.

CONCLUSION

In modernized South Korea, "the culture of militarism, which was maintained under the ideology of national division, was deeply implicated in the construction and maintenance of hegemonic masculinity." Under such circumstances, South Korean men expended considerable effort to respond to the ultimatum to "give one's all in the performance of 'surplus masculinity'." Men have always been responsible for fulfilling the key ideological task of constructing a loving family and strong nation.[29] Although gender relations in South Korea have passed through several transformative moments, gender inequality remains in place—and it is precisely under these conditions that the perception of masculinity and manliness as "innate and fundamental" has become further entrenched in South Korean society. As recent scholarship on masculinity has shown, "'the qualities of independence, action, intelligence, and sadism,' which have been defined as masculine traits," are "dynamic and change according to socio-political, psychological, and material variables."[30] However, despite these changing interpretations of masculinity, the economic crisis in South Korea has led to the growth of reactionary representations of strong men and patriarchs, indicating how deeply embedded male-centered dominant ideology is in South Korean society and film media. The rising prevalence of gratuitous violence and provocative sexual imagery in South Korean films beginning in the latter half of the 1990s is also intimately related to this reality. At the moment when the nation's future seemed deeply imperiled, representations of young men were once again summoned to the screen as manifestations of unconsciousness, popular demands emanating from the social base.

Yim's perspective on loser men within her films is deeply imbricated in the social conventions and norms of masculinity that are informed by these male-centric ideologies. By taking up the previously neglected narratives of loser men, she demonstrates that although men hold more power than women, they are similarly affected by the structural violence and oppression embedded within South Korean society. She also demonstrates that this violence and oppression penetrates deep into South Korean society, reaching schools, family, and workplaces. In *Three Friends*, Tae-moo, Se-in, and Seung-ho struggle through the violence and oppression they experience at home, school, and in the army. In *Waikiki Brothers*, musician Seong-woo chases his childhood dream and wanders on the margins of society. In *Rolling Home with a Bull*, angry and frustrated Sun-ho runs from his past and current problems. The characters in their twenties are overwhelmed by what the future may bring; the characters in their thirties give everything to achieve their life goals. Yet, all of them live outside of the approved trajectory of what is deemed a normal life. It is notable that all of these men are in some way engaged in artistic creation, be it comic-book writing, music, or poetry. However, in a society in which endless competition and material gain are valued above all else, their failures appear natural and inevitable.

Films do provide an engrossing illusion of reality. Indeed, "if films do not reveal life itself but rather a fiction that captures life," then Yim-Soon-rye's films prompt the viewer to ask themselves whether "there is any purpose to so closely scrutinizing someone's wretched and pitiful life."[31] Although her films depict the frustrations of men through a critical and socially aware lens, these men's lives do not meet depressing fates on dead-end streets. There is a risk of misinterpreting the ray of hope that shines in the film's final moment of despair as a moment of compromise and idealism. Describing the young men in *Waikiki Brothers*, one film reviewer wrote, "In our present world, where gaming the system to get by is considered an acceptable way to live, they fight back against reality by keeping their small band together and not giving up on their dreams."[32] As a female director, Yim places men with chaotic lives at the center of her films, provoking the viewer to consider the proposition that in our unforgiving society nobody's life can escape hardship. This consciousness springs from Yim's own life experiences. Yim's films are not about sympathy and empathy with social failures; rather, these films must be understood as her own self-reflection on a life lived at a slower pace than the rest of the world. Yim's films convey an acceptance and respect for how others live their lives. As such, her films are neither pure fantasy nor idealism; rather, her films present the most realistic response that can be offered by Korean film.

Chapter translated by Max Balhorn

NOTES

1. Young-mi Hwang, "Yim Soon-rye gamdok inteobyu *U jung sanchaek* buteo *Namjjogeuro twieo* kkaji" [Interview with director Yim Soon-rye: From *Promenade in the Rain* to *South Bound*], *Yeonghwa Pyeongnon* Vol. 25 (2013): 276.
2. Ji-yeon Park, "The first female director in Korea – Park Nam-ok's movie *The Widow*," *Jendeo wa Sahoe* Vol. 29 (December 2018): 68.
3. Hee-jung Sohn, Se-ho Park, "[Sureongeseo geonjin naettal] Munhwa pyeongnonga Sohn Hee-jung chucheon haneun hanguk gojeon yeonghwa, Lee Mi-Rye gamdok ui debwijak" (*My Daughter Rescued from the Swamp*) Cultural critic, Sohn Hee-jung's classic Korean film recommendations, the debut work of director Lee Mi-Rye] Korean Film Archive, 1 December 2020, video interview, 28:31, <https://youtu.be/K4ce_seelek> (last accessed 3 March 2021).
4. Sinemattekkeu, "*Woojoong sanchaek*" [*Promenade in the Rain*], *Idae hakbo*, 4 April 2005, <http://inews.ewha.ac.kr/news/articleView.html?idxno=10579> (last accessed 6 March 2021).
5. A-reum Song, "[Song A-reum ui sinema keuritikeu] Selpeu (Self) pirotro bijeun segye – 2010-nyeondae 'namseong yeonghwa' deul ui nollie daehae" [(Song A-reum's cinema talk) A world created by self-fatigue – A discussion about the logic of "male films" from the 2000s], *Le Monde diplomatique Korean Edition*, 4 December 2017, <https://www.ilemonde.com/news/articleView.html?idxno=8038&fbclid=IwAR2p3ooXeAe6IodSnQe17 plsmEQ_vO2cQiH6q7aYb-JKtQPjZYNkEqjgO9w> (last accessed 6 March 2021).
6. Myeong-jin Park, "Choeseon eul dahan jadeul eul wihan bimangnok – Yim Soon-rye ui *Uri saengae choego ui sungan*" [A record of all those who did their best – Yim Soon-rye's *Forever the Moment*], *Hwanghae Munhwa* Vol. 58 (December 2008): 372.
7. Sung-il Jung, "*Woojoong sanchaek*" [*Promenade in the Rain*], *Hankyoreh*, 18 September 1994, 15.
8. Samsung Entertainment Group (SEG) was officially launched in July 1995 with the goal of creating a "Hollywood-style entertainment business" by integrating its affiliates Samsung C&T, Samsung Electronics, Cheil Worldwide, as well as the film, video, broadcasting, and record businesses belonging to Star Max. An important achievement of SEG was the Seoul Short Film Festival, which was held four times from 1994 to 1997. As in the case of Yim Soon-rye, the film festival was a gateway for new directors with little or no experience in commercial film production or experience studying film abroad.
9. Nam-ung Hwang, "Akaibeu I sine tokeu_<*Achim gwa jeonyeok sai*>, <*Gang ui namjjok*>, <*U jung sanchaek*>" [Archive I Cine Talk: *From Morning to Evening*, *South River*, and *Promenade in the Rain*], *NOW*, 7 December 2018, <http://indienow.kr/?p=4261> (last accessed 13 March 2021).
10. Hyun-joo Kim, "'Daehak joleopjang=Iljari deunsik' ggaejyoudda" [The Equation of College Diploma and Occupation is Broken], *Segye Ilbo*, 22 July 2015, <https://www.segye.com/newsView/20150721001119> (last accessed 13 March 2021).

11. Kyung-uk Kim, *Hanguk yeonghwa neun mueot eul boneunga: 'Gukje sijang' eseo saenggin il* [What are Korean films looking at? What happened in *Ode to My Father*], (Seoul: Gang, 2016), 120.
12. Ibid., 115–17.
13. Kyeong-hye Han, "Abeojisang ui byeonhwa" [The changing image of the father], in *Namseong gwa hanguk sahoe* [Men and Korean Society], ed. Yeoseong hanguk sahoe yeonguhoe (Seoul: Sahoe munhwa yeonguso, 1997), 37.
14. Kwang-hun Lee, "Gogae sugin namja" [Men with Bowed Heads]. *Kyunghyang shinmun*, 21 November 1996, 5.
15. Hyo-jae Kim, In-bae Seung, Yeong-sin Yun, and Myeong-jin Lee, "Gogae sugin abeoji deul 'saelleorimaen jogi toejik sindeurom' hwaksan 2" [Fathers with bowed heads: Growth of the salary man 'early retirement' syndrome], *Chosun Ilbo*, 1 December 1996, 3.
16. Han, "Abeojisang ui byeonhwa," 40.
17. Ibid., 45–6.
18. Ruin, "Uiryo gisul gihoek gwa geundaejeok namseongseong ui balmyeong" [Medical Technology Planning and the Invention of Modern Masculinity], in *Namseongseong gwa jendeo* [Masculinity and Gender] (Seoul: Jaeum gwa moeum, 2011), 88.
19. Jo, "Gunin, Sanai, geurigo yeoja deul," 152.
20. Ruin, "Uiryo gisul gihoek," 87.
21. Seo-yeon Jo, "Gunin, Sanai, geurigo yeoja deul: Jendeohwadoen gunsajuui ui munhwajeok jaehyeon" [Soldiers, men, and women: Cultural representations of gendered militarism] in *Geureon namja neun eopda* [There are no such men], ed. Yeonsedaehakgyo jendeo yeonguso (Seoul: Oworui bom, 2017) 153.
22. In-suk Kwon, *Daehan minguk eun gundaeda* [The Republic of Korea is the military] (Gyeonggi Province: Cheongnyeonsa, 2005), 222.
23. Yun-a Kim, "Guwon gwa eungjing, saeroun abeoji ui deungjang" [Salvation and punishment, the arrival of the new father], *Cineforum* 11 (December 2010): 7–9.
24. For a detailed discussion, see Hee-jeong Sohn, "Korean Mega-hit Historical Films and K-Nationalism in the Era of Neo-liberalism," *Yeonghwa yeongu* 35 (September 2015), 109–42; Ji-mi Kim, "Gukga wa abeoji: Jasuseongga e daehan du gae ui pantaji" [The Nation and the Father: Two Kinds of Fantasies about Self-made Men], *Hwanghae munhwa* 91 (June 2016): 54–75.
25. Song, "Song A-reum ui sinema keuritikeu."
26. Ibid.
27. Do-yeon Kim, *So wa hamkke yeohaeng haneun beop* [Rolling Home with a Bull] (Gyeonggi Province: Yeollimwon, 2007), 215.
28. Young-hee Kang, "Yeonghwa gamdok Yim Soon-rye: Geeureume daehan chanyang" [Film director Yim Soon-rye: In praise of idleness], *Wolgan sahoe pyeongnon gil* (March 1998): 147–8.
29. Eunsil Park-Lee, "Paegwonjeok namseongseong ui yeoksa" [History of Hegemonic Masculinity], *Munhwa gwahak* Vol. 76 (December 2013): 175–6.
30. Jin-Kyoung Sim "Gyeonggye e seon namseongseong – Kim Hun ui soseol eul jungsimeuro" [Masculinities at the Border – Focusing on Kim Hoon's Novels], *Munhak gwa sahoe* Vol. 16, no. 3 (August 2003): 1257–8.
31. Hye-jin Hwang, "Geuraedo salmeun jisokdoenda: Jeong Jae-eun gamdok ui *Goyangi reul butakae* wa Yim Soon-rye gamdok ui *Waikiki beuradeoseu*" [Still, Life Goes on: Director Jeong Jae-eun's *Take Care of My Cat* and Yim Soon-rye's *Waikiki Brothers*] *Gongyeon gwa ribyu* Vol. 35 (December 2001): 125.
32. Ibid., 127.

CHAPTER 2

Politics of Slow: Yim Soon-rye's *Promenade in the Rain* (1994) and *Waikiki Brothers* (2001)

Kim Chung-kang

INTRODUCTION

Yim Soon-rye's debut film, *Promenade in the Rain*, follows the story of a young woman, Miss Park, who has been working in a run-down movie theater for several years. The theater is located on the outskirts of a small city in mid-1990s Korea. The story is set during one day of Miss Park's life, as she anxiously waits for a man who has promised to visit her. While she is waiting, the camera observes her as she performs her daily work, such as selling tickets in the theater, doing small favors for the audience, and occasionally operating the film projector. It seems that everyone knows everyone in this small theater, and the cinema itself looks like the kind of space in which people come to kill time. On the theater screen, an American film, *The Getaway* (1994), runs, and the people sitting in the stalls have probably been watching this same film several times in a row. Eventually, it turns out that the man Miss Park has been waiting for just wants to sell her a juicer. Disappointed, Miss Park impulsively goes out for a walk even though it is raining. After a while she comes back to the theater, dries her hair, and continues with her work routine again. The camera stops there.

This fifteen-minute short film enables viewers to observe what is going on in this small theater at a very slow pace. No close-ups are used, and the camera keeps its distance from the people in the film, as if the viewers are observing them through CCTV, though without any notion of a surveillant mood. This calm, observational mode, using a static camera, creates the feeling for viewers that they are spending "real" time with the characters within the film. The director appears to abstain from any type of judgment or emphasis. Through Yim's observant camera technique, the audience can naturally experience the everyday life of the people inside the theater. This uniquely slow-paced and distanced observation of her subjects is one of the distinct characteristics of Yim Soon-rye's filmmaking.

In total, Yim Soon-rye has written and directed four feature films, *Three Friends* (1996), *Waikiki Brothers* (2001), *Fly, Penguin* (2009), and *Rolling Home with a Bull* (2010), in addition to the short films *Promenade in the Rain* (1994) and *The Weight of Her* (2002). Yim has stated that the films she has made based on her own screenplays have always failed at the box office.[1] As a director, her commercially successful films have ironically been based on screenplays written by other people, while those she has personally scripted have gained higher critical acclaim. Perhaps this discrepancy in the quality of her work and its popularity is largely due to her own tendency toward cinematic "slowness," as exemplified by *Promenade in the Rain*, an approach which is far removed from any form of commercial cinema and more suited to critical tastes. Yim's work often features non-manipulative camera work to enable greater audience contemplation, and certainly it could be said that her films as a writer and director all show her patient control of the stillness, limited presence, and pace of the camera, while maintaining a qualitative distance between audience and subject.

The idea of "slow cinema" as I am referencing here by definition contrasts with blockbuster films' "over-investment in physical action, spectacle and violence."[2] As opposed to the dominance of commercial film within the global market and its pervasiveness across theater chains, "slow cinema" is often deemed to be a form of "art cinema," which circulates in the international film festival circuit to bypass the Hollywood commercial film production/distribution system.[3] Yim Soon-rye's early films were made in clear cognizance of this international arthouse circuit and in return were received positively at European film festivals, although she changed her attitude toward making "slow film" after a series of box office failures later on in her career.[4] "Slow cinema," in this sense, could belong to the category of festival film; however, beyond such broad compartmentalization it is difficult to define exactly what the formal or essential nature of the genre is. The audience perception of the speed (pace maybe a better word?) of cinema can hardly be objectively measured, as Lucia Najib has acutely pointed out, a "lengthy film for certain viewers might offer a plethora of exiting incidents . . . as much as an action-packed thriller may be perceived as tediously repetitive [by others]."[5] So, if we describe a certain film as "slow," such an assessment could only be a relative judgment. To justify Yim's films as slow cinema, then, will require a certain amount of concrete comparative and contextual analysis, to pinpoint how the speed and temporality of Yim's films can be identified as such.

To further qualify the formal character of Yim's film as "slow cinema," it would also be useful to explore what it means to be "slow" in modern Korean society. Regarding the speed of the film, Paul Virilio once argued that the kinetics of cinema are intrinsically related to the pace of modernity. Patterned images in an assembly factory, or those that display the speed of a highway, for example, consciously or unconsciously affect the viewers' mind, and lure the viewers into identifying with the simulacra on screen.[6] Virilio further points out that the kinetics of modernity amount to a "dictatorship of movement," designed for "corporeal discipline in the pursuit of the image of speed" in modern times.[7] In this respect, he coined the term, "dromology" to indicate a "government of differential motility, of harnessing and mobilizing, incarcerating and accelerating things and people."[8] The virtual space created on screen, then, is an image projected in relation to the certain totality of modern governance. In this sense, the speed of film cannot be detached from the politics of society.

Compared to the Foucauldian notion of power that was employed (and modified) by Virilio, Jean Baudrillard rejects the common understanding of media as that which "those in power [use to manipulate], seduce and alienate the mass."[9] For him, power is exercised only through a reciprocal relationship or through seduction, as the desire of people becomes "fresh blood" for power.[10] Thus, the dictation of speed in society or in film does not necessarily command the direction of the viewers, and yet it still functions to seduce them to aim to attain power. In a society where information proliferates and the digitalization of cinema pervades, however, Baudrillard argues that computer-generated images, digitization, and special effects, all of which were initially used to create "more reality" in film (what he terms "empty perfection"[11]), will eventually render the audience further removed from reality and propel them "toward banality and boredom."[12] And, in an age where digital film dominates society, technology-saturated productions have indeed arguably caused greater banality, whereas the old sensibility of cinematic materiality might, in contrast, be said to engender a certain greater notion of reality for viewers, which itself can provide a different type of seduction. This idea of reality, or lived experience, might be seen as one valuable sensibility that "slow cinema" can generate in the age of digital cinema.

In taking Paul Virilio's notion of the dictatorship of movement within the cinematic image as a significant diagnosis of the current digital age, this paper will discuss Yim Soon-rye's slow cinema as a commercially failed attempt to "seduce" audiences to rail against what time dictates. Based on Baudrillard's emphasis on cinema's possibility to cause a profound sensibility of reality (the "aura" of photographic reality), this chapter will argue that Yim's slow cinema was a specific attempt to shun the banality and boredom created by the increasingly digitized world. By focusing on two of Yim Soon-rye's early works, *Promenade in the Rain* (1994) and *Waikiki Brothers* (2001), I want to highlight the cinematic slowness of her films, and the ways in which Yim has created her own unique form of cinematic temporality. I use the term "aesthetics of slow cinema" to refer to her filmic style and the pacing of her screenplays and narrative structure. This "aesthetics of slow cinema," however (and as noted above), is not merely a reference to a set of stylistic characteristics. It also represents a critical approach to understanding Yim's portrayal of contemporary life, inasmuch as how the aesthetics of slow cinema could be resistant to the "historically determining mechanism[s] of power and pleasure."[13] As Yim has stated, her scripted films have always been relative failures at the box office, and so her way of dealing her own stories at such a slow pace certainly could not be considered as belonging to the mainstream of 1990s South Korea filmmaking, which had just begun to be molded on the profit-driven global standard, with its fanatical zeal toward overt technological development.

The "stillness" pervading Yim's films, then, is not just a matter of her stylistic singularity, but representative of her cinematic strategy to be slightly at odds with the mainstream trend and speed of society. Moreover, two of her early works, *Promenade in the Rain* and *Waikiki Brothers*, particularly represent the disappearing culture and quotidian life of the 1990s using a very slow and nostalgic tone. This technical and strategic employment of a slow filmic approach exposes the viewer to something akin to the emotional effect of old celluloid materiality, the "aura" of the photographic reality that Baudrillard emphasizes. This approach could also be considered in relation to how the "still or the use of stillness" manages and controls the psychology of the viewer, as Laura Mulvey has noted.[14] Yim's films, thus, offer a significant attempt to provide an alternative aesthetics, one that privileges its characters "slow" existence, in deliberate opposition to the speed-obsessed nature of Korean society.

AESTHETICS OF "SLOW CINEMA" IN YIM SOON-RYE'S EARLY FILMS

As noted at the outset, although one cannot definitely state that the slowness of film can be measured or diachronically defined, as many have asserted in the case of European New Wave film, the notion of slowness still commonly and usefully signifies certain aspects of the minimalist movement in art cinema. For instance, André Bazin highlights "modern cinema" for its ability to manipulate the film's time and duration as the "real" time of the audience, and the traits of slow cinema have even been characterized as a useful means to present unfiltered reality.[15] As Emre Caglayan argues, the frequent appearance of works of slow cinema in the arthouse circuit of the contemporary international film festival scene is quite institutional, and should not necessarily be regarded as a concrete quality of arthouse film's essential character.[16] It remains true, however, that the deliberate authorial control of time within the filmic work makes a huge difference to any given work's aesthetic and narrative sensibility, and can be used to cause specific emotional effects in audiences. Against this Eurocentric model of "slow cinema," Tiago De Luca has criticized that the diachronic development of a Western notion of slow cinema remains a quite arbitrary judgment, since the aesthetics of slowness were apparent in Asian cinema even before 1945, such as in the works of Ozu Yasujiro and Mizoguchi Kenji, prior to the development of the European New Wave.[17]

Despite this Asian tradition, the slowness of Yim Soon-rye's film reverberates more with her own cinematic interest in the French New Wave. Although her love of French film and four years at film school in France is not often mentioned in relation to her directorial style, Yim has confessed how much she was impressed with French cinema, and how its style differed in comparison to that of classic Hollywood film. She herself has said that the delicate portrayal of the "trivial everyday" in French film initially compelled her to go to France to study film.[18] In this sense, it would not be an exaggeration to say that her innovatively refigured mode of "cinematic time" might be grounded in the influence of the French New Wave or European arthouse cinema. Just as the idea of cinematic movement and stillness became a critical point of expression within the European New Wave, the deliberate use of slow movement by Yim could be read as the reconfiguration of such cinematic time, dictated differently and uniquely for her own purpose.

Irrespective of such possible external influences, it can certainly be stated based on the director's own comments that she has been particularly focused on controlling the speed or temporality of her work. Yim's way of dealing with cinematic temporality echoes the Bazinian idea that the director should restrict the use of subjective camera positions and instead use a more detached observant technique, to encourage the viewers' free contemplation and independent judgment. Yim herself had a clear consciousness about using this style in her early works. As she said:

> When I made *Three Friends* and *Waikiki Brothers*, I had few rules. First, do not use many cuts. Second, do not use much music. And finally, the camera is not positioned close to the actors/actresses. To give more space for the viewers' contemplation, I did not want to intervene too much. I tried not to use many professional actors or actresses. I wanted to minimize artificial movement as much as possible. But I forgot about this rule when I began to make commercial films.[19]

Yim's explanation of her approach to filming here is directly reminiscent of the Bazinian aesthetic approach to modernist films. In short, maintain an objective camera position and extend the temporality of the film by limiting the shot numbers. As Bazin celebrated Italian neo-realist innovation in both form and content, as a means to increase a notion of "reality" through the restricted use of montage and less-mediating camera work, the approach of Yim has the same potential to provide viewers with a space for contemplation, independent of the director's own narrative concerns. In this respect, the narrative content of Yim's early work is evocative of Cesare Zavattini's unrealized plan for a 90-minute film about a man's life, in which nothing in particular happens.[20]

Her intention to use the camera in this Bazinian mode is frequently revealed in her early films. Within these works, Yim impassively illustrates numerous fragments of the everyday lives of common people, and linearly aligns them in the narrative. The narratives are far from dramatic, and without event. For instance, the pace of scene change in *Promenade in the Rain* and *Waikiki Brothers* is very slow, and the camera remains largely observant and static, as described earlier in this chapter. In *Waikiki Brothers*, for example, the story starts with an opening sequence showing the on-stage performance of a four-man band wearing glittering violet costumes, with the leader Seong-woo sadly announcing that this is their last performance. After his announcement, the music continues, and the shot slowly moves back. As the camera dollies backward, it is revealed that the band is not performing at a concert full of adoring fans, and viewers slowly begin to see various elderly dancing couples, who are entirely indifferent to what the lead singer is talking about.

Centering around an old-fashioned band, *Waikiki Brothers* follows the life trajectory of the four members. Tired of their unpopularity, the band comes back to Seong-woo's hometown. There, the film contrasts the contemporary middle-aged, miserable Seong-woo with flashbacks to his high-school days when he dreamed of starting a Korean version of the Rolling Stones. Although Yim's camera meticulously follows Seong-woo throughout his largely miserable journey, the director ultimately offers a hopeful ending, finishing with the protagonist forming a new band with his teenage sweetheart in the remote port city of Yeosu. In the ending sequence, the camera again shows Seong-woo's on-stage performance, this time with his new group. Once again, the camera slowly moves back, and viewers again witness the elderly dancing couples in the hall before the camera finally stops.

In this manner, the narrative and visual structure in unison neatly deliver the story of this insignificant old-fashioned band and their repetitive daily routine. Viewers observe the trivial stories and episodes within the overall narrative and remain distanced from the characters. The remoteness of the camera that creates this objective space prevails throughout, and extreme close-ups, for instance, are almost entirely eschewed. Just as Bazin argued that "new subject matter demands new form,"[21] these trivial stories, which many might hardly consider as stories worthy of filming, are neatly transmitted through the observant camera of Yim. The decision to watch this seemingly non-dramatic life of trivial people therefore lies with the viewers.

Nevertheless, this does not mean that the film is bereft of emotive content. As Laura Mulvey points out, there still remain "lures and pleasures" for the spectator based on their active participation in deciphering the images that are presented to them.[22] For Mulvey, the example of Fassbinder's "frozen moments" usefully demonstrates how the use of stillness in a film can function to increase such tranquil "lures and pleasures" of the moment. And in Yim's early work, amid the overall sedate cinematic tone, there are certainly moments that serve to gradually intensify the viewers' emotional identification with the main characters. For instance, in *Promenade in the Rain*, after Miss Park realizes that the man who promised to visit her is only a juicer seller, she goes into the projection room to avoid him. Through the narrow window of the projection room, she watches *The Getaway* as the male and female protagonist dramatically meet. With vacant eyes, she looks at the scene. The viewers are left with the perspective of Miss Park and can only hear the loud operating sound of the projector. This stillness causes the viewers to position themselves with Miss Park. The viewers here are directly imbued with the emotion that flows on the cinema screen showing *The Getaway*, directly getting involved in the scene itself.

Similarly, in *Waikiki Brothers*, toward the end of the movie, Seong-woo plays a song alone after he is almost sacked by the hotel club while other workers are preparing to open up. For just a minute, and for the first time, the audience watches the middle-aged Seong-woo playing and singing a very personal song. The camera position starts with Seong-woo's teenage sweetheart, but as she begins to look at the protagonist, the camera moves back to show only the back of her. The position of the camera is set in the viewer's perspective in this way. At this moment, the viewers of the film become the intimate audience for Seong-woo's performance. Despite the fact that his ad-hoc performance is not staged for any audience within the context of the film itself, through this scene the viewer is encouraged to sympathetically understand why Seong-woo has been enduring his clumsy life as a musician. Tonal slowness, in this way, serves to powerfully influence the viewers' perception and their sympathy for the main characters. This scene also maintains the power to absorb viewers' attention through its deliberate use of stillness and the aesthetics of slow. This is the result of Yim's particular form of slow cinema that produces "intensities of time and speed [that] affect the body of a spectator or a user."[23]

As Yim Soon-rye mentioned, she no longer practiced this style in her later commercial films, as she somewhat abandoned her initial rules. However, even in these more populist and successful films, she has continued to manipulate the temporality of a film to dramatize and maximize emotion, just as many technologically savvy films do. For example, in *Forever the Moment* (2008), her most commercially successful film to date, there is certainly a conscious directorial moment in which Yim uses "stillness" to dramatize the feelings of the main protagonists. *Forever the Moment* is a film about a female national handball team based on real-life events. In this film, to keep the suspense that a sports game should maintain, Yim's camera constantly moves quickly, and she uses fast-paced editing to further enhance the feeling of action. But in the very final game, when the team loses on the final pitching ball, the film suddenly stops and this stillness remains for a dramatically frozen five seconds. Anxious viewers waiting to find out whether this pitching is successful remain trapped in this stillness, and only after a few moments do they realize in the last shot that the team did not get the point. As Laura Mulvey has stated, the development of technology has enabled viewers themselves to stop the moment and feel the stillness of the film, or the fragments of the moving image, and in such a manner the use of "stop motion" in this particular scene freezes time and prolongs the anxiety of the moment.[24]

Of course, the use of this type of cinematic slowness could be regarded as influenced by technological developments, as it is something frequently used in "CGI-saturated commercial cinema"[25] in the 1990s and exemplified by the "bullet time effect" used in *The Matrix* (1999). However, in her work Yim demonstrates how the speed of film can be used for emotional effect, and thus "stillness" is used to increase the expressive impact of the imagery and narrative, rather than just for effect, to show off the new digital visual control of time offered by computer technology. The use of speed in Yim's earlier films does not correspond to the movement and stillness deployed in *Forever the Moment*, yet Yim still consciously uses this slow motion, or frozen effect, to control the viewers' emotive response. The use of "stop motion" in this final scene is typically found in sports films to intensify the moment of movement. But because Yim uses this technique just once, at this key final moment, the emotional engagement of the viewer is particularly intensified. Notwithstanding Baudrillard's assertion that technology-saturated film tends to engender only "boredom or banality," Yim's controlled use of a technological effect at only the very last moment serves to imprint on the viewer an idea of the photographic "reality" of the scene, as well as dramatically underline the monumental failure of the handball team. The use of slowness by Yim, then, whether technologically assisted or in the more traditional Bazinian mode, consistently constitutes an attempt to be critically reflective on the temporal moment within her work.

STOP SIGN: ABOUT VANISHING CULTURE

The "slow cinema" of Yim Soon-rye reveals further meaning if we read her work in the historical and cultural context of 1990s South Korea, which was a highly transitional time. Thirty years of military dictatorship had finally ended after mass demonstrations in 1987, and the staging of the Olympic Games in 1988 created a mass fantasy that Korea had just crossed the threshold to become a developed and globalized nation. Within the newly established democratic regime, new media, computer technology, and new material culture proliferated into the social, cultural, and physical space of the nation at an extreme rate. As Paul Virilio offers, given the speed of a modern society "there is no 'industrial revolution' but only a 'dromocratic revolution.'"[26] In this respect, South Korean society was certainly moving toward insertion within the globalized neoliberal system with enormous speed.

In terms of the filmmaking industry within early 1990s South Korea, "Korean film," after an auspicious period of production in the early post-war period, was in more recent times notorious for producing only low-brow erotic cinema, and thus had been considered as a "vanishing industry" during a long period of stagnation between the 1970s and 1980s. In the 1990s, this "vanishing industry" began to recover its former ambition and reach new industrial and cultural potential. Economically speaking, the market share of national film was at a low of 15.59 percent in 1993. But the national market soon recovered, and by 2001 the national market share jumped up almost 50 percent.[27] In terms of filmmaking, huge technological developments were made, and new "Korean blockbuster" films dominated this resurgent era of national cinema.[28] So-called conglomerate companies began to invest in the film industry, encouraged by the prospects of Korean cinema as the leading cultural industry within the country.[29] President Kim Dae-jung also pronounced that the South Korean film industry should be the "strategic national industry."[30] Part of this new age entailed a new national emphasis on the "soft power" of Korea, and the cultural status of film was further elevated at great speed.

A key part of this was the immense success of *Shiri* (1998), and the involvement of chaebol companies such as Samsung (later CJ Entertainment), Daewoo, and other venture capital interests who unleashed a wave of so-called "blockbuster" films.[31] The involvement of these conglomerates opened up the possibility for filmmakers to test new film technologies that required big budgets. Additionally, the digitization of cinema made filmmaking technology much easier and accessible, and CGI was quickly introduced in Korea and rapidly adopted across commercial cinema. Positive public responses followed this use of new technology, as seen with the commercial success of *Ginko Bed* (Kang Je-gyu, 1996), which included an entirely computer-generated graphic section at the beginning section of the film. As a part of a new marketing strategy, the production company behind *Ginko Bed*, Shincine, provided excerpt trailers of the film through the internet.[32] Although this use of the web is nothing new today, at the time this was a highly novel attempt to use the internet for marketing purposes. The innovative use of new media for communication and publicity is further exemplified by the film *The Contact*

(Jang Yoon-hyun,1997),[33] which became highly popular among younger generations. At this time, many expected that this use of new media culture would open up a whole new landscape in filmmaking.

In terms of Yim Soon-rye's works from this period, while they do not belong exactly to any of these examples of mainstream filmmaking, she was not totally exterior to such trends. For instance, Yim's first short film, *Promenade in the Rain*, received an award at the Seoul Short Film Festival, which was sponsored by Samsung.[34] Empowered by professional networks formed through this film festival, Yim was able to secure financial aid from Samsung for her feature-length debut film, *Three Friends*, notwithstanding that it was a relatively a small-budget film. In making *Three Friends*, Yim used digital editing for the first time in South Korea, making use of the AVID system.[35] She was also able to work with Australian cinematographer Peter Gray.[36] Her next feature-length film, *Waikiki Brothers*, was also financed by CJ Entertainment, one of the biggest conglomerate media companies in Korea, although the overall budget was again only medium range. In terms of filmmaking technology, in *Waikiki Brothers*, Yim used new Dolby sound technology to create the signature sound of the band's old-style music, and for other special audio effects. In this sense, Yim occupied a niche as a director who made her works with a small budget, similar to independent filmmakers, and yet negotiated directly with the fast-changing filmmaking industry of South Korea in terms of finance and technology.

As such, while Yim Soon-rye's films emerged in the middle of this burgeoning neoliberal, digital "society of spectacle," the slow pace of her work and its refrained description of "small" people and the vanishing national culture provokes the viewer into feeling a different emotional connection with the period. Emre Caglayan has singled out the aesthetic characteristics of slow cinema in terms of "nostalgia, absurdism and boredom,"[37] and arguably these are precisely the defining aspects of Yim Soon-rye's work. When she was first recognized as "the new face" of Korean film in early 1990s, to the question asking what kind of themes she had in mind for the future projects, Yim replied:

> I am very interested in the modern history of Korea. Korea went through a compressed modernity, and in so doing we have had many lost things. [Despite] development, we have emotional and psychological loss. Korean history is a history of deprivation and loss. I want to deal with this oppressiveness and the norms that were formed in this historical process. [Korean society] pushes individuals to follow. . . So I want to portray the people who failed and fell behind in this history.[38]

Inasmuch as her interests lay with something vanishing, and being left behind, her early films deal with this focus as the main interest of the story. When Yim was planning her debut film, she thought about making a documentary film about the last circus group, Tongch'un Circus, which was about to disband and disappear into history.[39] In a similar manner, *Promenade in the Rain* is about a run-down, double-bill movie theater, and *Waikiki Brothers* is the story of an outdated cover band playing at cheap night clubs. In this regard, Yim has also stated that her desire is to make socially meaningful films based on themes which are peripheral within mainstream Korea, such as those focused on "animals, immigrant workers, minorities, and women."[40] This interest might be related to the fact that when asked about a director who had influenced her, Yim mentioned Bertrand Tavernier's early works that focused on "the perspectives of [the former French] African colonies and social issues."[41] So, where many other Korean arthouse directors have become more excited by the formal innovations of Jean-Luc Godard or François Truffaut, for Yim, her control over the films' narrative and overall theme is as important as any possibility for formal experimentation.

In terms of dealing with the peripheral life of people and lost national culture, her concerns could be compared to the Korean New Wave group, because many of these films also portray Korean society from a very critical viewpoint. For example, in response to the end of the military dictatorship in the late 1980s, in the 1990s the Korean New Wave group presented works focused on historical issues such as the Korean War (*The Taebaek Mountain*, Im Kwon-Taek, 1994), the Gwangju Massacre (*A Petal*, Jang Sun-woo, 1996), the issue of comfort women (*The Murmur*, Byeon Yeong-ju, 1995), and so on. These films all engaged with the silent history of modern Korea, which had been repressed under the military dictatorship, and so were often called Korean New Wave, though this categorization does not correspond to one particular aesthetic approach.[42] This conscious connection of cinema and the collective history of Korea, one which sought to clearly stake out a "leftist voice" within the national, cultural arena, came to be characterized by a broad notion of South Korean film realism that was believed to be the ideal localized form of art cinema.

However, Yim Soon-rye's way of dealing with the past is significantly different from that of the Korean New Wave group, which focuses on Korea's collective historical past rather than the individual lives within. Although one can guess that the historical time period of Yim's films is presumably contemporary South Korea, any direct revelation of date within the stories is vague, and so viewers are left with a very ambiguous cinematic temporality. Just as Tiago De Luca has pointed out that the post-martial law "slow" films made in Taiwan by Edward Yang and Hou Hsao-hsien move from a perspective of "historical-I" to a "private-I,"[43] Yim's way of dealing with the past focuses more on mundane everyday private life against an uncertain historical background. Yim's slow cinema strategically stops at the present and remains focused on the recent past, examining the very trivial moments of trivial people. To some degree her approach on the mundane resonates with the 1980s South Korean film, *Good Windy Day* (Lee Jang-ho, 1980),[44] a story of three friends from countryside who have taken on lowly employment as a delivery boy in a shoddy Chinese restaurant, a shaving boy in a small barber shop, and a clerk in a cheapy motel. However, in contrast to *Good Windy Day*, in which the three friends' lives become increasingly dramatized before a violent climax, Yim's work constantly observes people going about their lives with passivity.

In *Waikiki Brothers*, trivial episodes occur throughout the film while the Waikiki Brothers band constantly travel, because they receive requests to play from very remote places all over the country. Thus the narrative naturally takes the form of a road movie. By quietly tracing the journey of *the Waikiki Brothers*, this portrait of a band on the verge of collapse is sketched out with so many trivial everyday events in great detail. This portrayal of the Waikiki Brothers' life journey in film could be said to reflect what Tiago De Luca has referred to as the "materiality of quotidian events,"[45] a picture of everyday banality that functions as the natural backdrop to the film. For example, the band is invited to occasions such as a seventieth birthday party in a rural region, the Miss Pepper Lady Pageant, a Kimchi Festival, and so on.[46] In playing these events, the band encounter the other performers who share the stage. These are mostly third-rate singers and comedians who imitate famous stars with their own less-than-perfect performances. Yi Eong-ja, for instance, an impersonator of a famous comedian, Yi Yeong-ja,[47] works in a kitchen at a local diner. But she moonlights as a local club comedian, and does performances mimicking Yi Yeong-ja. Also featured is another impersonator, Neo Huna, doing an imitation of the famous singer Na Hun-a. Through these characters, the film unfolds various sub-stories about what is often regarded as "low-brow" or "cheap" culture. However, it does not provide any judgmental view and shows the enjoyable aspects of such culture. Also, a generous amount of time is given to portraying each character's shoddy performance. The film's narrative structure, in this way, is designed to highlight a series of unremarkable people on the periphery, whose ideas and lifestyles have lagged behind the dominant speed and flow of mainstream Korean society.

Although generally these small stories appear without much emotive tone, as if the film is simply portraying ordinary, everyday life, there is one dramatic, comic but sad story inserted toward the end of the film when Seong-woo's miserable situation is highlighted. After losing all his band members, Seong-woo plays guitar alone in a small karaoke room (*norae bang*) for a few drunk customers. These customers take off their clothes and force Seong-woo to strip down as well. Then the naked Seong-woo continues to play his guitar, which now barely hides his genitalia. On one level, this moment of absurdity is designed to provoke laughter from the viewers, accentuated by the television screen in the karaoke room, which shows a video of a woman in a bikini running along the seashore. However, the mood changes as the next shot shows the reflection of Seong-woo on the screen overlapping the images of him and his band members at the seashore. This reflection then transitions to Seong-woo's flashback, as he remembers running naked with his friends on the beach during his high-school days. The camera lingers on the TV screen at this moment, and the audio track is mixed to combine the karaoke songs with the sound of the waves that presumably comes from the image on the screen. This projection of Seong-woo's high-school memories on the TV screen is visually scratched and blurred, and this recreated video tape texture serves to create a certain feeling of old cinematic materiality. The materiality of the old video tape here serves to intensify the viewers' experience of the sentimental emotions of Seong-woo, who quietly sobs while continuing to play his guitar in front of the drunken customers.

The emotional impact of old memories and disappearing dreams is in this way both visually and sonorously rendered by Yim. The use of special visual effects and Dolby sound in this scene serves to create the whole evanescent mood on screen. The slow pace of the camera lingers on these ephemeral moments, and thus emotively depicts the broken heart of this miserable man and his love of old-fashioned culture. Here, Yim Soon-rye uses digital technology to reflect on the reality experienced every day by many Koreans. On one level it reduces the "realism" of the film, if the reality of realist film is a form of "filtered" or mediated reality based on a set objective distance, while also attempting to plunge the viewers into a character's real experience directly.

More significantly, this rather comic but sad scene also poses numerous questions for the viewer, such as should one bear such embarrassing moments, just because they are unsuited to contemporary life, and continue to dream of the past? As such, the scene provokes audiences to rethink what it means to keep pace with the speed of mainstream society. This portrayal of the peripheral life of Seong-woo and his associates, who have somehow managed to stick with their outdated lifestyle despite the fast-changing nature of Korean society, is well captured by Yim's camera, and her use of a "vintage" tonal "stillness" intensifies the empathy of the viewers. Yim's way of bringing emotion into her work is different from both the normative practice in Hollywood and the Korean films of the 1990s that were imbued in the discourse of catching up to new technologies with great speed. This variance notwithstanding, her films still aesthetically attempt to emotively effect the psychology of the viewers and could be considered as a "stop-sign" that critically illuminates the social "speed limits."

CONCLUSION

When Yim came back to Korea in the early 1990s from France, the culture of her homeland had changed unrecognizably. Thirty years of dictatorship had ended, and a growing democratic atmosphere had opened up new possibilities for the future of the country. But, at the same time, this transformation compelled Koreans to fully enter the era of neoliberal globalization, and directed them to constantly attempt to keep pace with a new world of global change. In terms of filmmaking, the new generation of directors were keen to make use of new technology, digitization, and new media amid the flood of information and innovative approaches that attended democratization. Additionally, filmmaking was considered an industry suitable to help realize the economic and cultural power of the nation. "Chaebol" companies joined the filmmaking system as financiers, which further highlighted the potential and possibility for those engaged in making blockbuster films.

In this new context of Korean history, the unique mode of cinematic time and space of Yim Soon-rye stands apart from most of the contemporaneous Korean film of the period, and appears to be of an older stylistic vintage and influenced more by foreign cinema. In short, Yim's work is focused on remote spatialities and slow temporalities, and concerned with what is disappearing rather than that which is new. Although many media scholars, including Jean Baudrillard and Friedrich Kittler, have predicted that the material aspects of media would disappear and become "flat" in the digital age, and that a world full of technology-saturated images would create only an increasingly banal experience for viewers, Yim's work offers strong evidence that new technology can also make a film look materially grounded, distinctively less hi-tech and deliberately out of time with the moment. In this new digital age of possibility, Yim Soon-rye's unique hybrid approach, based on new Dolby sound effects and special visual effects combined with the historical aesthetic innovations of the European New Wave Films, offers a moment of resistance against the forced acceleration of contemporary life in Korea. Slow cinema, which prevails within the works she has authored, could then be considered as Yim's signature aesthetic. But perhaps more importantly, this slow aesthetic provokes us to stop and think about what Koreans are doing with their own lives within their speed-obsessed society.

NOTES

1. Chu Chin-suk and Yi Sun-jin, ed., *Yeonghwa haneun yeojadeul* [Women make film] (Seoul: Sagyejeol, 2020), 68.
2. Thomas Elsaesser, "Stop/Motion," in *Between Stillness and Motion: Film, Photography and Algorithms*, ed. Eivind Røssaak (Amsterdam: Amsterdam University Press, 2011), 117.

3. Tiago De Luca and Nuno Barradas Jorge, "Introduction: From Slow Cinema to Slow Cinemas," in *Slow Cinema* (Edinburgh: Edinburgh University Press, 2016), 10–12.
4. Her debut film, *Three Friends*, was sent out to Vancouver International Film Festival and Berlin International Film Festival. She stated that she received a positive reaction from the Berlin, in particular. Yim Soon-rye and Chang Seok-yeong, "Sowoedwoen chadeul eul kwajang eopsi barabogi" [Looking at the marginalized people without exaggeration], *The Performing Arts and Film Review* 11 (1997): 63.
5. Lucia Najib, "The Politics of Slowness and the Traps of Modernity," in *Slow Cinema*, ed. De Luca and Barradas Jorge, 26.
6. Jean Baudrillard, *Forget Foucault* (Cambridge: Semiotext(e), 2007), 53.
7. Paul Virilio, *Speed and Politics* (Cambridge: Semiotext(e), 2006), 72.
8. Ibid.
9. Jean Baudrillard, *The Vital Illusion* (New York: Columbia University Press, 2000), 53.
10. Baudrillard, *Forget Foucault*, 65.
11. Gerry Coulter, "Jean Baudrillard and Cinema: The Problem of Technology, Realism and History," *Film-Philosophy* Vol. 14, no. 2 (2010): 9.
12. Ibid., 10.
13. Linda Williams, *Hardcore: Power, Pleasure, and the "Frenzy of the Visible"* (Berkeley: University of California Press, 1989), 46.
14. Laura Mulvey, "'Magnificent Obsession': An Introduction to the Work of Five Photographers," in *Visual and Other Pleasures* (Hampshire: Palgrave Macmillan, 2009), 145–6.
15. The Bazian concept of realism "invests in the objective and unfiltered representation of reality in cinema." See Emre Caglayan, *Poetics of Slow Cinema: Nostalgia, Absurdism, Boredom* (New York: Palgrave Macmillan, 2018), 12.
16. Caglayan, 22–4.
17. Tiago De Luca, "Sensory Everyday: Space, Materiality and the Body in the films of Tsai Ming-liang," *Journal of Chinese Cinemas* Vol. 5, no. 2 (January 2014): 157–9.
18. Yim Soon-rye and Chang Seok-yeong, "Sowoedwoen," 61.
19. Ibid., 69.
20. André Bazin, *What is Cinema, Volume 1* (University of California Press, 2004), 37–8.
21. Ibid., 30.
22. Mulvey, *Visual*, 144.
23. Røssaak, *Between*, 11.
24. Laura Mulvey, *Death 24x a second* (London: Reaktion Books, 2005), 18–23.
25. Najib, "The Politics," 27.
26. Virilio, *Speed*, 69.
27. Darcy Pacquet, "The Korean Film Industry: 1992 to the Present," in *New Korean Cinema*, ed. Chi-yun Shin and Julian Stringer (New York: New York University Press, 2005), 32–3.
28. Kim Kyeong-uk, *Blokbeoseuteo ui hwansang kwa hanguk yeonghwa ui nareusisiseum* [*The Fantasy of Blockbuster, and Narcissism of Korean Cinema*] (Seoul: Ch'aeksesang, 2002).
29. Pacquet, "The Korean," 36–40.
30. Park Young-a, *Unexpected Alliances: Independent Filmmakers, the State, and the Film Industry in Post-Authoritarian South Korea* (California: Stanford University Press, 2014), 3–4.
31. For more detailed explanations of the 1990s film industry, see Pacquet, "The Korean," 36–44.
32. "Yeonghwa eunhaeng namu chimdae inteonet tonghae dongyeongsang jegong" [*Ginko Bed* Provides a Moving Image through Internet!], *Yeonhap News*, 20 March 1996, <https://news.naver.com/main/read.naver?mode=LSD&mid=sec&sid1=103&oid=001&aid=0004110877> (last accessed 1 March 2021).

33. *The Contact* is a love story between a male radio program producer and a female telemarketer who happen to be connected through internet chatting. This type of new love story was a hot topic globally in the 1990s, as exemplified by the Hollywood film, *You've Got Mail* (1998).
34. The Seoul Short Film Festival was sponsored by Samsung from 1994 to 1997. This festival contributed to nurturing new film directors who were not trained through traditional apprenticeships in making film.
35. After using AVID for the first time in Korea, Yim Soon-rye taught many filmmakers about this new digital editing system, including Hong Kyeong-pyo (the cinematographer of Bong Joon-ho's *Parasite*). Yim Soon-rye and Chang Seok-yeong, "Sowoedwoen," 62.
36. Yim Soon-rye and Chang Seok-yong, "Sowoedwoen," 62.
37. Caglayan, *Poetics*, 6.
38. Yim Soon-rye and Chang Seok-yong, "Sowoedwoen," 62.
39. Ibid., 58.
40. Ibid., 66.
41. Chu Chin-suk and Yi Sun-jin, *Yeonghwa*, 56.
42. Kim So-yeon, "Minjok yeonghwaron ui pyeoni wa 'Korean New Wave' yeonghwa damron ui hyeongseong" [The Discursive Variation of Korean National Cinema and the Formation of Korean New Wave Cinema], *Daejung Seosa yeongu* 15 (2006).
43. The best example would be the slow cinema of Tsai Ming-liang, Yasujiro Ozu, Wong Kar-wai, and Zhang Yimou. Tiago De Luca, "Sensory," 159.
44. This was director Yi Jang-ho's comeback film in 1980 after years of alienation from the Korean film industry after the marihuana crackdown during the Park Chung-hee military dictatorship. It is often regarded as a "realist" film by many directors of Korean New Wave including Chang Son-u, Park Kwang-su, and so on.
45. Tiago, "Sensory," 41.
46. In Korea, there is a tradition of throwing a large-scale birthday party for parents when they reach the ages of sixty and seventy, to celebrate the longevity of their life. But with time it has become a tradition observed primarily in rural areas. So, this outdated party often takes place in a countryside setting, and no-name bands or out-of-season entertainers are retained to provide entertainment. Playing at such occasions arguably means that the band in question is barely surviving financially and is not working for purely artistic purposes. Playing at local festivals such as the "Miss Pepper Lady Pageant," that are often very small scale and in rural areas, carries a similar meaning.
47. Yi Yeong-ja is a widely known female comedian. And there are many Yi Yeong-ja impersonators in local clubs. Many of these performances resemble the original performance, and thus give a certain pleasure to the local club's audience, as if they are watching Yi Yeong-ja herself.

CHAPTER 3

The Cinematic *Naturecultural Turn* in South Korea: Ecofeminist Pastoralism in the Works of Yim Soon-rye

Lee Yun-jong

This chapter explores the theme of pastoralism within Yim Soon-rye's films of the 2010s. In particular, it pays attention to Yim's depiction of human communion with plants and nonhuman animals in relation to ideas of ecofeminism. I would thus call Yim's ecofeminist pastoralism the "cinematic naturecultural turn," borrowing Donna Haraway's metaplasmic term, "natureculture." By focusing on *Rolling Home with a Bull* (2010) and *Little Forest* (2018), this chapter looks into how the framework of ecofeminist pastoralism has grown relative to Yim's career and how these films resonate with the parallel contemporary South Korean pursuit for "healing" in nature. Yim's pastoralism is not simply a leisurely, relaxing retreat into the countryside but representative of an intricate course of humans becoming partners or kins with nature.[1]

In this sense, I would argue her vision of pastoralism is not only linked to the idea that a routine of hard work is needed to support a life of cohabitation with plants and nonhuman animals, but also with an identification of the difficulty of productively achieving the tightrope walk between the anthropocentric binarism of nature and culture, and a Buddhist–Daoist pursuit of a unity between human beings and the natural order.

In fact, Yim has not primarily focused on women's stories in her films and Haraway has not actually professed herself to be an ecofeminist. Yet, my ecofeminist approach to Yim Soon-rye's work can be connected with feminism in a broad sense. Aside from her work as a director and producer over the thirty years of her career, Yim has directed over ten feature films. This makes her the most prolific woman filmmaker in the South Korean film industry. Yet, Yim has not tended to feature female protagonists. Notwithstanding exceptions such as a high-school girl on the verge of undergoing plastic surgery in a lookist society in *If You Were Me* (2003), female handball players in *Forever the Moment* (2008), and a young woman returning to her rural home village in *Little Forest* (2018), Yim's films have primarily represented men in leading roles. Her focus has specifically been on alienated men struggling within changing South Korean society such as the three poverty-stricken, non-normative young men in *Three Friends* (1996); failed middle-aged musicians in *Waikiki Brothers* (2001); a non-drinker in an alcoholic society in *Fly, Penguin* (2009); a man traveling the country in *Rolling Home with a Bull* (2010); a father struggling with his daughter in *Sorry, Thank You* (2011); an anarchist filmmaker in *South Bound* (2013); and a TV-show producer who exposes a national scandal in *The Whistleblower* (2014).

Nevertheless, Yim's work can be considered as feminist in the sense that feminism is a form of political thought and movement that not only seeks the emancipation of biological women from patriarchal oppression but also aims to empower social minorities of various genders, races, and class positionings.[2] Judith Butler has remarked that feminism since its second wave movement in the 1960s has been extended from a theory about "the social transformation of gender relations" to "interventions at social and political levels that involve actions, sustained labor, and institutionalized practice" supporting answers to "the questions of survival posed by any vulnerable being."[3] Given that Yim's oeuvre has remained consistently attentive to those who reside in the shadows of South Korean society, whether women or men, her films fit into the rubric of feminism in that broad sense, which I would like to call "minority-oriented feminism."

As a feminist film scholar, I used to wistfully hope that Yim would feature more women-oriented stories and motifs in her work. At the same time, however, the progressive topics that define her oeuvre would likely have never emerged if Yim were a heterosexual, middle- or upper-class male elite of South Korea. Therefore Yim's attention to socially marginalized men and women squares with feminism's crucial agenda in Butlerian terms. Accordingly, film scholar Rob Wilson categorizes Yim's *Waikiki Brothers* as "global cinema wrought in a minor mode," alongside contemporaneous South Korean films such as *Failan* (*Pairan*, Song Hae-sung, 2001) and *Take Care of My Cats* (*Go-yang-yi-rul Bu-tak-hae*, Jeong Jae-eun, 2001). Wilson offers that

> Korean films [of the 2000s, have become] more expressive of minority [and] socially occluded perspectives and local voices, undeveloped characters, urban or rural hinterlands, drifting visual modes, narrative digressions, low-tech inscriptions of minor and marginal communities, and a more fully dialectical warping of voice and angle of vision.[4]

In this sense, Yim's consistent minority orientation in the 2000s can be considered to have converged with an ecofeminist perspective, moving further into ecologism as the 2010s have progressed. In the next sections, I will elaborate on how this convergence is geared toward the South Korean naturecultural turn in a mode of "healing in nature," and its representation in Yim's 2010s films.

NEOLIBERALISM, ECOFEMINISM, REALITY TV, AND HEALING IN NATURE IN SOUTH KOREA

Rob Wilson calls South Korean neoliberalism "killer capitalism," in which severe social antagonism between urban Koreans is represented through "lurid spectral effects and body-eating intensity of intimate mutilation," for instance, in the films of Park Chan-wook and Kim Ki-duk.[5] In South Korea the nationwide acceptance of "neoliberal competition," as a new way of life originated in the late 1990s with the nation's financial crisis, followed by the proscribed restructuring and deregulation of the country's economy by the IMF (International Monetary Fund). By the 2010s, the notion and practice of individualist competition among the younger generation of "homo œconomicuses" that proliferated into urban areas had become nearly all pervasive. Away from the urban "predatory and vampire-like habits of antagonism [that generate] an endless cycle of male resentment, a will to class and gender vengeance, and mutual violence,"[6] many South Koreans have come to optimistically dream of a life closer to nature in the early twenty-first century. This section thus explores how the conjunction between ecofeminist pastoralism and the naturecultural turn represented in Yim Soon-rye's films of the 2010s is tightly linked to the desire for rural retreat as an escape from the urban neoliberal rat race in Korea.

In fact, the aforementioned idealistic desire for nature has been harshly critiqued by such ecofeminists as Bandana Shiva and Maria Mies, who label "the urban workers' normal holiday" in the countryside "consumptionist tourism." For Mies and Shiva, these "consumptionist" tourists "use up and consume [. . .] wild nature or the land as a commodity, and having consumed it they leave only a heap of waste, as they do when they consume other goods."[7] While I, somewhat, agree with this insight, it is not directly applicable to South Koreans, because, as I will discuss in more detail below, here the interest in a natural retreat from city life exists at a different valence. One could also argue that the ideas of Mies and Shiva are fettered by their dichotomous divisions between men and women, nature and culture, the developed and the backward, city and the country, and so on. Although these binary perspectives influence Yim's pastoral mode of filmmaking (not to mention South Korean ideas about nature in general), her work remains not reducible to them, but rather more progressively related to Haraway's notion of natureculture. This progressive relationship pertains to the fact that Yim is an ardent animal-rights activist, who founded KARA (Korea Animal Rights Advocates) and undertook the role of its president from 2009 to 2020. In this vein, Yim's films of the 2010s can be considered ecofeminist works in a broad sense as well. Before moving on to a detailed analysis of *Rolling Home with a Bull* and *Little Forest* in the next sections, it first has to be noted how the national passion for "healing" has become fused with South Koreans' desire for rural retreat in the 2010s, how this fusion is reflected in their cultural products (including Yim's films), and how these products can be critiqued, considered, and valued from an ecofeminist standpoint.

As a Korean sociologist, Seo Dong-jin demonstrated in his 2009 book that by the early twenty-first century South Koreans were widely obsessed with self-improvement, habitually engaging in after-school or work edification to prove themselves as better "neoliberal subjects," and desperately gain some kind of advantage in the urban rat race.[8] Given this circumstance, with little guaranteed reward many city dwellers enthusiastically longed for a new life in the countryside. The emergence of Koreanized healing-oriented reality TV shows in the 2010s such as *3 Meals a Day* and *Hyori's Bed and Breakfast* is particularly notable, partly because they are still popular today, and partly because through these programs I construe the emergence of national fervor that parallels the Harawayian "naturecultural turn."

Donna Haraway is a key feminist scientific philosopher, who has attempted to deconstruct the binary divisions between men and women, organisms and machines, colonizers and the colonized, Caucasians and non-Caucasians, and nature and culture. Her particular approach to the topic started with her 1985 work, "A Cyborg Manifesto," the aim of which was to "foreground specific positioning, multiple mediation, partial perspective, and therefore a possible allegory for feminist scientific and political knowledge."[9] More recently, a sociologist, Maria Mies, and a philosophic physicist, Vandana Shiva, co-authored a 1993 book, *Ecofeminism*, in which they intervened into "the destructive tendencies that threaten life on earth [borne out of] the capitalist patriarchal world system."[10] In particular, Mies and Shiva take issue with environmental developmentalism and human reproductive science, both of which are implemented primarily by white men on the natural world, women from the global south, and the colonized.

Ecofeminism (like feminism) is defined by a diverse range of progressive agendas and orientations on topics from gender, nature and science, to reproduction, developmentalism, and modernization. Nevertheless, arguably there persists within the discourse a reductively essentializing tendency, since many ecofeminists directly equate nature with women, mystifying it both through metaphorical imagery such as that of "Mother Nature" suffering matricide at the hands of patriarchal intellectuals, and directly equating men with science to demonize both. In reinforcing such essentialist divisions between a feminized nature and a masculine science/culture, women and nature are rendered as merely helpless victims who bear no responsibility for the damage inflicted upon the globe. However, in reality all humans, whether men or women, are equally a part of the same ecosystem. In a similar way, instead of seeking to essentialize women and nature, Haraway and Merchant have emphasized ideas of human "kinship" and "partnership" with nature in their twenty-first century studies of the anthropocene, that is, the geological era of anthropos/humans causing environmental crisis through their nature-developmental drive.[11]

In her previous work, *Companion Species Manifesto* (2003), Haraway first introduced the term, "natureculture" to show the "co-evolution of nature and culture" through offering "[i]nverting meanings; transposing the body of communication; remolding, remodeling; swervings that tell the truth."[12] More recently, Haraway proposes a new metaplasmic epochal term, "Chthulucene," to replace anthropocene, to better reflect the idea that "human beings are with and of the earth, and the biotic and abiotic powers of this earth are the main story."[13] Part of the reason for this reframing for Haraway is that

> [t]he chief actors [of the current ecological crisis] are not restricted to the too-big players in the too-big stories of Capitalism and the Anthropos, both of which invite odd apocalyptic panics and even odder disengaged denunciations rather than attentive practices of thought, love, rage, and care.[14]

Instead of disregarding the term anthropocene, Merchant stresses the role of "environmental humanities" in helping to overcome the planetary crisis through ideas of "sustainable livelihood" and a new human "partnership ethic" with nonhuman nature.[15] As such, while Haraway urges humans to realize their kinship with all earth-beings in a naturecultural sense, Merchant emphasizes partnership between human and nonhuman nature, and between environmental developers and victims of the anthropocenic disasters such as Hurricane Katrina. My view is that such ideas of human-natural kinship or partnership have been imaginatively depicted within Yim's *Rolling Home with a Bull* and *Little Forest*. Before analyzing these films in detail, I would like to touch upon a particular South Korean naturecultural turn within various cultural manifestations, not least the wider framework of Yim's works during the 2010s.

In the aftermath of the financial crisis of 1998, South Korea completely reorganized its export-oriented industrial capitalist system into a finance-capitalist form by adopting and enshrining neoliberalist tenets at the heart of its national economic policy as a condition of borrowing loans from the

IMF. By the end of the 2000s, flexible labor, the deregulation of import markets, and privatization of public sectors came to be the social and economic norms of the country. To survive the heated neoliberal capitalist competition that has refigured the nation as a "winner-take-all society,"[16] one must "discipline" oneself into a "homo œconomicus" who "invests" oneself in education, innovation, and "self-governance" to prove oneself as a better "ability-machine" in the market of "human capital."[17] Foucault contrasts the classical definition of homo œconomicus as "the man of exchange, the partner, one of the two partners in the process of exchange" with the American neoliberal reconceptualization of it as "an entrepreneur of himself," whose life it is "possible to calculate, and to a certain extent quantify, or at any rate measure, in terms of the possibilities of investment in human capital."[18] By the 2010s this endless process of calculation, quantification, and measurement in the market place of human "ability machines" had so exhausted South Koreans, especially young adults in urban areas, that the nation's suicide rate soared up to "5% in 2017."[19]

In such circumstances, it is unsurprising that the idea of personal "healing" has boomed. The widespread fame of this fad is such that even *The Wall Street Journal* reported in 2018 that "healing is a uniquely South Korean concept that [only] bears some distant relation to the original English word." Some have linked the increasingly emergent desire to leave the city and subsequent new trend of urban migration to countryside, which emerged in South Korea in the 2010s, with this healing phenomenon. According to a news report, "[t]he data compiled by Statistics Korea showed 490,330 people moved to rural areas in 2018," while "one-fifth of South Korea's 51 million population lives in Seoul."[20] However, this survey shows that the South Korean desire for rural migration is not simply motivated by economic reasons, as "alternative lifestyle-related motives such as seeking a 'country life' (29.4%), 'skepticism about urban life' (14.7%), and 'health' (10.7%) were frequently answered as the reasons for these moves by Korean urban-rural migrants."

The South Korean frenzy for healing through rural retreat from urban competition has been further fueled by numerous reality TV shows. Starting with the successful talk show *Healing Camp* (SBS, 2011–2016), the televised healing fad has gradually evolved through various formats of entertainment program from talk shows to contestant competitions to survivalist mocumentary to specific reality shows which are virtually nature documentaries in form. Just as the disguised or unobtrusive cameras observe plants and animals going about their daily lives in "real" nature documentaries, cameras in South Korean reality TV shows focus on the "natural" activities of the people enjoying their new healing circumstances. During the 2010s, it was notable that the most highly viewed reality television formats in South Korea shifted from those featuring celebrities being at home with their children

(*The Return of Superman*, KBS, 2013–present), or carrying on with their single lives (*I Live Alone*, MBC, 2013–present), to those featuring celebrities staying in the countryside and cooking and eating (*3 Meals a Day*, TVN, 2014–2020), hosting traveler-guests in idyllic Jeju Island (*Hyori's Bed and Breakfast*, TVN, 2018–2019), or traveling around the peninsula by camping car (*House on Wheels*, TVN, 2020–2021).

This nature-documentarization of Korean reality television reflects the wider "naturecultural turn" in South Korea during the 2010s. Moving beyond commonsensical human exceptionalism, the shift deconstructs the binary division between humans/culture and nonhumans/nature by treating human animals as observable object, just like the nonhuman animals and plants in nature documentaries. The South Korean naturecultural turn also reflects the city dwellers' desire to "evade" the "discipline" that is constantly inflicted upon neoliberal homo œconomicus, and helps them to attain the feeling of healing associated with pastoral lifestyles remotely. The "evasion" in this context brings the viewers the same "popular pleasure" that John Fiske has characterized as the "physical, evasive, offensive pleasures" that occur "in the body of the [viewer] at the moment of [watching] when text and [viewer] erotically lose their separate identities and become a new, momentarily produced body that is theirs and theirs alone, that defies meaning or discipline."[21] Interestingly, Fiske finds that such "evasive" pleasures in popular culture "produce the energy and empowerment that underlie the production of meaning (possibly resistive) of self and of one's social relations that may eventually result in politically active resistance" to the patriarchal capitalist "disciplines."[22] In this respect, the resistive pleasures that the South Korean viewers gain from such nature-documentarized reality television can be defined in terms of "evasion" from the demands of the socially inescapable competitive urban neoliberal lifestyle.

The illusion of the neutral observing of the camera and assumption of an accordingly impartial audience has been previously criticized as a format that actually conversely encourages viewers to engage in an extreme form of voyeurism that parallels the spectatorship practice associated with pornography.[23] However, in contrast to the particular form of pornographic pleasure, the audiences for these nature-documentarized reality shows are instead engaged in something more akin to the aforementioned notion of "evasion"; that is, a form that produces resistive pleasures from everyday routines in patriarchal capitalist society.[24] In this sense, this example of "healing" from South Korean popular culture directly parallels the Fiskian notion of evasion, and the popularity of South Korean reality shows undoubtably stems from their ability to salve the national passion for healing. This dynamic exists in a direct continuum with the thematic focus of Yim Soon-rye's films from the 2010s.

YIM'S PASTORALISM I: HUMAN–ANIMAL COMPANIONSHIP IN *ROLLING HOME WITH A BULL*

In the 2010s, Yim Soon-rye directed four features and one short film, all of which were, coincidentally or not, naturecultural-themed ecofeminist works. *Rolling Home with a Bull* (2010), *Sorry, Thank You* (2011), *South Bound* (2013), and *Little Forest* (2018) depict the development of some form of "natural" kinship experience between humans and animals, plants, and the agrarian landscape, while *The Whistleblower* (2014) focuses on a concern for the exploitation of female reproduction. The four nature-focused films are notably slow-to-medium-paced, no doubt mindful of the South Korean desire for relaxation, soothing, and healing. In contrast, *The Whistleblower* is a fast-paced thriller investigating the real-life scandal of human stem cells that were extracted from female-human eggs. By analyzing primarily *Rolling Home with a Bull* for its thematic focus on the Harawayian notion of human beings bonding with a companion species, and *Little Forest* as a paradigmatic ecofeminist work portraying a woman's personal development in nature, this section shows how Yim's works from the 2010s reflect the wider naturecultural turn that emerged in relation to the South Korean "healing" boom.

In chronological terms of her filmography, Yim opens the decade with *Rolling Home with a Bull* (hereafter *Rolling Home*) in 2010 and closes with *Little Forest* in 2018. In the early 2010s, several other South Korean films explored human–animal relationships, and particularly prevalent were those that focused on the theme of female humans taming wild male beasts such as *Howling* (*Haulling*, Yu Ha, 2012), *A Werewolf Boy* (*Neukdae sonyeon*, Jo Sung-hee, 2012), and *Mr. Go* (Kim Yong-hwa, 2013). While these films were basically in line with the changing South Korean perceptions of human–animal relationships as well as the growing companion-species consciousness, they were still too bound up with notions of anthropocentrism or a patriarchal perspective that manifests skepticism toward female organizers, or leaders in a broader sense. In contrast, Yim's *Rolling Home* is relatively unconstrained by anthropocentrism or gender prejudice, and notwithstanding that the film centers around a rather homosocial bond between a man and a bull, in its depiction of this idealized companionship between a human and a nonhuman animal it clearly reflects a concern with foregrounding the naturecultural links between humans and other animals.

While both *Rolling Home* and *Little Forest* reflect the ideas of natureculture, Yim constructs her own style of pastoralism that is not merely predicated on a rural idyll but on an assiduous human effort to cohabit with nonhuman forms of nature. Additionally, as with *The Whistleblower*, these two films develop narratives by centering on one main character. This is in contrast to most of Yim's oeuvre, in which multiple protagonists are generally featured, such as with *Three Friends* (1996), *Waikiki Brothers* (2001), *Forever the Moment* (2008), and *Fly, Penguin* (2009). *Rolling Home* was unfortunately a commercial flop, and remains the least-known work by Yim. In contrast, *Little Forest* garnered both critical and commercial success.

Yim thus gained a respectable two commercial successes with *The Whistleblower* and *Little Forest* from the four feature films she directed in the 2010s. And while *The Whistleblower* quickly sold 1.75 million tickets as a commercial picture, the slow-paced *Little Forest* was a sleeper hit selling over 1.5 million tickets in South Korea, despite its relatively low budget. The commercial success of *Little Forest*, which was nearly equivalent to that of *The Whistleblower*, is notable as it resonates with the popularity of other media that functioned to satiate the national desire for being healed in nature. Given this, one might reasonably ask what caused the uneven popularity between *Rolling Home*, *South Bound*, and *Little Forest*, all of which present new contemporary pastoral approaches to national life. I presume that the unevenness among their reception pertains to the peculiarity of South Korean moviegoers' fantasy of pastoralism. In other words, the disparities within Yim's depiction of cinematic pastoralism in the three films make disparate appeals to Korean audiences. In addition, the free-spirited patriarch protagonist of *South Bound* may have proven particularly hard for a younger generation of Koreans to relate to. Portrayed as originally being a political dissident who struggled against the military dictatorship in his youth, and who later in life fought against statists and corporatists in the city, once relocated the main character of the father finds himself in a lone struggle against the land developers on his island. In this regard, while the father's struggle is absolutely ecological, his pugnacious combative brand of pastoralism was arguably entirely unattractive to the healing-oriented audiences.

In terms of *Rolling Home*'s failure to cater to these audiences, Yim blamed herself for miscasting the film's leading actor, Kim Yeong-pil, and failing to incorporate his thespian acting style within her cinematic vision. In this respect, it is clear that Kim's performance does at times disrupt the screen chemistry between him and the female lead, Kong Hyo-jin,[25] whose stature as one of the top actresses in South Korea was startlingly overshadowed in the film. However, I rather find *Rolling Home*'s commercial failure to be in the film's esoteric, Zen-Buddhist philosophical underpinning. Based on the eponymous Korean novel by Kim Do-yeon, the film not only reflects the South Korean cinematic naturecultural turn in terms of its narrative theme, but also offers a series of stunningly beautiful landscapes of the nation, from the mountains, valleys, fields, and coastline to the towering skyscrapers of Seoul. Both a road movie and buddy film between a man and a bull, *Rolling Home* constantly presents the human and bovine companions amid splendid natural scenery within extreme long shots. As such, the aesthetic of the film is somewhat like that of a traditional East-Asian landscape painting that features a tiny dot of a person with or without animals in the middle of vast natural scene. Indeed, one Korean critic has particularly commented upon Yim's preference for medium-to-long and fixed camera shots over moving cameras as a means to magnify the objective effect of the observant lens, just like a documentary film,[26] something that squares with the aforementioned nature-documentarization of reality television. In contrast to the more tumultuous *South Bound*, *Rolling Home* offers a quiet and tranquil spectacle, almost to the extent of conveying a Buddhist meditative experience to its audiences. While the film, therefore, delivers a healing encounter to the viewers, it also somewhat pedantically focuses on the metaphysical lesson that everything, whether pleasure or pain, depends on the state of one's mind. In this regard, despite the palliative power of its style and content, the abstruse Buddhist philosophy of *Rolling Home* failed to appeal to cinemagoers.

In the film, the protagonist, Seon-ho, during his journey with his bull, unexpectedly reunites with his former girlfriend, Hyun-su. She has lost touch with Seon-ho following her marriage to his best friend, Min-gyu, seven years ago, and is now widowed. Having lived as a brokenhearted bachelor for many years, Seon-ho fiercely vents his anger at Hyun-su when he first encounters her in a funeral hall and during her visits to him on his travels. At one point, Hyun-su finally asks him if he has really suffered or if his mind has merely brought the perception of suffering. It is a remarkably important question, but vexingly metaphysical as well, and interestingly this question scene was not in the source novel, but created by Yim, who co-authored the screenplay with Bak Gyeong-hee. The scene seems to have been inserted to help viewers understand Buddhist notions of loss and pain more easily than in the novel, which on one level is extremely symbolic and allegorical, despite being superficially simple. Also in broader terms, although *Rolling Home* is in many ways a faithful adaptation of the source material, Yim makes several other distinct changes. While the novel features the companion animal, a cow, and Seon-ho, a novelist, Yim changes this to a film about a bull and a poet, respectively. Additionally, in the film she gives Korean names to the characters Seon-ho, Hyun-su, and Min-gyu, which have been changed from Paul, Mary, and Peter, who are intentionally named after the American folk trio Peter, Paul, and Mary in the novel. Referencing this, in the film, the three friends are occasionally refer to as Peter, Paul, and Mary in flashback scenes to the band's popular song, "Five Hundred Miles." Furthermore, Yim prefers working in a simpler realist aesthetic and accordingly has confessed that she is not so much interested in allegory or symbolism but inclined toward a strict realist style.[27]

With respect to this concern of the director, the novel is a much more metaphysical encounter than the film adaptation, and at many points within the text it is hard to distinguish whether the events described are dreams or realities. The book takes its narrative form from a serial Buddhist painting,

Ten Ox Herding Paintings, in which a boy monk embarks on a quest with an ox to become enlightened by undergoing ten phases of religious training. In the Buddhist context, the ox symbolizes the meaning and essential nature of being, so each of the ten pictures illustrates the boy variously searching for the ox, tracking its footprints, discovering it, catching it, taming it, riding it, ignoring it, then being ignored by it, returning it to its place of origin, and finally entering into a public square together. Following the phases of the ten pictures, the narrative of the novel *Rolling Home* is structured through Paul's quest with the cow. Initially, Paul leaves his mountain home with the cow to sell her so that his elderly father can replace her with a mechanical plow, and so that he can also spare more time to write novels. However, instead of selling the cow, he begins a journey throughout South Korea along with the cow through which he develops a great affection for the animal, and then also becomes reconciled with Mary in the end.

Notably, the film illuminates the deepening kinship between Seon-ho and the bull by turning it into a sort of male homosocial bond. This creates a contrast with the novel which emphasizes the more complicated dynamics of affection, love, and sexual attraction and stresses the overlapping triangles between Paul, his father, and the cow; between Paul, Mary, and the cow; and between Paul, Mary, and Peter. By equating the man's and the animal's sex, the film constructs a more neutral idea of naturecultural utopia in contrast to the novel's focus on Paul's quest for his true self and spiritual peace of mind in a Buddhist sense. Accordingly, Seon-ho in the film is depicted as more human than Paul is in the novel, in that the former is not as calm, thoughtful, and spiritual. In terms of audience connectivity, for most of the film Seon-ho is arguably too angry, anxious, resentful, and whiny to be attractive to offscreen viewers. He is infuriated with his life, in which he has never been awarded nor recognized as a poet, and constantly beleaguered by his parents, relatives, and peers as an aging lovelorn singleton who never got over Hyun-su. At the outset of the film, Seon-ho is asked by his parents to stop drinking and oversleeping from frustration, to take more care of the bull as would a diligent farmer, and to get married, even if this means marrying a foreign migrant through a commercial brokerage. These personal dynamics of Seon-ho's life are not addressed in the novel at all, and, in this vein, the film emphasizes the character development of Seon-ho relative to the reality of contemporary rural life in South Korea. Perhaps the most crucial point about this setting-up of Seon-ho's personal circumstance is that it contrasts with that of Paul in the novel, who does not undertake his journey to becoming a situationally changed man but a spiritually enlightened one. Also, unlike in the novel, what changes Seon-ho in the film is neither Hyun-su nor the people he encounters on his journey but simply his developing relationship with the bull, whom he names Han-su following the suggestion of a little local girl. During his odyssey, Seon-ho is continually worried about Han-su's frequently bleeding nose, something that occurs due to the fatigue caused by the constant travel, so he tries his best to attend to the bull's comfort and welfare by providing food, drink, sleep, rest and even the opportunity for sightseeing. In Seon-ho's physical contiguity with Han-su as well as his emotional, affective contact with him through his eyes, nose, mouth, torso, tail, and sound, the partnership is depicted as that of equal travel companions. In contrast to the erotic touch that the male novelist adds to describe Paul's complex relations with the cow, Yim instead demonstrates that human–animal companionship is best based on non-erotic affection and she foregrounds the "co-evolving" friendship of the bull and man in the film.

Given the realist tone that pervades the film, Yim was probably initially motivated to adapt the novel into a film not for its topic of Buddhist enlightenment but because of its theme of human–animal companionship. In an interview, Yim also mentioned that she was drawn to Buddhism not for its metaphysical profundity but for its philosophy equating nonhuman animals with humans.[28] And, given that the avid animal-rights activist Yim professes that animal care is her second favorite job next to filmmaking,[29] it is probably no coincidence that *Rolling Home* was her first project focused on cinematizing human–animal companionship after her establishment of KARA (Korea Animal Rights Advocates) in 2009. To follow up this project, she then collaborated with three other directors to make an anthology film on the issue of animal rights entitled, *Sorry, Thank You* in 2011. In this film, Yim writes and directs a segment portraying the conflict and reconciliation between a father and his cat-obsessed daughter, whose passion for protecting stray cats is decried by both him and her female work colleagues. As described at the start of the chapter, this interest in human kinship with animals and the natural world became a consistent topic within Yim's work after *Rolling Home*, such as in *South Bound* and *Little Forest*, and it is the latter of these two films that we discuss next.

YIM'S PASTORALISM II: ECOFEMINIST KINSHIP/ PARTNERSHIP WITH NATURE IN *LITTLE FOREST*

If the focus of *Rolling Home* is a form of naturecultural companionship between a human and an animal that offers a cinematic materialization of Haraway's *Companion Species Manifesto*, *Little Forest* shows how a female college graduate constructs a similar naturecultural relationship with a dog, and with her wider environmental surroundings in a rural mountain village by following Haraway's exhortation to "make kin, not babies!" and taking to heart the idea that it deeply "matters how kin generates kin."[30] Within the film the theme of kinship, whether between humans (such as the protagonist's relationship with her childhood friends) or between humans and their nonhuman natural environment, is given more weight than in the original Japanese film. This Korean version appealed to local audiences who strongly connected with the "healing" ways in which the protagonist, wounded by her experiences of dreary urban life, gradually recovered by entering into a partnership with nature and becoming empowered by human and nonhuman friendships.

While the original Japanese version is composed of four segments, each an hour in length corresponding to the four seasons, and each based on processes of harvesting, cooking, and eating fresh seasonal vegetables, the Korean counterpart particularly accentuates how the protagonist makes food with her friends and shares it with them. In general narrative terms, Yim's remake is faithfully structured after the Japanese original, in which a young woman returns from the city to her rural home, wherein she is overcome by the memory of her widowed mother who suddenly left her behind when she was just a high-school girl. Thereafter she not only starts to farm and cook just as her mother did but is also reunited with her childhood friends and neighbors. In the initial Japanese film adaptation, based on a comic book by Igarashi Daisuke, the protagonist becomes aware of her responsibility to the local community, which is fulfilled not only by her starting a new family through marriage but also by preserving the local rural traditions. Rather than direct the idea of pastoralism toward the specific cause of the immediate rural community, Yim's remake instead inclines toward showing a healthy, organic life in nature, an orientation that served South Korean cinemagoers' interests well.

Yim's *Little Forest* vicariously represents a South Korean notion of contemporary pastoralism, one for which young urban Koreans deeply longed and sought via their pursuit of "healing" in the 2010s. In this vein, the lifestyle of the main protagonist Hye-won in *Little Forest* encapsulates the pastoral fantasy that most urban South Koreans have in mind; growing vegetables to cook and eat, sharing this food and platonic affection with their friends in a serene natural environment. This is shown within *Little Forest* in how Hye-won's life is dominated by her relationships with her childhood friends Jae-ha and Eun-sook, through her growing companionship with Jae-ha's dog, Ogu, and in how she is surrounded by neighbors and relatives who also provide comfort, care, and attention.

However, the pastoral life led by Hye-won is not simply depicted as idyllic and leisurely but as based on diligent hard work, which includes chores such as farming, repairing the house, shoveling the snow, and chopping firewood. In addition, a certain amount of courage is required in the country just to sleep through dark nights dominated by animal roars and to tolerate natural hazards such as typhoons, storms, and heatstroke. Although constantly busy with her physical labor in this cinematic vision of nature, both Hye-won and her friend Jae-ha, who graduated from universities in the city and then went on to initially lead professional lives there, now prefer living in the countryside. Their current happiness as farmers in rural nature is portrayed as based on their exhaustion with the individualistic neoliberal competition that defines contemporary urban life, and demonstrated by elements such as their frequent flashbacks to the anguish of city life. Even Eun-sook, one of the three main characters who works in a small bank nearby and dreams of leaving her home is tired of currying favors with her superior at work. The three friends frequently meet up at Hye-won's house, where they complain about their work, discuss their love lives, and help each other with chores. Their friendship is portrayed as commensurate more with an idea of familial kinship rather than the standard girl–boy–girl love triangle frequently found in Korean drama. In short, while there are conflicts between them at times, these are shown to rarely disturb their close ties, just as within an ordinary family.

Beyond her newly found familial ties with her childhood friends, Hye-won also makes kinship relations within the realm of nonhuman nature. She takes care of and is taken care of by Ogu, the white puppy that Jae-ha brings to keep her company as she maintains a single household life in the isolated country home. Hye-won's bonding with Ogu grows through her always talking, embracing, and playing with him; she even wakes up in an anxious state on a stormy night to hold him tight. In the film, she also communicates with an ox, chickens, potato sprouts, worms in the soil, cabbages, onions, and marsh snails in mountain streams. Further, she grows to think of herself as a plant growing from the seed that her mother sowed in the village. Here the film makes the analogy between Hye-won and a green crop in the soil of her village, both of which are a "little forest" to her mother. Healing her wounds from her inhumane existence in Seoul through her new life in her home village, Hye-won decides to become eternally rooted there, and just like onions that have to be transferred from fertilized soil after being initially sown, Hye-won leaves Seoul to come back home again. In these ways, Hye-won in *Little Forest* is framed as indeed a part of nature, a plant sown in her home village, and kin to the organisms in her mother's "little forest." Hye-won's communion with nature in the film can therefore be read in a true ecofeminist sense, as it not only moved young female moviegoers but also widely echoed the sentiments and aspirations of male and female audiences across various age groups, inasmuch as so many South Koreans dream of escaping from the urban neoliberal nightmare to start new natural lives in similar pastoral settings.

CONCLUSION

This chapter has analyzed *Rolling Home with a Bull* and *Little Forest* as Yim Soon-rye's representative ecofeminist works of the 2010s in Harawayian terms of natureculture. As mentioned above, a majority of films made by Yim during this period are ecofeminist: if *Rolling Home* offers a model of Harawayan human–animal, nature–culture companionship along with *Sorry, Thank You*, *Little Forest* deals with the rediscovery of self in nature and the construction of kinship with/in nature, and not only with human and nonhuman animals but also with plant life and the wider environment as in *South Bound*. Then, in the case of *The Whistleblower*, it is concerned with the scientific appropriation of stem cells extracted from female-human eggs, which is undoubtedly an ecofeminist topic in terms of female biopolitics. Although both *Rolling Home* and *Little Forest* were produced relative to the wider national cultural tenor of naturecultural pastoralism, they still failed to comfort Korean moviegoers who desired to escape the urban disciplines of contemporary life. The retreat of Hye-won sets out a mode of life not bounded by constant self-control and social discipline but filled with affective relationships with the human and nonhuman natural world. While Yim frequently portrays naturecultural pastoralism in her films from the 2010s, the specific pastoral lifestyle embodied in *Little Forest* tallies with the South Korean desire for being healed through nature.

The close reading of *Rolling Home with a Bull* and *Little Forest* provided in this chapter has shown how Yim's work embodies a particular idea of naturecultural ecofeminism. Within her films, not only has Yim Soon-rye portrayed naturecultural pastoralism, but in scenes such as the flashbacks of *Little Forest*, she has demonstrated how neoliberal competition has worn away the souls of South Korean city dwellers. This breadth of portrayal notwithstanding, Yim herself agrees with the evaluation of the film as being overwhelmingly a "healing movie." Yim's notions are entirely reflected in the way in which her characters find healing and happiness through achieving kinship and partnership with nature and in pursuing pastoral lives. While Yim's pastoralism might be the majoritarian way of life in South Korea, it can still be said that her minority-oriented filmmaking in the 1990s and 2000s has been progressively extended to include ecologism and feminism in the broadest sense in the 2010s.

Yim's film style and approach to narrative are less flashy and glamorous than those of her male contemporaries such as Lee Chang-dong, Im Sang-soo, Park Chan-wook, and Bong Joon-ho. Instead, Yim has consistently pursued a straight, inornate, and rather old-fashioned mode of unobtrusive filmmaking, reflected in both storytelling and cinematography, particularly based on slow-paced editing. In her early career, Yim balanced critical acclaim and box-office success with her own, unique interests in alienated social outliers such as within films like *Three Friends*, *Waikiki Brothers*, *If You Were Me*, and *Fly, Penguin*. In the 2010s, Yim has progressively turned to naturecultural cinema, while maintaining her adherence to her signature discreet film style, through the successive films *Rolling Home*, *Sorry, Thank you*, *South Bound*, and *The Whistleblower*, with *Little Forest* highlighting both the critical and commercial potential of her approach. As Yim's most recent film, *Little Forest* successfully narrows down the scope of her diverse naturecultural ecofeminist concerns and satisfies audiences' widespread aspiration for "evasion" from the drudgery of urban life.

Given the success of *Little Forest* and her trajectory of films since 2010, I believe it is possible that Yim has ushered popular South Korean cinema into accepting a new progressive range of ecofeminist issues. Particularly in the current era of Covid-19, ecology and ecologism are no more simply about climate change, nor are they distant from our everyday lives, but are with us all the time. It is thus indeed a matter of urgency that filmmakers increasingly and creatively confront ecological and ecofeminist issues in their work.

NOTES

1. Donna J. Haraway, *Staying with the Trouble: Making Kin in the Cthluscene* (Durham, NC: Duke University Press, 2016), 12.
2. As an editorial board member of a South Korean journal of cultural studies, *Culture/Science*, I proposed and edited a special issue of the journal titled *Stretching Feminism* in the fall of 2020. To stretch the agenda of feminism from the emancipation of biological women to the disruption of the tight global nexus chains between patriarchy, capitalism, and colonialism, particularly in East Asia, I have not only written the introductory article entitled, "Towards a Stretchy Feminism" for the issue in Korean but have also rewritten and presented the same-titled paper in English in the annual conference of the Association for the Asian Studies held in March 2021. See Yun-Jong Lee, "Feminizeumui Hwakjangseongeul Jihyanghamyeo [Towards a Stretchy Feminism]," *Munhwa/ Gwahak* [*Culture/Science*] Vol. 104 (Fall 2020), 23–48.
3. Judith Butler, *Undoing Gender* (New York and London: Routledge, 2004), 204–5. Butler's concept of "vulnerablity" is broached in *Undoing Gender*, but it is more deeply explored in her more recent work, *Notes Toward a Performative Theory of Assembly* (Cambridge, MA: Harvard University Press, 2018).
4. Rob Wilson, "Killer Capitalism on the Pacific Rim: Theorizing Major and Minor Modes of the Korean Global," *Boundary 2* Vol. 34, no. 1 (2007): 115–3, 119.
5. Ibid., 123.
6. Ibid., 124.
7. Maria Mies and Vandana Shiva, *Ecofeminism* (London: Zed Books, 2014), 134.
8. See Seo Dong-jin, *Jayuui Uiji Jagigyebarui Uiji: Sinjayujuui Hankuk Sahwoeeseo Jagigyeblalhaneun Jucheui Tansaeng* [*Volunteering Will, Will to Self-improvement: The Birth of the Self-Improving Subject in Neoliberal South Korean Society*] (Seoul: Dolbege, 2009).
9. Donna J. Haraway," *Simians, Cyborgs, and Women: The Reinvention of Nature* (New York: Routledge, 1991), 3. See particularly Chapter 8, "A Cyborg Manifesto: Science, Technology, and Socialist-Feminism in the Late Twentieth Century," 149–81.
10. Mies and Shiva, *Ecofeminism*, 2.
11. See Haraway's *Staying with the Trouble* and Carolyn Merchant's *The Anthropocene and the Humanities: From Climate Change to a New Age of Sustainability* (New Haven: Yale

University Press, 2020). While Haraway proposes a term, "kinship," in *Staying with the Trouble*, Merchant uses "Partnership."
12. Donna Haraway, *The Companion Species Manifesto: Dogs, People, and Significant Otherness* (Chicago: Prickly Paradigm Press, 2003), 20–1.
13. Haraway, *Staying with the Trouble*, 55.
14. Ibid., 55–6.
15. See Merchant, *The Anthropocene and the Humanities*.
16. See Robert H. Frank and Philip J. Cook, *The Winner-Take-All Society: Why the Few at the Top Get So Much More Than the Rest of Us* (New York: Penguin Books, 1996).
17. Foucault, *Birth of Biopolitics*, 228–33.
18. Ibid., 223, 225, 230.
19. See the website "Our World in Data," <https://ourworldindata.org/suicide> (last accessed 2 March 2001).
20. "Nearly Half a Million S. Koreans Move to Rural Areas in 2018," *Yonhap News Agency*, 27 June 2019, <https://en.yna.co.kr/view/AEN20190627003700320> (last accessed 2 March 2001).
21. John Fiske, *Understanding Popular Culture*, Second Edition (New York: Routledge, 2010), 42.
22. Ibid., 44.
23. For instance, Korean popular culture critics such as Jeong Deok-hyeon and Kim Heon-sik have problematized the voyeurism magnified in South Korean reality shows in newspaper columns many times since the early 2010s. Their logic interestingly parallels that of an ecofeminist, Maria Mies, who remarks that the "pornographic gaze, which thrusts together desire and violence, is the basis for much commercial advertising, for the flood of magazines, videos, TV and other films etc." Mies further comments that "[l]ike the yearning for nature, the yearning for the dissected, naked female body is wholly consumerist [which] cannot be satisfied by interaction with a living person but only by the response to lifeless pictures." Again, I partly agree with Mies's keen perception, yet I would like to point out the difference between the pornographic gaze and the inattentive gaze directed at a nature documentary. While the former is geared toward "sexual arousal" despite its lack of interaction with the object of the gaze, the latter advertently withholds any arousal, whether sentimental or sensational. I see this neutral position rather being developed into the feeling of either "being healed" or empathy, unless the gaze is too intrusive. See Mies and Shiva, *Ecofeminism*, 135.
24. Although Fiske illustrates the popular pleasures with more active user involvement such as rock 'n' roll head-banging, "flashing lights of discos, [use] of drugs (both legal and illegal)," and female readership of romance novels, rather than the inattentive viewership of nature documentaries, the seemingly passive viewership of reality television programming actually demands the active participation of the viewers who "erotically [lose] their separate identities and [indeed] become a new, momentarily produced body that is theirs and theirs alone, that defies meaning or discipline." See aforementioned quotes.
25. Hwang Yeong-mi, "Yim Soon-rye Gamdok Interview: <Ujung Sanchaek> buteo <Namjjokeuro Twieo> kkaji" [An Interview with Yim Soon-rye: from *Promenade in the Rain to South Bound*] *Yeonghwa Pyeongron* [Film Criticism] Vol. 25 (2012), 270–90, 289.
26. Gang Seong-ryul, "Yim Soon-ryle, Nalji Motaneun Penguindeurui Daebyonja" [Yim Soon-rye, a Spokesperson of Unflyable Penguins], *Gongyeongwa Review* Vol. 67 (2009) 222–8, 228.
27. Ibid., 280.

28. Gang Yeong-hee, "Gang Yeong-heega Mannan Saram: Geeureume Daehan Chanyang, [People Whom Gang Yeong-hee Meets: In Praise of Idleness]," *Sahwoe Pyeongron Gil* [Social Critiques], Vol. 98, no. 3 (1998), 146–55, 151.
29. Kim Jin-guk, "Munemi Gogae Neomdeon Sankol Soneyo" [A Rural Girl Crossing the Munemi Hill Turns into a Film Director Crossing Europe: Director Yim Soon-rye], Europeeul Neomneun Yeonghwa Gamdogeuro: [Yeonghwa Gamdok Yim Soon-rye], *Hwanghae Munhwa* Vol. 84 (September 2014), 258–79, 283.
30. Haraway, *Staying with the Trouble*, 203.

CHAPTER 4

The Woman with a Movie Camera: Dismantling the Male Gaze in Yim Soon-rye's *The Whistleblower* and *The Weight of Her*

Margaret Rhee

> **Interviewer:** "And do you feel you have some special responsibilities as a successful and well-known female director?"
>
> **Yim Soon-rye:** "I think my responsibilities as a director are not really in the production stage but more outside of my films, I participated to the movement #metoo and I helped to build the "Centre for Gender Equality in Korean Film", an organization designed to combat inequality in the film industry, because I belong to the first generation of female filmmakers in South Korea and I feel this responsibility."[1]

As one of the few leading female filmmakers in Korea, Yim Soon-rye occupies a pioneering role in the country as her filmmaking and activism sheds significant light on the interventions of the female auteur. Yim has directed, written, and produced over a dozen films including highly recognized and acclaimed feature films such as *Waikiki Brothers* (2001), *The Whistleblower* (2014), *Little Forest* (2018), and others. Along with these feature films, she was a participating director for the Korean Human Rights Commission omnibus film *If You Were Me* (2003) which focuses on diversity issues in South Korea.[2]

When questioned on her feminism in the online interview cited above, Yim commented on her role as a female director, and qualified that her responsibilities are "outside of my films." As such, Yim references her activism around gender and the filmmaking industry, and the #metoo movement in Korea, and rightly highlights these explicit ways in which she has enacted social change. Along with her activism, her films also highlight how Yim helps viewers see through a feminist lens in powerfully nuanced and subtle ways. Feminism, as an ideology, movement, and identity refers to the dismantling of patriarchal culture and practices. Yim's formative activism in the film industry and #metoo are vital and her films also demonstrate how gender equality is cinematically interwoven via the lens of the female director with a movie camera.

Yim's films offer compelling, dramatic, and oftentimes humorous storytelling which also undercuts misogynistic and patriarchal culture through inventive cinematic strategies. In this chapter, I refer to her films as feminist due to the cinematic strategies employed that address patriarchal society, though Yim does not identify herself as a feminist director explicitly. As this collection demonstrates the long overdue respect to female directors such as Yim, I aim to add to this by recognizing the expansive and particular cinematic interventions she makes as a female auteur. In his article "Time's Up for the Male Canon," Shambu Girish offers a feminist critique of the male dominance of auteurism and how auteur status is often a mechanism for furthering the few men awarded this status.[3] Yim as a feminist auteur adds to the discourses of Korean film feminism discussed in scholar Park Hyun-seon's article "South Korean Cine-Feminism on the Move."[4] Yim's films—whether explicitly about gender such as in *The Weight of Her* (2003) or not explicitly about gender-based themes in *The Whistleblower*—show a formative South Korean auteur illuminating feminist cinematic interventions.

Specifically, I focus on the male gaze, labor, and the incorporation of the camera in Yim's films *The Weight of Her* and *The Whistleblower*. Labor and the body are key themes in both films, and Yim dismantles the "male gaze" with the incorporation of the camera as a feminist metaphor and object in her films. In *The Whistleblower*, the film subtly negotiates the politics of women's labor, bodies, and the male gaze through the inclusion of the camera in the film, while *The Weight of Her* tells the story of the struggles of South Korean women high-schoolers and the pressures of a patriarchal society on their bodies and appearance. These pressures around the ideals of a "normative" body have a devastating impact on the professional opportunities and psyches of young women, so leaving male dominance intact. In *The Weight of Her*, I track how the male gaze operates to demonstrate how the female characters' bodies are subject to a gaze under the shadow of the growing economic and aesthetic pressures in a patriarchal pre-IMF Korean society. Here Yim subverts the male gaze by breaking down the walls of conventional cinema through an inventive turn of the camera upon herself, shedding light on South Korean female labor.

The second part of the chapter provides an analysis of the male gaze in regard to women's labor and bodies in *The Whistleblower* (2014). While *The Whistleblower* depicts women as minor characters, their role in the workplace and as egg donors demonstrates the politics of the male gaze, labor, and body through the lens of biotechnology. In *The Whistleblower* Yim uses close-ups of embryonic cells, which evokes a haunting specter of patriarchal norms and power in Korean society. Comparatively examining the two films offers a special opportunity to analyze cinematic strategies employed by a female auteur and a possible intervention as a feminist. Specifically, I point to a minor character in *The Weight of Her* who exhibits non-binary and non-normative gender presentation which is policed in the oppressive setting of the high-school classroom. This same character seems to reappear in *The Whistleblower* in a drastically different depiction of a young gender non-conforming woman or non-binary individual who has a successful career as a camera person. I refer to the character as a gender non-conforming woman or non-binary individual due to not knowing the gender identity of the character. However, the gender non-conformity also transforms the binary between man and woman in the films and is further evidence of Yim's visionary lens. Yim retells and retools the optics of the male gaze within South Korean society through the camera within film.

THE CAMERA AND THE MALE GAZE

> The camera tracks.
> The camera pans.
> The camera is positioned in her hands.

The power of cinema relies on the invisibility of the camera and its absence on screen. Spectatorship is maintained through the pleasure of disappearing into the film in the dream factory. However, when the camera behind the screen appears in front of the camera, it penetrates the screen and renews our understandings of reality without phantasy. The camera, the very instrument that writes the language of cinema, can serve a different and feminist purpose when held by female directors and when incorporated into the scene of the film. Filmmaking with its mechanics of production is largely a male endeavor and a labor industry with men in control of the camera. However, as a female auteur Yim's films illuminate interventions in what we see when a woman is armed with a camera.

Key to this chapter and analysis of Yim's films includes an engagement with the term "the male gaze" as theorized by Laura Mulvey in her formative article "Visual Pleasure and Narrative Cinema" (1975).[5] Mulvey refers to the way in which the camera lens has functioned to "gaze" upon the woman's body for the pleasures of "looking" and voyeurism that take place in film through a male lens. Oftentimes, as argued by Mulvey, this translates to the female body being objectified, sexualized, and evaluated according to patriarchal standards, and extends to the spectators of film. As Mulvey writes:

> In a world ordered by sexual imbalance, pleasure in looking has been split between active/male and passive/female. The determining male gaze

projects its phantasy onto the female form which is styled accordingly. In their traditional exhibitionist role women are simultaneously looked at and displayed, with their appearance coded for strong visual and erotic impact so that they can be said to connote to-be-looked-at-ness.[6]

Mulvey writes about the "pleasure in looking" and how active/male and passive/female is the organization of the film and patriarchal culture. It is primarily the camera that incorporates the male gaze in cinema, and some examples include shots that are leveled at, pan, and close up on women's bodies as if the lens were the eye. Hence the spectators watch alongside the camera, and objectify the women's bodies.

However, what happens when a woman holds the camera? Is the male gaze then different? Can it break and fall apart? Before moving to the utility of the male gaze in Yim's poignant films, consideration of critical engagement with Mulvey's initial theorization of the male gaze is in order. There have been critiques of the male gaze in regard to the positionality of race and sexuality from scholars such as bell hooks with her argument of "oppositional gazes" and Patricia White's critique of the film politics and projecting.[7] While these necessary and useful criticisms mainly pertain to the male gaze itself, Mulvey's theory still offers important cinematic insights into how female directors can utilize and intervene into the male gaze within film.

Within Korean film scholarship, "Escaping the Gaze: The Three Looks in *The Handmaiden*" by Leo A. Ortega outlines the gaze in Park Chan-wook's *The Handmaiden* to demonstrate how female eroticism is represented, objectified, and freed through camera angles, and the shifting of the female gaze.[8] Moreover, the way in which Korean male characters observe and gaze at women has been criticized by feminist film critics including Chung Hye-seung who pointed out the explicit depictions of rape and violence, for example in Kim Ki-duk films such as *Bad Guy* (2002).[9] By considering the male gaze in Korean cinema, we can turn to the ways in which Korean women are depicted and how Korean female auteurs provide new ways of "looking." The male gaze in cinema becomes a site for intervention when a female director utilizes it as Yim does in her films, and sheds light on Korean women in particular. I want also to briefly gesture to Laura Kang's recent book *Traffic in Asian Women*, which demonstrates that the figure of "Asian women" functions as an analytic and has been "distinguished and effaced as subjects of the traffic in women, sexual slavery and violence against women."[10] Kang analyzes Korean comfort women within Japanese occupation and she points out how Asian and Korean women in particular provide specific understandings of Asian women as an analytic. While not centrally focusing on film, Kang's feminist writings ask questions about the ways in which Asian and Korean women as characters and as directors may provide key interventions within the objectified gaze of cinema.

Specifically, Yim's films unpack the male gaze through the exploration of labor and the body, and in doing so, the films illuminate economic opportunities for women and the politics of gender within the compressed modernity of Korean society. The depiction of women and work in film has been analyzed by Barbara Mennel, in European film specifically. She argues, ". . . female characters who embody labor function as sites for critical negotiation over gender roles, agency, and subjectivity in the framework of this argument."[11] The changing depiction of working women illuminates the times when women are not only objects but subjects, and highlights the complexity of these gendered negotiations. However, Mennel does not discuss these depictions in regard to the male gaze, although she cites the body within the formulations. In Yim's films *The Weight of Her* and *The Whistleblower*, labor is the crux in which gender relations and negotiations of the body and power are expressed through the operations and interventions of the male gaze in cinema.

IF YOU WERE ME/THE WEIGHT OF HER

All Cho Sun-kyung wants is a job.

The Weight of Her includes the story of a high-schooler Cho Sun-kyung who is harassed and objectified by her teachers, fellow classmates, men, and larger society in terms of her weight and appearance. Her classmates suffer these same patriarchal circumstances. Sun-kyung is a large, overweight young woman, and we see her struggles negotiating normative ideals of body and beauty within Korean society. Predominant is the pressure to achieve a normative feminine beauty which is understood as a means of social mobility and job placement, and this leads Sun-kyung to the desire and obsession to obtain the costly cosmetic procedure of *sangappul*, double eye folds. The stakes of the normative body and appearance include misogynistic pressures of policing women's bodies, as well as connections to labor and access to professional opportunities. The message is that a normative appearance—thin, beautiful, and with "double eyelids"—leads to a secure future for these young women.

The Weight of Her is actually part of an Omnibus production *If You Were Me*, commissioned by the National Human Rights Commission and focused on the theme of discrimination. *If You Were Me* included filmmakers such as Park Chan-wook, Yim, and up-and-coming directors, featuring vignettes or sketches weaved together to explore one key concept. *If You Were Me* looks at many areas and experiences of discrimination in Korea, including the oppression of Nepalese migrants, and the discriminatory practices and cultures of Korean women in Yim's *The Weight of Her*.[12]

Figure 4.1 Sun-kyung gazing at examples of eyelid surgery on a digital monitor in *The Weight of Her*

The Weight of Her depicts the particularities of the oppression of Korean women and shows these real pressures within the film. Sociological studies on Korean society have identified "attractiveness" as an indicator of social status, so many Koreans believe they need to change their appearance to get a good job, get married, or become an entertainer.[13] Moreover, this patriarchal culture is further enforced as employers "require photos to be included in résumés, and determine if they are willing to work hard by asking them to lose weight or undergo plastic surgery."[14] The normative appearance includes the idea that individuals who don't conform are seen as "lazy or incapable" based on their appearance, with weight bearing especially heavily on young women like Sun-kyung.[15] In 2019 the Moon Jae-in administration called for "blind hiring," in which personal questions and photographs are considered illegal for companies with more than thirty employees,[16] and *The Weight of Her* depicts these social shifts through utilizing the male gaze.

The film opens in a high-school classroom with the news that Sun-kyung's class partner Song (Eun-mi) has lost 12 kilos. The entire class erupts in surprise and awe. Their female teacher tells the students that a priority should always be to look in the mirror in order to get a job, further emphasizing appearance as part of education. Some of the students are identified as needing to lose weight, and Sun-kyung as the endearing protagonist, larger in size, is one of them. Another early scene opens with Sun-kyung in the high-school bathroom and, in her attempt to look attractive and do well in school, gazing at her eyes to apply eyelid tape, fumbling with her hands, and running late to class. In an English class which attests to a subtle critique of the Western and capitalist influence, the male middle-aged teacher asks if anyone can read the board. He notices Sun-kyung still fumbling with the eyelid tape while in her seat. The male teacher walks up to her and implores her to "invest in some surgery" and to lose weight as the class erupts in laughter. Sun-kyung responds that the teacher is also overweight, and he replies, "For men, it doesn't matter if they are fat."

In a humorous back and forth, the dialogue attests to the ways in which weight and appearance pressures bear down on young Korean women. In this scene, the male gaze operates overtly as viewers see the male teacher gaze at Sun-kyung, and in turn we gaze at her too. Through his gaze, he defines and ridicules her because of her body that does not adhere to normative standards, and this cinematic strategy of the male gaze is implemented numerous times in the short film to emphasize patriarchal control. In many ways, Sun-kyung learns to gaze back at herself through this lens via her viewing of the mirror in the attempt to produce a crease on her eyelids.

From the classroom to home the gaze turns inward, as Sun-kyung asks her mother for eyelid surgery. Her mother replies that this is too expensive. We learn more about the challenges to Sun-kyung's quest for funds for eyelid surgery, as the *mise-en-scène* of the home appears to be a modest apartment with three individuals living there. Sun-kyung's father is absent throughout the film, and it appears that she has a single mother who is not attentive. The mother refuses all of Sung-kyung's attempts to change her body—diet camp is out of their family's price range—and encourages her to take some of her older sister's diarrhea pills, and says that she is pretty in her eyes. Beholden to her class status, Sun-kyung has no access to funds for the many procedures and practices women need in order to look attractive for a job in a patriarchal society. Without her mother's support, Sun-kyung attempts to take matters into her own hands and tries to get a job. However, at every instance, her body is again judged and policed while a young female who is normatively thin and feminine receives interest, attention, and positions. In a world organized by weight, appearance, and gender, the unrealistic and patriarchal pressures produce the "weight of her."

Additionally, the male gaze operates intensely in the classroom. Students are publicly weighed and evaluated in the classroom as Sun-kyung and her fellow classmates are gazed upon and criticized in a humiliating and denigrating weighing session at school. In this scene, a different male teacher from the English course gazes at each female student, criticizes their weight, and warns that they won't be able to get a job or get married. While thin women such as Sun-kyung's class partner Eun-mi is praised for her body, she is also offered a disconcerting kiss by the teacher, highlighting the unwanted attention that comes in exchange for praise and acceptance. When Sun-kyung is weighed, the teacher moves her feet roughly with a stick as if she were an animal, and tells her that over 50 kilos won't get her a job. The camera features a long shot of the male teacher and the line of presumably female students who await their turn to be evaluated, so emphasizing the patriarchal control through the male gaze.

It is not only "overweight" young women who are criticized; anyone outside of normative femininity is policed. After Sun-kyung is ridiculed for her eyelid tape in the earlier classroom, another student is policed for their gait when the male teacher gazes at the student and is offended by their "masculine" walk, and orders them to walk again (though the male teacher acknowledges that their weight is acceptable, at least). Here I refer to "all-female" in the context of the "all-girls" school but note that non-binary or transgender identity is not identified. Nevertheless, the scene demonstrates how gender conformity is enforced. As a gender non-conforming student in the all-girls school, the student presumably is female but this is not confirmed. They are also reprimanded for their deep voice. Although the student protests, "I was born like this," their resistance may seem futile within the classroom steeped in patriarchal culture.

While the male (adult) gaze operates with regard to the young high-school students, the film begins to showcase how the male gaze is overturned as Sun-kyung gazes at herself through the male gaze. At many moments of the film, we see an earnest, naive Sun-kyung's attempts to change herself without much success. In a pivotal and haunting scene at home, Sun-kyung gazes at her computer and looks at examples of eyelid surgery. As she scrolls, rows and rows of cosmetically (operated) eyes gaze back at her. This scene features multiple eyes, and the emphasis of the male gaze that follows Sun-kyung in her home prompts her own gazing back at the cosmetic eyes. In her understandable desire to conform to society to survive, Sun-kyung gazes back with desire for the eyes to be her own. As Foucault writes on the gaze and the panopticon, it is almost as if young women like Sun-kyung are gazed upon and disciplined by society, and begin to gaze back at themselves and others through this patriarchal lens.

Forwarding to the end of the film, the male gaze permeates the scene again as we see Sun-kyung interviewing for a job with other young women demurely standing in a row, and being gazed at by middle-aged men. Sun-kyung is ridiculed by the all-male hiring committee for her plastic surgery and the sunglasses she wears to hide it, and she runs out of the interview room. The last scene of the film includes a return to a karaoke setting of a private bar room and the men celebrating the end of their successful job interviews. Different young feminine women are led into the room by a female "madam" to help the men "enjoy the night." The film ends with the men proclaiming the great job they've done and toasting, "To our company and pretty ladies." The storyline and conclusion are clear: the men get jobs with the power to hire and gaze at women. In this world, young women like Sun-kyung seem to have no agency.

FINAL CUT

However, the film does not end there.

As the end credits roll, we see Sun-kyung exit a cafe and the camera pulls back as we hear "Cut." We now see a production set and a film crew. An older male passer-by asks "Who is the director?" When the crew points to Yim who is in the scene, directing and gazing through the camera lens, the man proclaims he can't believe a "fat ajumma" is a film director. "No way!" he exclaims. While the scene is comical, the fourth wall of the narrative is broken as Yim is revealed to be a director to the surprise of the male passer-by. In this brilliant feminist cinematic move and searing critique of patriarchal society, we see how Yim turns the male gaze back on herself and illustrates that even with her power and employment as a director, she is still questioned, insulted, and policed based on her body and size. While Yim herself is near the camera as the director of the film, the power of the camera does not seem to protect her from discrimination. As with Sun-kyung, the man's comments objectify her body and deny her professional accomplishments as a director. In this powerful intervention, Yim demonstrates the discrimination women experience based on their bodies and labor.

I turn to the camera included in this scene during the end credits to point out the significance of its inclusion within the scene. If camera shots help demonstrate the male gaze and the politics of cinema, the camera appearing in front of the camera, along with the director herself, helps intervene in the seamlessness of cinema that is often constructed as monolithic and male. Including the camera in the scene breaks open the film, deconstructing the production of the scene for the viewer, and breaking the male gaze. During the end credits of *The Weight of Her*, the camera is unable to fully protect a woman director from the slings of misogynist comments, yet ultimately Yim as the director tells the story, deconstructing a misogynist culture. The appearance of the camera signifies deconstruction and is a feminist intervention. It is through the vulnerability of including herself as the director who, despite her profession, is still privy to discriminatory comments and policing by patriarchal culture, that Yim's end credits reveal how the film boldly intervenes.

THE WHISTLEBLOWER AND THE CAMERA

While *The Weight of Her* was explicitly about gender, *The Whistleblower* is subtlety so, yet both films feature the camera as a metaphor that deconstructs monolithic nationalistic truth which in turn upholds the male gaze and a focus of the male gaze. *The Whistleblower* is based on the true story of national

Figure 4.2 The character Yi-seul pictured in the background holding a camera in *The Whistleblower*

scientist celebrity Hwang Woo-suk and the fraudulent claims of stem cell advancements in Korea. The whistleblower (Shim Min-ho, played by Yoo Yeon-seok) reveals the truth as part of a large institutional case of fraud.[17] At first sight, the Hwang case evokes key themes such as nationalism, celebrity, biotechnology, and not necessarily gender nor women. However, as the details of the case are uncovered, the role of women as bearers of the oocytes, their untimely deaths, and the labor of women assistants within the science lab offer significant contours of gender within the highly publicized case. This case reverberated not only nationally but internationally, shedding light on Korea's national standing.

This juxtaposition of the camera and the male gaze operates powerfully in the film *The Whistleblower* as the camera deconstructs a monolithic and patriarchal ideal of truth in the name of Korean nationalism. This nationalism may be imbricated with the same patriarchal pressures bestowed on young women in *The Weight of Her* while exalting scientists who are fraudulent like Hwang. As analyzed earlier in this chapter, the camera is symbolic in how it opens up the film and represents power and truth. While in *The Weight of Her* the camera appears only during the end credits when the film pulls back to reveal Yim directing with the production crew, the camera appears frequently in *The Whistleblower*, highlighting monolithic truth as a type of male gaze.

In *The Whistleblower* the main character, Yoon Min-cheol, is an investigative reporter working for the *PD Notebook* TV news program (called *PD Chase* in its fictionalized film version), and played by Park Hae-il who starred in Bong Joon-ho's film *Memories of Murder*. Min-cheol begins to uncover the "truth" surrounding Hwang (called Dr. Lee in his fictionalized film version); his portable camera appears as a character. Through anonymous tips and via a disconcerting account of a man's wife dying after donating her eggs, Min-cheol goes to the site of the clinic to find out more. We see him sitting at the restaurant across the street, casually eating udon. When he sees a nondescript van pull up, he holds the small camera in his hand to open and shoot, and the film provides a close-up of the small monitor which films women running hurriedly into the clinic. Instead of a male gaze, the camera footage aims to document the truth of the women's current circumstances.

However, even with this documented evidence, his fellow producer and his boss, once they learn that the clinic is in collaboration with Hwang who is a figure of "national pride," discourage him from continuing his investigation. Thus, the appearance of the camera within the film in the hands of the *PD Notebook* producer sheds light not only on the realities of evidence or the deconstruction of "national" truth, but also on the challenges of resistance to hegemonic patriarchal culture, despite the camera.

Additionally, Yim challenges the male gaze in *The Whistleblower* as a male character is subjected to a gaze of admiration and power. For example, Hwang Woo-suk is gazed at by multiple audiences throughout the film, and in the opening section he speaks to college students who gaze at him with admiration. Dr. Hwang is not objectified, nor othered, prodded, or policed for his body like the young women in *The Weight of Her*. Instead the male gaze upholds his status as a leading scientist even if this was fraudulent and unearned. The film opens with him on stage, close-up, and shot from the rear of the cavernous room to demonstrate the vast dimensions of a space that holds the many individuals who have come to hear him speak. At the end of his speech, we see flashes of camera lights which signify a male gaze of yet more admiration and power.

Throughout the film Hwang is constantly on a stage, speaking, and gazed at by others. On stage, Hwang recounts an occasion when a *New York Times* journalist told him that "world science communities and media are watching me [Hwang], for successfully creating clinical stem cells from patient somatic cells." The testimony from Hwang includes the words "watching me" and testifies to the significance of the male gaze that upholds men, and instead he asks "humbly" to "keep an eye on Korea instead of me." While Hwang takes photos with disabled children as the cameras flash "national pride," the truth of his fraudulent biotechnological experiments are yet to be uncovered. The male gaze here is at the opposite end of what the women experience in *The*

Weight of Her when gazed upon by individual men of power, which signified the denial of professional opportunities. Thus, the patriarchal culture we see in *The Weight of Her* is the same one that produces someone like Hwang, who holds a powerful position in his labor as a scientist, even if fraudulent.

The Whistleblower unpacks this fraudulent science through nationalistic media depicted as the purveyors of fake news. For example, the scientist is often featured on news media alongside the running titles which represent the official national doctrine. There is a juxtaposition with the grainy footage from *PD Notebook* from a small camera. In the film, the camera, not the news media, is the instrument of truth. The camera represents documentation and truth-telling and does so by deconstructing film through its appearance.

In *The Whistleblower*, the person who holds the camera is a minor female character named Kim Yi-seul—the assistant producer at *PD Notebook*. More significantly, Yi-seul is not normatively feminine; she does not wear dresses or accessories, and instead presents as gender non-conforming, androgynous, and highly competent at her job even as a young producer. In fact, she is nicknamed the "Ace" within *PD Notebook*. There is no male gaze on Yi-seul, and she is seen not for her body but for her mind. Her personality is spunky, smart, quick-witted, and keen. While young, she is respected and supported by her male coworkers and not objectified. Yi-seul holds the camera and records the witnesses throughout the film. While a minor character, Yi-seul is significant in the counter-position that a woman or gender non-binary person can hold a job in the professional world of news and investigative reporting.

In nearly every key scene that depicts filming, Yi-seul is holding the camera. Moreover, in work meetings, she presents to her fellow producers and they listen to her, respect her, and call her the department's "ace." More specifically, as the case around Hwang unravels, Yi-seul holds the camera and is asked by Min-cheol (they are a great team) to interview doctors and experts who criticize Hwang. The camera records the evidence and testimony. As the camera pans out, it depicts Yi-seul holding and filming with the camera that provides information against the scientist. As well as holding the camera, Yi-seul also gestures and briefly gives her opinion after the filmed testimonies.

The women workers at the science lab in *The Whistleblower* are dressed smartly in feminine but conservative blue shirts, professional slacks, and white lab coats. These women do not occupy the top scientist roles but are employed as professional women associates. They all appear to have normative weight and a feminine appearance. While there is no overt male gaze on their bodies, they are asked to donate their eggs and their bodies. In one pivotal scene, the women lab workers in their pristine white coats are standing in a circle and reading papers from their workplace about donating their eggs. They protest among themselves as an indication of the devaluing of their professional status and their bodies. Much as with dissection in early sixteenth-century Europe that drew from women's bodies, the women in the lab are gazed at by the scientist and by culture, not only in an objectification but to be cut open and to give part of their bodies in their labor. With the close-up of the eggs through the scientific gaze, the male gaze permeates into the very intimate insides of the woman's body through the guise of science.

In contrast, Yi-seul with her short hair, gender-neutral clothes, and her boyish voice is the opposite of these women, as she frequently scorns and frowns in response to the injustices she hears from men. When they also investigate the cloned dog Molly who in real life was the only accurate case of the truth of the experiments by Hwang, Yi-seul films Molly holding the camera steady with her two hands. This is a different camera that is heavier and bigger, without a tripod. Yi-seul films the truth about Molly, a dog who is not doing well due to the cloning and is later diagnosed with cancer. The heavy camera symbolizes the heaviness of the truth that Yi-seul holds and the stakes of the documentation. While both are compassionate, Min-cheol, even when hearing the news about cancer, wants the DNA for the investigation. Yi-seul figures out, even though she is not initially believed, that the embryonic stem cells were in fact misidentified as stem cells. Yi-seul's speculation is initially determined to be invalid, but ultimately, she was correct—the scientist conned the whole world. Later, when her thesis is proved right, her partner acknowledges her in a respectful way.

"They never made a single stem cell," testifies the whistleblower Shim Min-ho (Yoo Yeon-seok) and yet the scientist managed to con the world and specifically his lab: "Who here has seen a stem cell. But no one has seen one . . .," says one of the women lab workers to Dr. Shim's wife. Later, Dr. Shim's wife is shown the fraudulent stem cells presented as truth and she believes Dr. Hwang. Following the encounter, she tells her husband that "I saw it with my own eyes," as the fake cloned stem cells were in storage. She still believes Dr. Hwang and this illuminates how the truth is distorted when she views the eggs through the male gaze.

Scholarly articles have articulated the stakes of gender in the issues surrounding the case of Hwang. For example, So Yeon-leem argues,

> the patriarchal structure of family, the myth of economic growth, and the restricted activities of feminist organizations are possible contributors to the invisibility of Korean women. On the other hand, in the practices of bodily technologies such as cosmetic surgery and reproductive technologies, Korean women have been highly visible."[18]

Scholars have pointed out the "socio-cultural factors that motivated a group of women voluntarily to donate their eggs for Hwang's research, despite the hazards of possible side-effects."[19] Yim's film, through her cinematic techniques, exemplifies the intersectional stakes of biotechnology fraud which made women's bodies, professions, and lives vulnerable.

THE STRUGGLE FOR THE CAMERA

At the climax of the film, Yi-seul and Min-cheol approach the scientist and are invited to the university to interview him. The interview is easy to secure, and Min-cheol wonders why the scientist is so open to getting his eleven stem cells tested. However, upon leaving the university building, they realize why, as they are bombarded with media and protestors set up by the scientists. A protestor tries to grab Yi-seul's camera, and a struggle ensues. The scene illuminates the struggle between truth and fraud, and the media's role within the national scandal.

The camera that Yi-seul has slung to her body, and which the protestor tries but fails to pull from her, represents the deconstructed truth at stake. Moreover, Min-cheol also shields Yi-seul when leaving the building and seeing the journalists' cameras. While Min-cheol may do this because of gender, or age and professional hierarchy, the act of covering Yi-seul from the cameras also evokes a protection from the male gaze, knowing how the news cameras would gaze upon her. Min-cheol protects her body by covering her and she is not seen or objectified.

While Yi-seul is a minor character, when armed with a camera she illuminates a feminist take on the stem cell research. Ultimately, Yi-seul provides this truth-telling through offering an analysis broadcast via the web. As she posts the photos that reveal the truth on the web, which changes public opinion about the stem cell research and *PD Notebook*, her colleague says, "You really are the ace." When the injustice of her boss being fired occurs, she says "This is frigging nuts." Yi-seul always speaks out and is the one who reveals the truth through digital media, which changes public opinion in terms of questions of equality.

The plot changes when Dr. Lee Jang-hwan (Dr. Hwang's fictional equivalent in the film) testifies against *PD Notebook* in the national news, and again the mass media headlines demonstrate how national news is not truth. When everyday people watch the news, they exclaim, "Don't they know Dr. Lee is our nation's hope?" The film foreshadows Hwang's demise with some sympathy as he speaks to his cloned dog Molly toward the conclusion of the film, "Everyone looked up to me, I couldn't do it." "I couldn't stop," he says, because the public wanted more from him. "I missed the chance to stop. I missed it." This scene highlights the structural gridworks of South Korean culture that created him, such that Hwang is not solely culpable for his fraudulent behavior. Through this, the film demonstrates that the issue is not just about one individual but about a societal structure that allowed the fraud, and enabled the women's eggs to be used for national research at the sociocultural intersection of biotechnology and national desire.

After a series of struggles, *The Whistleblower* concludes with a successful airing of the program on *PD Notebook* that identifies Hwang as fraudulent. Earlier I indicated that Yim's cinematic technique includes mass media footage which represents nationalistic truth (even though this is not the actual truth but rather reflects the male gaze). In the opposite way, when the *PD Notebook* episode airs it is not seen as a mass media program that is seamless. Instead, the viewer hears and see the edits, the camera, and the production of media. Thus the media is rendered un-seamless as the revelation of production cuts into the media broadcast and depicts the complex space between real and fake through the multiple monitors. Yim offers a representation of truth that is un-seamless and media making as a feminist act of deconstruction. Much like the pivotal end credits scene in *The Weight of Her* that openly reveals the production of the film, the airing of the *PD Notebook* episode dramatically shows the process of media production. In this way, Yim deconstructs the idea of an overarching hegemonic truth through media and ruptures a male gaze that insists on the logics of patriarchal power.

CONCLUSION

Both *The Weight of Her* and *The Whistleblower* demonstrate Yim's cinematic strategies and directorial visions that deconstruct logics of hegemonic truth and the male gaze through explicating labor. In *The Weight of Her*, Yim foregrounds the discriminatory experiences of young women by a culture focused on their objectification and oppression of their bodies, and highlights their inability to move forward in their employment prospects. Yim innovatively breaks the filmic wall by inviting spectators to view the production of the film, and as a female director, Yim utilizes her own body and labor to deconstruct the idea of a monolithic and "seamless" film through revealing the camera within the frame of the film. By revealing the insides of the production, and providing a comical but significant scene regarding her position as a director, Yim further deconstructs the male gaze. Similarly, though in a different way, Yim deconstructs hegemonic or monolithic truth which manifests as the male gaze and nationalism in *The Whistleblower*. Through the insertion of the camera into the film, specifically in the hands of an androgynous character-producer Yi-seul, the camera symbolizes truth-telling in the setting of a nationalistic society that upholds fraudulent truths. Through these cinematic strategies, both *The Weight of Her* and *The Whistleblower* demonstrate the masterful power of director Yim

Soon-rye's vision of an egalitarian society through the reclamation of the female body, labor, and vision—all while armed with her camera.

NOTES

1. Adriana Rosati, "Interview with Yim Soon-rye: I belong to the first generation of Korean women filmmakers and I feel this responsibility," *Asian Movie Pulse*, 14 April 2020, <https://asianmoviepulse.com/2020/04/interview-with-yim-soon-rye> (accessed 1 March 2020).
2. *If You Were Me* directed by Jeong Jae-eun, Yim Soon-rye, Yeo Kyun-dong, Park Kwang-su, Park Jin-pyo, Park Chan-wook (Seoul, S. Korea: Chungeorahm, 2003), DVD.
3. Girish Shambu, "Time's Up for the Male Canon," *Film Quarterly*, Berkeley: UC Press (21 September 2018).
4. Park Hyun-seon, "South Korean Cine-Feminism on the Move," *Journal of Japanese and Korean Cinema* Vol. 12, no. 2 (2020): 91–7.
5. Laura Mulvey, "Visual Pleasure and Narrative Cinema," *Film Theory and Criticism: Introductory Readings*, ed. Leo Braudy and Marshall Cohen (New York: Oxford UP, 1999), 833–44.
6. Ibid., 845.
7. bell hooks, "The Oppositional Gaze: Black Female Spectator," in *The Feminism and Visual Cultural Reader*, ed. Amelia Jones (New York: Routledge, 2010), 94–105. Patricia White, *Women's Cinema, World Cinema: Projecting Contemporary Feminisms* (Duke University Press, 2015).
8. Leo A. Ortega, "Escaping the Gaze: The Three Looks in *The Handmaiden*," *Cinemedia: Journal of the SFSU School of Cinema* (2017); Chung Hye-seung, "Beyond 'Extreme': Rereading Kim Ki-duk's Cinema of Ressentiment," *Journal of Film and Video* Vol. 62, no. 1–2 (Spring/Summer 2010), pp. 96–111.
9. Chung, "Beyond Extreme".
10. Laura Hyun Yi Kang, *Traffic of Asian Women* (Durham, NC: Duke University Press, 2020): 1–25.
11. Barbara Mennel, *Women at Work in Twenty-First-Century European Cinema* (Champaign: University of Illinois Press, 2019).
12. For other scholarship on *If You Were Me*, see David Scott Diffrient's "*If You Were Me*: Human rights discourses and transnational crossings in South Korean omnibus films," *Transnational Cinemas* Vol. 2, no. 1 (2012).
13. Ruth Holliday et al., "Gender, Globalization, and Society in South Korea," *Body & Society* Vol. 18, no. 2 (2012): 58–81.
14. Isabella Steger, Jung Soo-kyung. "Korea's President Wants to Ban Photos, and Questions about Your Parents, in Job Applications," Quartz, 3 July 2017, <https://qz.com/1016682/south-koreas-president-wants-to-ban-photos-and-questions-about-your-parents-and-schools-in-job-applications> (accessed 9 June 2021).
15. Ibid.
16. Kelly Kasulis, "South Korea's new 'blind hiring' law bans personal interview questions," *The World from PRX*, GlobalPost, 23 July 2019, <https://www.pri.org/stories/2019-07-23/south-koreas-new-blind-hiring-law-bans-personal-interview-questions> (accessed 9 June 2021).
17. Jeyup S. Kwak, "Korean Cloning Scandal Movie Examines Patriotic Instincts," *The Wall Street Journal*, 29 September 2014, <https://www.wsj.com/articles/BL-KRTB-6674> (accessed 17 April 2021).

18. Lee So-yeon and Park Jin-hee, "Rethinking Women and Their Bodies in the Age of Biotechnology: Feminist Commentaries on the Hwang Affair," *East Asian Science, Technology and Society: An International Journal* Vol. 2, no. 1 (2008).
19. Kim Sun-hye, "Hwang Woo-suk and his Patriotic Egg Donors: The Mechanism of Voluntarism," in *Narratives and Perspective in Sociology Understanding the Past, Envisaging the Future*, ed. Cheung Siu Keung, Harold Traver, Li Xiuguo, Hong Kong Shue Yan University. Proceedings of the 8th Annual Conference of Hong Kong Sociological Association (2007).

CHAPTER 5

Dropping-Out and Truth-Telling (Both Acts Rather Unpopular): Sovereignty, Biopolitics and Critique of the Nation-State in Yim Soon-rye's *South Bound* (2013) and *The Whistleblower* (2014)

Kim Kyu-hyun

This chapter focuses on Yim Soon-rye's films *South Bound* (2013) and *The Whistleblower* (2014), problematizing the way "politics" is reflected in such a cinematic text as a concern, a problem, or a message. It is intended as an act of critical intervention that challenges or at the very least questions the conventional understanding of the sphere of "politics" (the usual Korean term for politics is *jeongchi*, composed of the two Chinese characters used for "governance" or "rule") as understood in South Korean popular culture. In the latter, the sphere of the political tends to be construed as an exclusive discursive domain of the hyper-masculine educated elite, media opinion-makers, "keyboard warriors," and other anonymous "angry citizens." This domain is then all too easily conflated with the "national public sphere" that determines in substance who gets to be included or excluded as a political agent.[1]

To put it another way, in contemporary South Korean popular culture, hyper-masculinized rage against the "establishment" or the "system," or a "movement," in which mobilization of the "people" into crowd assemblies, a pattern sometimes disturbingly similar to the mobilization of "people" under the Japanese colonial rule or the Park Chung-hee military dictatorship, is often constituted as the hegemonic means of infiltration and domination of the sphere of politics. In truth, this narrow sphere of "politics" cannot adequately capture politics, not "governance" (*jeongchi*), but "relations of power" (*gweonryeok gwangye*), of everyday Korean lives in its variegated permutations. To give concrete examples, in South Korea, to speak out urgently against the physical abuse of cats and dogs, or to put a Post-It message in the Gangnam subway station with a brief scribble that reads, "I Could Have Been You, I am So Sorry" in the aftermath of the so-called "gender killing" incident of 2016, must be acknowledged as significant and meaningful political acts. It is no less "political" than debating in public whether Roh Moo-hyun was truly a great president of ROK or voting for a particular candidate because he or she belongs to a "progressive" political party.

South Bound and *The Whistleblower* do display, I concede, the conventionally hyper-masculine or patriarchally nationalist rhetoric. However, at the same time they also illustrate the modes of resistance, criticism, and elision of such rhetoric that render these two films just perceptively but not overwhelmingly "off-kilter" compared to other socially or politically engaged genre films (comedy, melodrama, or investigative films noirs, and so on) currently produced in South Korea. Since hyper-masculine nationalism appears mostly in the form of pervasive rhetoric (and less in the actual behaviors of the characters), one might construe this as evidence that Yim's true intentions might have been in the resistance, critique, or elision of this rhetoric in the substance of lives depicted in the films. However, since hyper-masculine nationalism in fact functions most powerfully as a rhetoric seeking to colonize the public sphere and "lifeworlds (*Lebenswelten*)" of the residents of South Korea, one could also argue that these films ultimately become subservient to it, without the characters and storylines engaged in the corresponding counter-rhetoric. This chapter hopes to show that, while these two films inevitably show the traces of compromise with Korean nationalism and its attendant ideologies/discourses of patriarchy, masculinity, and devouring of the "public" by the state, there are also sufficient elements in them that suggest post-nationalist possibilities of addressing fundamental questions of human lives in the South Korean context, including those involving the environment, gender equity, and human (and animal) rights.

Needless to say, politics and cinema have always been intimately intertwined with one another, from the earliest incarnations of the latter as a distinct artform. D. W. Griffiths's *Birth of a Nation* (1915) sought to develop its cinematic language to the next level, all the while disseminating what is today recognizable as an overtly racist message. The path-breaking aesthetics of the silent classics of the Soviet Union such as *Battleship Potemkin* (1925) cannot be understood separately from its ideological commitment to the Communist revolution, although one need not have been a Communist or a socialist to be enthralled by the (formally) revolutionary *mis-en-scene* and editing techniques propounded by Sergei Eisenstein. There can hardly be any doubt that, as Claire Molloy and Yannis Tzioumakis suggest, there is an "enduring connection between cinema and politics where films continue to play a role in the dissemination of political messages, shape the collective memories of past events and inform political agendas."[2] However, as any serious observer of the global commercial cinema scene would notice immediately, the relationship between politics and cinema is seldom "straightforward." Even for those cases in which a motion picture was explicitly produced to serve as a propaganda piece, the film in question might be subject to the kind of readings never intended by the filmmakers and generate an entirely different political meaning for particular viewers.

South Korea is a vibrant democracy today, having achieved its transition to a civilian democracy from a military dictatorship through a series of landmark citizens' movements and painstaking structural reforms in the late 1980s and early 1990s. This process also inevitably politicized South Korean cinema. Critical features and documentaries dealing with the subject matter and perspectives hitherto shut out by the state censorship flourished, and these elements eventually worked their way into the mainstream commercial feature films. By the 1990s, the retreat of the military dictatorship and its "militarized modernity," regimented, mobilized, and hyper-masculine, had begun to shift the mainstream culture of Korean society, best exemplified by the expansion of women's political voice.[3] However, I would argue that widespread democratization and successful inclusion of the multitudes of voices into the cinematic realm has had its downside, or more precisely, has created its own spaces of exclusion, or blind spots. I do not wish to dwell on the film industry's alleged lack of inclusion and democratic consciousness. If anything, the episodic evidence suggests that South Korean films have done an arguably better job of opening up their class, ethnic, and cultural boundaries to the marginalized and excluded—foreign migrant workers, temporary workers, sexual minorities, the disabled, and so on—than the rest of Korean society.

Yet in many popular cultural products, not just cinema, democratization is sometimes codified as just one more instrument of national construction or development. This is reflected in the designation of student activists killed in the course of street demonstrations or those who immolated themselves in public acts of suicide as *yeolsa*, a term meant to be used for a patriot who has sacrificed themselves for the nation-state (in its original designation, the king). In terms of mass self-mobilization and expression of nationalist pride, even more than the 1988 Seoul Olympics, the World Cup soccer games of 2002 indicated a new level. Since then, various political institutions and agents have attempted to tap into and manipulate the energy of mass self-mobilization to push through their agendas, or even worse, substitute the top-down, "militarized modernity" of the previous decades with the newfound populist hegemony of the "people."[4]

Equally alarming are the ways in which certain efforts on the part of members of the national public sphere to expand the boundaries of the political have been met with resistance, condescension, or hostility. "Politics" in South Korea still very much remains the province of the state bureaucracy, the national assembly, and discursive institutions such as the news media. The citizens and their "everyday concerns" need to be mobilized into visible collective actions such as "candlelight protests (*chotbul siwi*)," which some Korean opinion-makers have consistently romanticized as a true expression of the "will of the people," before they are taken seriously as legitimate political action.[5] The New Korean Cinema, especially in its generic manifestation as films noirs and crime thrillers, has attempted to draw upon this new surge of democratic consciousness among filmgoers, often portraying the elite businessmen, attorneys, police, national assemblymen, and even the Blue House bureaucrats as corrupt villains. Ryoo Seung-wan's *Veteran* (*Beterang*, 2015) and *The Unjust* (*Budanggeorae*, 2010) are two representative examples of a police action thriller and a film noir, respectively, making use of this modality of political criticism and civic engagement to propel their narratives and build emotionally powerful set-pieces. And yet, as we can see, for instance in Kim Byung-woo's *The Terror: Live* (*Deotereolaibu*, 2013), a "subversive" political critique against these agents of government and the economic elite could itself degenerate into a cliché. Such devices exist mainly to push emotive buttons on the part of the viewers rather than to genuinely stimulate the latter toward critical reflection of their own agency in the political process. These "political thrillers" could provide Korean viewers with a fantasy experience in which their own responsibility as sovereign citizens is erased, leaving them to enjoy the spectacles of fistfight, explosion, car chase, and other violent mayhem as well as those of the powers-that-be brought down, without ever acknowledging their complicity in putting these powers-that-be in their positions in the first place.

Yim Soon-rye, who debuted with a brilliant and still devastating critique of South Korean (militarized) masculinity, *Three Friends* (1996), has always been at the forefront of advocation for human rights, as her participation in the *If You Were Me* project (*Eo-tteon si-seon*, 2003), produced by the National Commission on Human Rights, indicates. In the latter portmanteau film Yim contributed a gently ironical and self-deprecating take on "lookism," specifically the way (male) Koreans tend to look down on women who do not fit in with their image of standardized beauty. She playfully inserts herself into her episode as a director, à la Alfred Hitchcock, observing the life of a young high-school graduate struggling to get a job against the frowning, negative appraisals of her body weight, small eyes, and other "unattractive" features. She even inserts a pointed shot in which an onlooker comments, "[Yim] does not look like a movie director." She also turned a sharp yet compassionate eye to the evolution of social life in a regional community, specifically the hot springs resort town Suanbo, in the feminist-tinged musical drama *Waikiki Brothers* (2002).

It is likely that, upon adapting the popular Japanese novel *South Bound* (2005) by Okuda Hideo into a Korean film, Yim was expected to bring her compassionate, localist sensibility to the project. In the novel, Uehara Jirō, an eleven-year-old boy, living with a family barely managed by an allegedly former radical paterfamilias, is forced to relocate from Tokyo to Iriomote Island in Okinawa. On the island, Uehara's father gets involved in the environmental protection movement against the forces who want to develop the local areas for tourism. Still, the novel is primarily constructed as a *Bildungsroman* with Jirō as a protagonist, observing his father and other family members rehabilitate their ties of kinship through hard-bitten circumstances of having to survive on Iriomote Island. While the island is not exactly presented as an idealized, utopian site, it remains a literary trope in which the Uehara paterfamilias's stance of "dropping out" from society is partially, if not entirely, vindicated.

The Korean film version, as many have noted, is centered on the Uehara father, called Choe Hae-gap (played by Kim Yun-seok), rather than his son, although its narrative—starting with Nara's (Jirō's Korean equivalent, played by Baek Seung-hwan) trouble with the school bullies, the boy's involvement with Choe's younger friend Man-deok (played by Kim Seong-gyun) who gets embroiled in a quasi-terrorist plot to punish the national assemblyman Kim Ha-soo (played by Lee Do-gyung), a villainous figure behind the plan to turn Choe's hometown island, Deulseom, into a gentrified resort, which in turn results in the Choe family returning to their father's old home in the island, uprooting their lower-middle class lives in Seoul—follows the novel rather closely. Again, in the film version the state is rendered a clearly visible presence, in the form of two hapless government agents (played by Joo Jin-mo and Jeong Moon-seong) assigned to keep Choe, as a potential "subversive," under clandestine surveillance. These two government agents serve as comedic foil as well as a form of Greek chorus in the film. They are two of the more interesting characters in the film, showing an arc of personal growth as they end up developing sympathies with Choe's fight against the corporate developers and using their skills as surveillance agents help the latter and his family in coping with the thugs sent by the corporate villains.

Indeed, the stronger presence of the state in this Korean film version is impossible to miss, even if much of it is presented as sources of humor. Choe's character in the film is an independent documentary filmmaker shown to be screening a film which criticizes the government practice of using fingerprints in issuing national identification cards. In an early, character-establishing scene, Choe is seen arguing against a group of irate soccer fans in his wife's eatery, when he abruptly turns off a soccer match between a Korean and a foreign team broadcast on TV:

A soccer fan: Aren't you a Korean too? Don't you have any patriotic spirit?
Choe: What bullshit. What kind of patriotism returns every four years [just in time for the World Cup games]?

Choe is also clearly hostile to his former "comrades" in the student movement, seen to have become well-established as institutional political figures, either as national assemblymen, journalists, or citizen's activists. Their conspiratorial outlook and willingness to manipulate Man-deok for their scheme to bring down Kim Ha-soo are met by suspicion and later outright condemnation by Choe. The latter shows little respect for the police schools, or government institutions including the national pension service (even though one local policeman, similarly to the surveillance agents, eventually becomes his ally).

It is open to debate whether we would want to characterize Choe's stance as negatively defined apoliticism ("Leave me out of any politics and state-related affairs!") or anarchism ("There should be no institutionally legitimate form of state authority and I recognize none of such forms of authority.") Either way, he is taking an active political stance by rejecting and struggling against the sinews of state power: apoliticism, not to mention anarchism, is no less an expression of political stance than a thoroughgoing commitment to a particular political ideology or any form of power distribution such as a constitutional democracy. One must paradoxically make a great effort—and actively struggle against state power—to reject or escape state power in a modern nation-state, much less one like South Korea constantly under the threat of war. To "drop out" from politics in the Korean context (also in the Japanese, American, or European contexts) means not a passive, peaceful, "do-nothing" life but a life driven by sustained struggles, as indeed Choe's life is in the film, against the state's biopolitical governance, its constant surveillance, mobilization, and enforcement of the "duties of the sovereign citizens."

While the South Korean media, in a truncated summary of the film, seems to have settled on "anarchist" to describe Choe's political ideology, director Yim's sympathy with the latter's unpopular stance in *South Bound* is consonant with her sustained interest not so much in those suppressed by the state for overtly ideological or political reasons but in those rejected, unacknowledged, and unaccepted by the state, beginning with many Korean women. The designation "anarchist'" suggests that Choe's positionality is incorporated into the existing matrix of political positions as defined by one's proximity or engagement (or lack thereof) with the South Korean state. It excludes the agents, or simply "bodies," without any public recognition of their agency, that nonetheless exist in Korean society and are often recalled in public discourse to serve as fodder for discursive contestations. Political theorist Giorgio Agamben, drawing upon Michel Foucault's concept, has explored the relationship between "bare life" and "biopolitics," the life that precedes its recognition as a member of a political community predicated on the claims of national sovereignty. He provocatively suggested that the concept of "human rights" in modern politics is in fact a consequence of the realm of politics expanding to encompass "bare life." In the modern world, political subjectivity is defined through national sovereignty, including democratic politics geared toward expanding political rights of the citizenry. Few can escape the biopolitical reach of the nation-state (and conduct their lives as "purely" bare lives), whether it is democratic or fascist-totalitarian in nature. This unprecedented level of biopolitical reach, instead of giving rise to totally enfranchised human citizenry, resulted in global problems such as those of refugees who fall in the interstices of international politics and, most frighteningly, mass killings of "stateless" people during the Holocaust and the "extraordinary rendition" of detainees from the American Guantánamo Bay prison. Agamben quotes from Hannah Arendt in articulating this conundrum for modern politics:

> The conception of human rights . . . based upon the assumed existence of a human being as such, broke down at the very moment when those who professed to believe in it were for the first time confronted with people who had indeed lost all other qualities and specific relationships—except that they were still human.[6]

Echoing Arendt's observation that human rights as we understand could only be sustained by nation-states (which, he notes, might not have indicated her acceptance of such a situation as a norm), Agamben analyzes the most fundamental historical source for the universal conception of human rights, the Declaration of the Rights of Man and of the Citizen (1789). While this document indeed explicitly recognizes "bare life," i.e., that a person (*l'homme*) born into the world and possessed of no other qualification serves as a source of human rights, it also codifies, in its section on the rights of the citizen (*citoyen*), national sovereignty as the site and instrument through which these human rights are to be realized.[7] Now a modern state, superseding by many orders of magnitude the at-the-time hyper-aggressive French Revolutionary state of late eighteenth century in its reach and capacity of the technologies of surveillance and discipline, maintains the fiction that "*birth* immediately becomes *nation* such that there can be no interval of separation between the two terms."[8] Agamben argues that Nazism and the Holocaust were the most abject example of a modern state employing this (il-)logic to declare millions of people as simply "non-humans" in legal and political terms, thus justified in killing them *en masse*. His theory compels us to contemplate the dangerous possibility of a modern democratic state that refuses to question this conundrum of "human rights" as conceptualized under the historical context of prioritizing national sovereignty behaving as indifferent, oppressive, or even murderous toward some "excluded" living bodies as much as its "fascist" or "totalitarian" counterpart.

Yim Soon-rye's adaptation of *South Bound* makes the problems of the modern state and national sovereignty more explicit than Okuda's source novel. As I have observed, Choe Hae-gap's stance is more overtly critical of the state. Instead of rhetorically mouthing the usual disparagement of "politics as usual," Choe pushes the surveillance agents to tear up and throw away their own national I.D. cards, and aggressively rejects political machinations of his former "movement (*undonggweon*)" comrades. Throughout the movie, Yim clearly illustrates multiple instances of micro-exercises of power from the Korean state to which any ordinary Korean person would be subject. Her film is exactly "political" in the areas that a mainstream Korean film is "non-political," i.e., those sites that depict school lives of children, rigidly hierarchized and prone to masculine violence, the everyday survival of the rural elderly, the manners in which the police would or would not act on what they construe to be an instance of "illegal" behavior, and so on. The fact that her film was considered "irresponsibly" hostile to the state by some Koreans is indicated by the complaints lodged to the film by various government agencies including the Korean Broadcasting Service and National Pension Service.[9] One of the strengths of *South Bound* is that, while these depictions of the workings of the Korean state are meant to be taken as humorous at their face value, they do remind viewers of the constant presence of the Korean state in their everyday lives in such a way that they cannot reduce everything they see into positions on the spectrum of "left" and "right."

However, in the end, *South Bound* feels compromised, possibly due to the fact that Yim was constrained from presenting her unfettered interpretation of the source novel. It appears that the film's star, Kim Yun-seok, imposed his own vision of the character and the film (he also served as a co-screenwriter), prompting Yim to leave the project, only to return and complete it following the distributor Lotte's mediation among her, Kim, and the producers (who had apparently put their trust in the lead actor). Watching the film, it is difficult to avoid the impression that Choe Hae-gap is increasingly portrayed as a political hero in the conventional "movement activist" mode. His wife, An Bong-hee (played by Oh Yeon-soo), a patient, loyal spouse throughout the film, re-enacts their student-day struggles by making Molotov cocktails and throwing them at the police in the climactic confrontation. Kim is a talented and persuasive actor, but his Hae-gap has few moments of self-reflection: frankly, he sometimes comes off as a self-righteous patriarch, not that much removed from a typical "586" *kkondae* (the Korean equivalent of an American "boomer"). This is also reflected in his relationship to male violence. While he thankfully refrains from attempting to instill in his son the typical Social Darwinist mores of hyper-competition ("play dirty to win"), he himself ultimately resorts to acts of micro-aggression as well as physical assault as a means of resolving a problem at hand. In the end, Hae-gap is portrayed as a suitably patriarchal "political leader" for a new generation of Korean kids, presumably more environmentally conscious and communally oriented than his opponents. The ending of the film also appears to place the task of rearing her siblings on the shoulders of the oldest daughter Min-joo (played by Han Ye-ri), a typical behavior for socially irresponsible parents.

Yim's next feature film project, *The Whistleblower*, is a densely plotted, documentary-style exposé of the notorious Hwang Woo-suk scandal (2005–2006) in which the allegedly pioneering research into stem cell replication by a renowned scientist at Seoul National University was revealed to have been a hoax, despite his team's research results having been accepted as legitimate by *Science* magazine and other international academic institutions. Eventually Hwang and his team were revealed to have committed many serious violations of medical and scientific ethics.[10] In some ways, Yim, who had shown a consistent level of commitment to human rights concerns over the years, was the logical choice to tackle the dramatization of this instance of the abuse of scientific authority. The film, scripted by Lee Chun-hyeong, adopts the modality of a political thriller with an investigative reporter as its protagonist (cf. *All the President's Men* [Alan J. Pakula, 1976]; *The Pelican Brief* [Alan J. Pakula, 1993]), here modeled after an amalgamation of producers of the real-life investigative news program *PD Notebook* and played by Park Hae-il. The film fabricates the character of a key whistleblower (Shim Min-ho, played by Yoo Yeon-seok) who starts the ball rolling by confessing to the fictionalized *PD Chase* program producer Yoon Min-cheol (Park) that the movie's Hwang equivalent, Dr. Lee Jang-hwan (played by Lee Kyoung-young), had faked the result of cloning human stem cells.

As such, *The Whistleblower* tries to have it both ways as a critique of hypermasculine nationalism and a rehabilitation of that nationalism by way of promoting citizens' democracy. The nationalist rhetoric is rather obviously emblazoned in the earlier exchange of dialogue among the *PD Chase* producers that starts with the question, "Between truth and national interest, which do you think is more important?", in turn answered by the statement, "truth will ultimately lead to promotion of national interest," and culminating in the declaration that "truth *is* national interest." One gets the sense that either the screenplay originally had a clearer trajectory toward rehabilitation of scientific nationalism, or the nationalist rhetoric was deployed strategically as an alibi against the potential criticism that *The Whistleblower* is denigrating pursuits of national interest. Indeed, this was the very kind of attack that Hwang's supporters and followers levied against the journalistic investigators and critics of Hwang in the scientific community during the unfolding of the scandal.

However, Yim makes sure that her film consistently subverts the standard expectations of a crowd-pleasing blockbuster in which nationalist heroes fighting against corrupt government agents and the economic elite are valorized. First of all, as was so in the real-life scandal, a large proportion of the "democratic citizenry" is seen as almost blindly venerating and supporting

Dr. Lee/Hwang, who actively engages in media politics, including a disturbing, theatrical manipulation of the imagery of disabled children to portray himself as a national hero (as expressed in his dialogues, "Please do not look at me, Lee Jang-hwan, but at the Republic of Korea," "I will make these children, future leaders of the Republic of Korea, stand on their feet [by curing their disabilities]," and so on). The Korean "people" turn against Min-cheol and his crew: they hurl eggs at them, and even hold a scene of candlelight vigil in support of the errant scientist. Moreover, Yim, unlike what a director of a typical investigative thriller might have done, starts the narrative by focusing on the illegal sale of human ova and by painstakingly showing how ethically grave Lee's violation of the female bodies of his own research team was.

While Min-cheol and his annoyingly perky female assistant Yi-seul (played by Song Ha-yoon) are conceived as largely conventional characters, engaging in humorous banter and light insults, the psychological and social toll on Min-ho, the whistleblower, and his wife Hyeon-gyeong, for attempting to speak truth to power, is depicted in an intimate, *cinéma-vérité* style, with layers of revelations in the narrative concerning the true nature of duplicity and cover-up involved in keeping Dr. Lee's project afloat. Likewise, Yim, without demonizing Dr. Lee as an evil, sociopathic villain, dedicates an unusual amount of attention to his potential and real victims: not only the disabled children and their duped parents, the violation of whose emotions surely cannot be adequately compensated by the law, but also animals subject to cloning experiments. The film depicts with compassion Molly, a cloned dog once touted as a trophy evidence for Dr. Lee's brilliance, now riddled with cancer and dying alone, neglected by its human caretakers. The sequence in which Min-cheol and Yi-seul locate and observe Molly's sad state is indeed one of the most heartbreaking scenes in the entire film. In the way Agamben's

Figure 5.1 *The Whistleblower:* the characters find Molly the Dog

modern state might be capable of subjecting certain bodies that do not fit in with its category of "healthy bodies" deserving to be "members of the nation" to the category of "mere lives" bereft of sovereign rights, the South Korean government and its sponsored client Dr. Lee/Hwang could couch ruthless exploitation of the female, the disabled, the young, and the non-human bodies under the rubric of "pursuing national interest."

As I have pointed out above, however, *The Whistleblower* does not quite stay focused on its gendered and "bare" lives. Although the film does faithfully recreate the vistas of many "ordinary citizens," such as the young scientists writing on the website BRIC and contributing their share to the exposure of Hwang's deceptions, it ultimately gives primacy to Park Hae-il's investigate journalist as a male democratic hero, again very much in the mold of the cultural imaginary of '80s democratization politics. The film does not end with a serious reflection on the relationship between truth and politics but with Min-cheol defiantly walking toward his next news source, invested with the role of "cleansing" the national community of the corrupt and lying "bad apples" like Dr. Lee. This formula repeats itself in *The Whistleblower* as well as in *South Bound*. What gets effaced is the truly tough question about the ethical responsibility on the part of the democratic citizenry.

I certainly do not wish to downplay the significance of mass protests, including the candlelight protests, and other particular forms of democratic political expression in South Korea. *The Whistleblower* illustrates the danger of such acts of self-mobilization degenerating into a form of personality cult (unfortunately even one devoted to some genuinely popular political leaders such as the late Roh Moo-hyun) or an "angry mob." Judith Butler, among others, has presented an incisive critique of how this type of "gathering of people in a public square" could challenge our conceptions of popular sovereignty and the attendant assumptions about what type of collective actions may be designated as "democratic." In the contemporary world, many exclusivist, discriminatory, even some overtly fascistic movements freely make use of the rhetoric of popular sovereignty ("will of the people") to justify their policies. Butler's response to this conundrum is that we acknowledge that many popular assemblies, sometimes organized around the principle of simply "showing up (appearance)," are performative (that is to say, not always discursive) in nature, and therefore do not always correspond to the ideational construal of them as "expression of the will of the people." At the same time, precarity of the conditions for those who appear collectively must be recognized as the core trait of such acts. In other words, the question of "who gives the rights to these people to do this?" should never distract us from "what is happening to these people?"[11]

The widely accepted American social imaginary that Butler means to problematize is the idea of an absolutely autonomous individual who in reality lives under the conditions of accelerating precarity. At worst, the American Republican right wing completely negates the everyday existence of precarity for American people in favor of the rhetorical invocation of "American democracy" and "rights of the individual," no matter how destructive in material life the latter rhetoric becomes. U.S. Senator Ron Paul's suggestion, cited by Butler, at a 2011 presidential election fundraising conference that those who cannot or choose not to pay for privatized health insurance should *just die*, was allegedly met with a shout of joy that rippled through his audience. Butler astutely observes that this "joyous shout" would be akin to the one "that usually accompanies going to war or forms of nationalist fervor."[12] One could argue that Yim's two films engage in the soft (and perhaps compromised) but resilient critiques of hyper-masculine nationalism by engaging with the South Korean equivalent of the myth of autonomous individual for Americans, the "default democratic citizen," a masculine, militarized "Korean" existing merely to pursue national interest. Both *South Bound* and *The Whistleblower* attempt to illustrate negative outcomes of the "democratic" agents faithfully (naturalized, for instance, in the form of a military salute barked with a call, "Loyalty! [*Chungseong!*]" by the Korean police, soldiers, and, if needed, female K-pop idols) executing their nationalist agendas in those circumstances no longer attributable to the authoritarian dictatorship. In addition, Yim refuses to demonize or denigrate the villains of the films, government agents engaged in the surveillance of ordinary citizens, Dr. Lee and his followers, and so on, recognizing that "we" could easily become "them."

Butler has argued for a bodily dimension of political action, arguing that politics cannot be reduced to its discursive components. Likewise, the dialogues and narratives of both films under discussion here express merely a part of what these films reveal as "political." The "little touches," i.e., affective microeffects of the film's visual language, as well as articulations of the characters that at first glance do not seem to advance the film's ideological agendas, are what gives Yim's works their distinctive flavor. Perhaps the very affective ambivalence of the ways in which these films play out their politics might be what makes their messages more complex, thoughtful, and interesting, even if these films for precisely that reason refuse to become pleasurable fantasies of venting political anger at the powers-that-be. To cite an example, in *South Bound* Hae-gap faces down a motley crew of baseball bat-carrying thugs, an excavator, and development company honchos descending upon his home, determined to demolish it according to the "law." His country home momentarily turns into a site of recreating the anti-authoritarian democratic struggle of '80s, wherein Hae-gap's superior masculinity and strength of ideological beliefs elevate him to the status of an *undonggweon* hero. Yet, as the sequence plays out, Yim deflates Hae-gap's heroism by having him rather quickly overcome by the thugs. Due to his ingenious plan, the excavator is also disabled, and the fight ends in an uncomfortable draw. The site is soon abandoned, drenched in rain, for Hae-gap's family and kind neighbors to pick up the pieces. The overall mood is melancholy, and when Hae-gap's little daughter wails upon finding her pet goat dead, the viewer is induced to feel anger at least partly at Hae-gap. Was this bloody, "macho" display of his heroism really necessary? I for one felt that the ambivalent quality of this sequence would be far more appropriate for a narrative about a Korean man deciding to "drop out" and actively or passively taking him out of the nation-state's reach, rather than that of the Molotov cocktail-throwing finale of the film. If he wanted to be a "hero" to those unenfranchized and excluded (rather than settling down with the self-righteous replay of his "glory days" as a student activist) in South Korea, he should have realized that beating up the "bad guys" cannot lead to a real solution.

Figure 5.2 *Southbound:* the aftermath

In conclusion, *South Bound* and *The Whistleblower* straddle the conventional genre-oriented domain of the formulaic articulation of "angry" democratic citizenry against the corrupt, greedy, or incompetent institutions and the elite, on the one hand, and that of a subtler type of political critique, in which the usually suppressed and unarticulated post-colonial and post-nationalist desires of South Koreans, seeking to decenter or elide the hegemonic hyper-masculine narratives of the South Korean nation-state, are acknowledged, on the other. This balancing act is not always successful, sometimes resulting in "neither here nor there" outcomes, but few other Korean directors have so consistently explored these interstitial spaces between the conventional democratic nationalism of New Korean Cinema and the alternative modes of articulating one's political and social being in the context of modern Korean history. Herein lies, in my view, one of the true strengths of Yim Soon-rye's filmmaking.

NOTES

1. I have previously discussed the formation of the national public sphere in nineteenth-century Japan that sought to cut across class and status differentiations and concurrently gave rise to a modern nation-state in my book *The Age of Visions and Arguments: Parliamentarianism and the National Public Sphere in Early Meiji Japan* (Cambridge, MA: Harvard Asia Center Publication, 2007).
2. Claire Molloy and Yannis Tzioumakis, "Introduction," in *The Routledge Companion to Cinema and Politics*, ed. Yannis Tzioumakis and Claire Molloy (London, New York: Routledge, 2016). 1.
3. The term "militarized modernity" is borrowed from Moon Seung-sook's *Militarized Modernity and Gendered Citizenship in South Korea* (Durham, NC: Duke University Press, 2005). See, for instance, Yun-Jong Lee's "Between Progression and Regression: Ero Film as Cinema of Retreat," in *Revisiting Minjung: New Perspectives on the Cultural History of 1980s Korea*, ed. Sunyoung Park (Ann Arbor: University of Michigan Press, 2019), 223–46, for a discussion of how South Korean films in the period prefatory to democratization, i.e., the 1970s and '1980s, focused on eroticized female bodies, vacillating between a progressive critique of mainstream social mores and regressive self-orientalization in service of patriarchal nationalism. This mode of erotic cinema had precipitously declined in 1990s, yet had left legacies in the *auteur*-driven New Korean Cinema works of Jung Ji-woo, Min Kyu-dong, and others.
4. The notion that a democratic society could voluntarily submit to the type of mass self-mobilization tantamount to a form of "mass dictatorship" has been explored by historian Jie-Hyun Lim. See, for instance, "Mapping Mass Dictatorship: Towards a Transnational History of Twentieth-Century Dictatorship," in *Gender Politics and Mass Dictatorship*, ed. Jie-Hyun Lim and Karen Petrone (New York: Palgrave Macmillan, 2011). See also Jie-Hyun Lim, Paul Corner, eds, *The Palgrave Handbook of Mass Dictatorship* (New York: Palgrave Macmillan, 2016). Likewise, political scientist Jang-jip Choi argued, as of 2012, that the successful democratization of South Korea's institutions and practices had failed to dismantle concentration of power in the state and a small minority of the elite sectors, and thereby to introduce and stimulate pluralism and genuine multivocality in Korean democracy. See Jang-jip Choi, *Democracy after Democratization: The Korean Experience* (Palo Alto, CA: Stanford University Press, 2012).
5. See, for instance, Kim Jong-bub, "Chotbul siwi eui sahoemunhwajeok byeonhwa wa euimi" [The Socio-Cultural Meaning and Its Changes in Candlelight Demonstrations], *Tongbuka yeoksa* [History of Eastern North Asia], Vol. 34, no. 1, 2019, 245–74; Jung Jai Kwan, "Chotbul siwi eui jeongchihak: misijeok bunseok, geosijeok jujang, dacheungjeok bigyo yeongu" [The Politics of Candlelight Protest: Micro Analyses, Macro Claims, Multi-level Comparative Studies], *Hanguk gwa gukje jeongchi* Vol. 35, no. 4, 2019, 141–69. The more recent post-2016 studies of the candlelight protests tend to focus less on their overt political effect, for instance their contribution to the impeachment of President Park Geun Hye in 2017, than on the socio-cultural character of a "loose" coalition among disparate interest groups and agencies of South Korean society. These studies do not necessarily consider the candlelight protests as inherently manifesting "progressive" characteristics.
6. Hannah Arendt, *The Origins of Totalitarianism*, p. 299, quoted in Giorgio Agamben, *Homo Sacer: Sovereign Power and Bare Life* (Stanford, CA: Stanford University Press, 1998), 126.
7. Giorgio Agamben, *Homo Sacer*, 126–30.
8. Ibid., 128.

9. "KBS do 'Namjjokeuro ttwieo' taekeul . . . Yeongsang-sosik geumji" [KBS, too, Pushes Back at *South Bound*, Banning Reports of Its Images or News], *Gobalnews*, 7 February 2013, <http://www.gobalnews.com/news/articleView.html?idxno=1021> (last accessed 25 March 2021).
10. For an overview of the Hwang Woo-suk scandal from a scientifically informed legal and ethical perspective, consult Han Aeran, "The Ethical and Regulatory Problems in the Stem Cell Scandal," *Journal of International Business and Law* Vol. 4, No. 2 (2007), <https://www.degruyter.com/document/doi/10.1515/JIBL.2007.009/html> (last accessed 30 March 2021).
11. Judith Butler, *Notes Toward a Performative Theory of Assembly* (Cambridge, MA: Harvard University Press, 2015), 1–12. It is worth noting that Butler critiques Agamben's political theory along with Hannah Arendt's for having bound themselves to the legal-philosophical language of the *polis* and therefore assuming that the sphere of politics must be as exclusivist as the classic philosophers had conceived them. In other words, the "bare lives" that Agamben posits is, according to Butler, still not entirely reduced to "mere being:" "To be outside established and legitimate political structures is still to be saturated in power relations, and this saturation is the point of departure for a theory of the political that includes dominant and subjugated forms, modes of inclusion and legitimation as well as modes of de-legitimation and effacement." She then affirms one of the phrases Arendt uses, "the right to have rights" as a corollary to "the right to appear," assertion of one's visibility and hence existence. Butler, *Notes*, 77–84.
12. Butler, *Notes*, 12.

CHAPTER 6

Sensory Connections Between Food and Femininity in Yim Soon-rye's *Little Forest* and Lee Seo-gun's *The Recipe*

Bonnie Tilland

In Yim Soon-rye's 2018 film *Little Forest*, viewers witness young protagonist Hye-won spend four seasons in the countryside home she grew up in, living in rhythm with the planting and the harvest, and preparing and eating foods in accordance with their proper seasons.[1] As winter deepens, she hangs persimmons on the eaves of the house to dry, something she had watched her mother do. The scene resonates with a scene from an earlier film, *The Recipe* (2010), in which young protagonist Hye-jin hangs *meju* (fermented soybean cakes) to dry on the rafters of her house.

In terms of genre, pacing, and plot the two films could hardly be more disparate, and the fact that both were directed by female filmmakers should not on its own justify a comparison (after all, male filmmakers are not compared solely based on their gender). However, both films share a sensory focus on food and its connection to female identity, which is further complexified by the gender identity of the respective filmmakers. This chapter begins with a discussion of the thematic foci of female filmmakers in South Korea, and how the expectations placed on them have shaped their career trajectories. The sensory focus of Yim's *Little Forest* is also compared with other films in her oeuvre, followed by an analysis of food and femininity in the greater South Korean media landscape, including in Lee Seo-gun's *The Recipe*. While *Little Forest* is a rich film through which to explore multiple aspects of South Korea, including the urban–rural divide and the intense neoliberal pressures upon South Korean youth—as well as Yim's own activism around these issues—the primary focus of the chapter is the relationship between the sensory experiences of preparing and eating food and women's identity in the film. Yim explores the sensory and affective connections between feeding oneself, feeding others, and feeding the community. Female relationships—mother and daughter,

Figure 6.1 Haewon hangs persimmons outside her countryside home to dry (*Little Forest*, Yim Soon-rye, 2018)

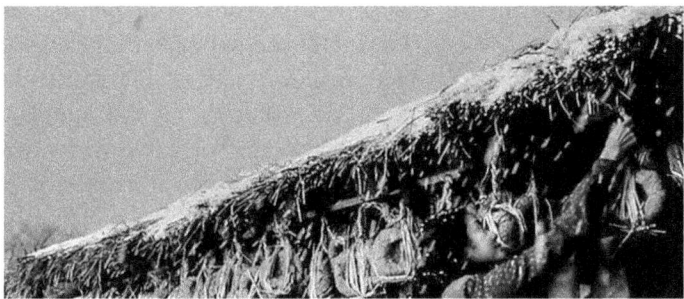

Figure 6.2 Hye-jin hangs meju (fermented soybean cakes) on the rafters of her countryside house to dry (*The Recipe*, Lee Seo-gun, 2010)

and female friends—are privileged, with an understated romance with a male friend fitting in with the female relationships, rather than disrupting them. *Little Forest* has quite a different focus on women, the senses, and food to Lee's *The Recipe*, in which food is transformed into magic through romantic love.

The novelty of Yim's layered sensory approach to food and feminine identity in *Little Forest* is brought into relief when one compares it with other food representations in recent films, from the fried chicken in *Extreme Job* to the "jjapaguri" of *Parasite*. Whereas Yim has slowly built her sensory world over decades, Lee popped up with the uncategorizable *Rub Love* in 1998, only to disappear and resurface again for 2010's *The Recipe*. The genre-defying *The Recipe* features bean paste stew as the center of a mystery, endowing women's food preparation with magic. In contrast to Yim's sensory smorgasbord, the star dish of Lee's (much less popular) earlier film appears and disappears, rather like the director herself. Lee's interest in food and relationships is also present in Park Chul-soo's *301, 302* (1995), on which she was the writer. In that film, neighbors in an apartment complex enter into a dysfunctional friendship that revolves around food, with the woman in number 301 cooking obsessively and binge-eating and the woman in 302 suffering from anorexia. Baron analyzed the horror created by excessive and repulsive food scenes in which food connects to sexual trauma and alienation, noting that "whereas utopian films use meals to illustrate the building of community, this dystopian film will probe neuroses and show that the inability to accept food and the drive to force others to eat are signs of severe dysfunction."[2] While it is difficult to separate writer Lee's influences from director Park Chul-soo's for *301, 302*, food is again a preoccupation in *The Recipe*, though this time it is intensely utopian. Filmic connections between women and food on the one hand, and dichotomies between on-screen instant/convenience food and traditional/local food on the other, illustrate a sensory approach to cinema that articulates the experiences and focal points of South Korean female filmmakers.

As other chapters in this volume demonstrate, Yim Soo-rye has earned her title of "South Korea's best-known female filmmaker" through her nearly three decades of filmmaking. Her focus on slice-of-life stories has stayed consistent throughout her career, and despite relatively low budgets, many of her films have achieved mainstream success and loyal followings (particularly 2008's sports film *Forever the Moment* and 2018's *Little Forest*). She is the only female auteur consistently associated with the Korean New Wave in film of the late 1990s through mid-2000s. Previous analyses of Yim's work have focused on time and space in her films,[3] her strong stance on animal rights and anti-discrimination activism,[4] and youth psychology.[5] While all of these are ripe for analysis, it is her sensory focus in her films that sets her apart from other filmmakers working in South Korea today. Yim's most recent film, *Little Forest*, is based on the earlier Japanese manga and subsequent Japanese feature film,[6] but she brings particular South Korean sensory conceptions and food knowledge to her version. Mori's adaptation sprawls over two parts (spring/summer and fall/winter), with less dialogue and more narration, and the natural landscape taking on an even greater role.[7] In Yim's more abbreviated adaptation, female bonding takes center stage, and while viewers do not know for sure whether Hye-won's mother returns at the end of the film, there is more of a sense of psychological closure in Yim's film. Yim's directorial choices cannot be reduced to her gender, but there is a notable lack of a male gaze sexualizing Hye-won and other female characters, or reducing them to tropes.

If Yim Soon-rye's decades of filmmaking resulted in success and recognition—even as she continues a humble life outside of Seoul in the mountainous area of Yangpyeong—the director of 2010's *The Recipe*, Lee Seo-gun, followed a more familiar path for female filmmakers in South Korea: accolades, and then obscurity. Lee is fourteen years Yim's junior but they started their engagement with South Korean film worlds around the same time. After returning from film school in Paris, Yim was one of the producers on Yeo

Kyun-dong's crime comedy *Out to the World* (1994), before directing her own first feature-length film (*Three Friends*, 1996). Lee was the screenwriter for Park Chul-soo's shocking food-centric thriller *301, 302* (1995) at the tender age of twenty, returning to Korea after studying film in New York. A newspaper article of the time described Lee as one of the *yuhakpa* (study abroad faction), as opposed to those who came up through the domestic Chungmuro studio system.[8] Like Yim, Lee received awards for a short film (*Suicide Party*, in 1996; for Yim it was *Promenade in the Rain* in 1994) before directing her first feature film. Lee's first feature film, *Rub Love* (1998), confused audiences and failed at the box office. Lee emerged again in 2010 with *The Recipe*, which was produced by veteran director Jang Jin (*Guns and Talks*; *Welcome to Dongmakgol*),[9] by which time Yim had made three more feature films (*Waikiki Brothers*; *Forever the Moment*; and *Rolling Home with a Bull*) and two shorts. *The Recipe* screened at several domestic film festivals and was highly anticipated in part due to its star-studded cast: actor Ryu Seung-ryong played the TV news program journalist tasked with figuring out a mystery, and actress Lee Yowon was the mysterious female lead, Hye-jin. Lee Dong-wook played Lee Yowon's love interest. While he would become one of South Korea's most in-demand actors, in 2010 he was a relative unknown. Jang Jin's role as producer was played up, to the extent that some media outlets mistakenly referred to him as the film's director. The film's star power and producer could not save the film from overall poor reviews and disappointing box-office sales. Film critic Djuna, in their review of the film, wrote that the mystery's momentum was frequently interrupted by an ultimately boring love story[10]—a view seemingly shared by many, despite substantial commentary on the film's lush food imagery.

While Yim's *Little Forest* allows food and sensory engagement with it to lead, Lee's *The Recipe* subsumes sensory experience to tragic romantic love. And yet, despite this generic conventionality, feminist readings are possible, with many small touches that suggest a female filmmaker behind the scenes. Although one review complained that the brilliant Lee Yowon only appeared on screen for about a quarter of the film—despite promotional posters exclusively showing her face[11]—her tragic story becomes all-consuming, with the male journalist becoming obsessed with solving the mystery. In documentary-like footage in the first part of the film, various men appear on screen and say boorish things about the mysterious and beautiful young woman who passed away with a clay pot of *doenjang* (fermented bean paste) in her hands, but in the end the journalist is pursuing the mystery not out of a romantic or sexual obsession with the young woman, but due to the mysterious pull of the perfect *doenjang jjigae* itself. The young woman, Hye-jin, spends the film in a state of deep grief—happy only in flashbacks, as viewers know the love story is doomed from the start—but her grief still cannot sully the nurturing power of her *doenjang*. When the CEO happens upon the restaurant where Hye-jin is temporarily working and has his senses of taste and smell restored by her cooking, he quickly falls in love with her. Yet unlike fairytales or plenty of other cinematic examples, the rich man does not attempt to possess her, but instead respectfully honors her request to drive her to the village where she and her lover met, though she knows that he has perished at sea. The final moments between the smitten CEO and the grieving Hye-jin before the car plunges over a ravine are spent in the company of thousands of butterflies attracted by the magical *doenjang*, a profoundly sensual and sensory experience.

YIM SOON-RYE, LEE SEO-GUN, AND SOUTH KOREAN FEMALE FILMMAKERS

The consideration of food, the senses, and femininity in these films by Yim and Lee inspires curiosity over the conditions the filmmakers have worked under, and how this contributes to their themes and trajectories. Until the mid-1990s, the South Korean film production system demanded that aspiring filmmakers first serve as an apprentice to an established (male) film director.[12] Yim and Lee both debuted with their feature films in the late 1990s, and while they served as producer and screenwriter on the films of established male directors—both more common roles for women in film than directing—they established their reputations through winning prizes for short films first. Notably, both also studied film abroad before returning to South Korea, as making one's way through the Chungmuro studio system was a difficult prospect for any new filmmaker at the time, let alone a female filmmaker. In Yim's case, as she moved beyond her debut feature and began to establish herself, she received some criticism for not focusing on "women's issues."[13] After her first feature film *Three Friends* focused on male high-school students, some criticized her continued focus on men in the next film, *Waikiki Brothers*. In fact, more of Yim's films feature men in leading roles than women, with *Little Forest* and *Forever the Moment* as notable exceptions, and male–female balance in the reunited couple in *Rolling Home with a Bull*. Rather than interpreting this as a lack of interest in feminist issues, the themes Yim tackles include militarism, economic inequality, body image and lookism, social marginalization and corruption—revealing her consistent concern over gender equality and social equality more broadly defined. After decades, Yim Soon-rye is increasingly anticipated at domestic and international film festivals alike, but as she persistently pursues projects that first and foremost interest her rather than overly concerning herself with the film-going public, many of her films stay under the radar. While *Forever the Moment* was an unexpected hit in 2008, *Rolling Home with a Bull* in 2010 had little impact. Yim's directorial voice is established, and no one would expect populist melodrama in her works, but other female directors who have begun careers more recently still tell stories of being instructed by production companies to direct melodramas focusing on "women's identity" first, before being allowed to direct films in their desired genre.[14] A related problem that Paquet identifies since the late 2000s "has been the increased concentration of films made within the umbrella of major local studios such as CJ and Lotte, and the subsequent loss of power of individual producers." South Korean female filmmakers have also been relatively neglected on the international film festival circuit, even as they have had success at domestic Korean film festivals.[15]

In the case of Lee Seo-gun, the trajectory is that of a screenwriting prodigy failing to make a significant impact with first feature film *Rub Love*, and then failing to make a mark a second time more than a decade later, despite the backing of established filmmaker Jang Jin as producer. One review from 2010 praises the pureness of *The Recipe*, and its creative transformation of a "hickish" (*chonseureupda*) ingredient like *doenjang* to a magical potion, but ultimately cautions viewers that "you shouldn't expect novel ideas, a smooth plot, or characters that make an impression."[16] A review from 2019 praises the film in retrospect for awakening the senses through *doenjang*—suggesting that viewers were just not ready for a film in which bean paste is removed from Korean tradition and made youthfully sensual—and compares it with another "food film" (the Japanese *Kamome Diner*) and also with the importance of the sense of smell in *Parasite*.[17] A very short review from 2019, reintroducing *The Recipe* to coincide with its screening on the CGV cable channel, mentions Lee Seo-gun once, but mainly laments the film's failure at the box office in 2010 despite "director Jang Jin's time and effort."[18] Many of Jang Jin's signature elements are indeed present in the film, including witty banter and magical realist elements—such as the lighting in the scene in which the wanted criminal eats the *doenjang jjigae*, and the snow that falls in slow motion—but the pacing, plot, and genre shifts are Lee's. If the film-going public was not ready for Lee's re-interpretation of *doenjang*, as the one reviewer surmised, it is telling that another 2019 review of Lee's previous work, *Rub Love*, drew similar conclusions about Lee's timing in 1998.[19] The story of a bleak Seoul in the year 2028, and the "erased memories of the killer Nana and the comic artist Cho Han" (to quote the film promo posters), could not console a viewing public suffering from the social turmoil caused by the IMF crisis. The review also referred to a critic at the time calling *Rub Love* a "postmodern puzzle made up of unfamiliar images outside of the soil [*toyang*] of Korean cinema." One of the few extant (though very brief) English-language reviews of Lee's first film calls it "a genuine original," and predicts that "Lee, who wrote the script for *301, 302*, clearly has great things in prospect."[20] Given the reviews and reflections on Lee's films in 2019, perhaps it is now time for her to make a reappearance for a third feature film. As a South Korean female filmmaker, Lee subverted the expectation to make melodramas and films on "women's issues" first and genre film later, starting with the decidedly unusual *Rub Love*. Once that film was evaluated as too "out there," she attempted a melodrama with a gustatory twist with *The Recipe*, but that too failed to meet expectations. While Yim has steadily made slice-of-life films even with the expectations of the South Korean film world and viewing public pushing against her, Lee Seo-gun represents another more discouraging outcome for South Korean female filmmakers. She emerged, then re-emerged, and now generally cannot be found among lists of South Korean female filmmakers. To be sure, male filmmakers have also failed, and failed spectacularly, but it is hard not to conclude that such unique films may have propelled a male filmmaker further, despite their undeniable flaws.

SENSORY TEACHINGS IN YIM SOON-RYE'S FILMS

Yim Soon-rye's films largely deal with those who have "failed" in their lives in one way or another, from the three socio-economically disadvantaged youth in her first feature film *Three Friends*, to a washed-up band in *Waikiki Brothers*, to former handball champions in *Forever the Moment*, to a couple who failed in their relationship in *Rolling Home with a Bull*, among others. *Waikiki Brothers*, *Forever the Moment*, and most recently *Little Forest* are also notable for their particular sensory focus. *Waikiki Brothers* does not focus on music particularly intensively, but rather the relationship between the band members; nonetheless, the auditory element is significant. *Forever the Moment* is a sports film and features the tactile physicality of the relatively obscure sport of handball. *Little Forest* delights in the gustatory pleasures of preparing and eating fresh food. Yim is engaged with the senses, but not in a coldly aesthetic way nor in a wholly emotionally invested way. In interviews, Yim has spoken about her films as practicing empathy rather than too-close sympathy with characters, as well as intending for her films to "open up the possibilities of a discourse between the film and the viewer."[21] She is also interested in the relationship of the individual to their social world—and notably in *Little Forest* and *Rolling Home with a Bull*, the natural world as well—and thus does not focus on traditional character development or character sketches. Yim's films tend toward reconciliation between characters or a broader tolerance acquired by the end of the film, and the sensory experiences of characters through their surroundings and interpersonal relationships serve as teachings. In *Rolling Home with a Bull*, these teachings are explicitly connected to a Buddhist worldview. In *Little Forest*, Hye-won observes the changing of the seasons and the growing of plants after being disconnected from these during her years in the city, and is healed enough by the scenery and fresh food to begin to understand her mother's actions. Her understanding of her mother's actions does not arrive in any sudden revelatory moments, but rather through

Hye-won's shifting perspective made possible through her changed relationship with the natural world and experience of the seasons.

As a widely acclaimed "food film," *Little Forest* engages with "the sensory" more tangibly than any of Yim's other films, though *Rolling Home with a Bull* has parallels. As with other food-centric films, it plays with synesthesia, "the way that different senses elaborate on each other, rather than being considered separate domains of experience."[22] Sutton, an anthropologist of food, instructs us to try to recall a smell or a taste on its own without a connected visual image, claiming that these senses are most often connected to memories of a place or an interaction. Throughout *Little Forest* viewers witness Hye-won recall interactions with her mother from earlier in her life, and even when she does not want the bittersweetness of these memories, the tastes and smells keep bringing them up unbidden. Moreover, the close-up shots of bubbling stews on a cold day, cold noodles with chunks of ice and cucumbers on a hot day, and dancing *bonito* flakes on *okonomiyaki* bring up separate sets of memories and taste/smell associations for individual viewers. In addition to the links between the gustatory, olfactory, auditory, haptic, and memory through the visual medium of film, Hye-won's verbal descriptions of tastes and elaborations of recipes also add a textual element; this resonates with tea practitioner/scholar Zhang's discussion of how she lost track of the taste of tea while trying to make a documentary about it, but recalled the tastes when writing down notes in text about her tasting experience.[23] This attention to synesthesia also helps explain the film's success across demographic categories: while it is first and foremost a slow and carefully crafted film with similarities to other Yim Soon-rye films, *Little Forest* also satisfies "food porn" impulses in an age of social media, and methodical yet hypnotic scenes of Hye-won preparing dishes while narrating the steps she takes bring to mind video blogging of recipes—albeit with much more skilled and lush cinematography than such videos usually involve. Notwithstanding certain similarities, *Little Forest* is an antidote to the quickly produced, often interchangeable content of video blogs, aiming to convey a message about slowing down and engaging in the natural world and in meaningful connections with friends. A strong contrast is drawn between Hye-won living in Seoul in flashbacks and Hye-won in her natural habitat in her countryside town: in Seoul she appears run down, making instant food such as packaged ramen noodles only to fill her up while studying, whereas in the countryside she recreates her mother's recipes and experiments with her own creations without concern over time limits and schedules.

At the beginning of *Little Forest*, Hye-won returns, in winter, to the house in which she grew up. After lighting a fire in the wood stove, the first thing she does is cook herself a meal, a simple soup made with napa cabbage and green onions she digs out from under the snow in the yard. In a flashback viewers see Hye-won in work uniform in a convenience store, grabbing a mouthful of food from the inventory here and there when she has a spare moment. At the end of her shift she sits with a pre-packaged boxed lunch and digs in to the rice, only to spit it out a moment later, repulsed by its chemical taste. Back in her small apartment, she receives a voice message from her boyfriend letting her know that he has passed the grueling teachers' exam, while she has failed yet again. Opening her small fridge for bottled water to wash the unpleasant taste of the rice down, she eyes the sad contents—a lone apple and old packaged food. Back in her hometown, she tells a childhood friend that she came back "because she was hungry." A few days after her return, she ravenously eats her paternal aunt's cooking despite their strained relationship, but going forward seems to absorb the culinary creative energy of the house her absent mother has left behind. Anything she wants to eat she makes from scratch—when she wants a drink she makes the rice liquor, *makkeoli*, herself—and as winter turns to spring she begins to plant as well. Occasional letters without a return address arrive from her mother, but they are only recipes, not explanations for why she left. Hye-won only gradually gains the recognition that the recipes are intended to welcome her back to her childhood home and bring her into her rightful power and ease with herself.

LITTLE FOREST VS. *THE RECIPE*: FOOD AND GENDER IN THE SOUTH KOREAN MEDIA LANDSCAPE

In contrast with Yim's *Little Forest*, food in *The Recipe* is linked with women's magic but does not explicitly play a role in connecting generations. Instead, it highlights women's sensuality. To be sure, *Little Forest* also does not focus on traditional recipes passed across generations, but only the psychic culinary connection between Hye-won and her mother, which then is naturally transformed into expressions of care from Hye-won to her friends. The connection is not about traditional Korean food, but rather all the food that can be made through living in close collaboration with the land and out of love for family and friends. After a flashback in which Hye-won's mother makes her crème brûlée—the camera focusing on Hye-won's mother's hands crushing the nuts at the bottom, pouring in the custard, and torching the top—Hye-won makes the same crème brûlée for her friend as an apology after an argument. In *The Recipe*, in contrast, the story insistently returns to the bean paste stew (*doenjang jjigae*), attempting to break down its parts (the salt, the water used in cooking, the fermented beans, and any errant plants or insects that may have become involved in the fermenting process) to determine what makes Hye-jin's stew so magical. In a review of *The Recipe*, Djuna observes that while the mystery—unfolding across creative mockumentary-style footage and even surprising interludes of animated sequences—seems that it may connect back to Hye-jin's childhood or end as a tale of an enchanted restaurant, in the end it is a simple romance.

> Hye-jin is young, and the man she is connected to romantically is also young. The two are geniuses who have learned [the culinary craft] on their own, without connection to the past or the older generation. It seems that Lee Seo-gun wanted to depart from the familiar image and fixed concept of *doenjang* and make a younger and more contemporary story.[24]

In trying to solve the mystery, the TV producer experiences traditional foodways and culinary magic in the course of his research, attending traditional fermented food workshops, tasting mountain stream water, and visiting a blind potter who made the pot in which Hye-jin stores her extraordinary *doenjang*. But while it is revealed over the course of the film that Hye-jin has grown up in a village known for its *meju* (bean cakes for making *doenjang*), her magic comes purely from her love for a young man in town known as "the goblin," who is himself an expert in making *makkeoli*. The magic this strong love produces also helps others, even as Hye-jin grieves when her beloved does not return after going back to Japan for his grandfather's funeral. A CEO who has lost his sense of smell due to childhood trauma visits the restaurant where Hye-jin makes *doenjang jjigae*, and magically his sense of smell is restored. Unlike *Little Forest*, the senses in *The Recipe* are not focused on teaching and transmitting knowledge, but rather on healing, against a magical realist backdrop of love and fermentation. While *Little Forest* also deals with healing, it focuses on the transmission of care and sensory knowledge in the countryside space, whereas *The Recipe* focuses on the healing powers of romantic love.

Although *Little Forest* and *The Recipe* are profoundly different from one another in most respects, they are united by two common elements: a strong dichotomy between instant/convenience foods and traditional/local foods; and themes of connection between the feminine and the sensory. Between *The Recipe*'s release in 2010 and *Little Forest*'s in 2018, the culinary landscape in South Korea underwent a great deal of transformation, with ever-expanding snack and convenience food options; restaurant menus adjusting to keep pace with the rise of single-person households and with it, solo diners; and a sustained focus on "well-being" foods (see Lee for a discussion of the greater "healing" and "well-being" context in relation to *Little Forest*, this volume), both traditional and globally influenced. South Korea's changing culinary desires have been reflected in media, including the rise of *meokbang* ("eating broadcasts"),[25] diversified cooking shows,[26] and food-centric variety shows.[27] In *The Recipe*, the TV journalist becomes obsessed with uncovering the secrets behind Hye-jin's *doenjang jjigae*, pursuing every lead to deep corners of South

Korea's countryside. Unsurprisingly, the journalist learns that Hye-jin grew up in Jeollado, the southwest region traditionally known for culinary abundance. The TV journalist at times engages in some gently comedic gender role swapping, such as when he eagerly takes notes at a fermented food workshop, the lone man in a sea of aproned housewives. In the end, the TV journalist is left without a reportable story, as the secret ingredient of Hye-jin's *doenjang jjigae*—which so enchanted a wanted criminal that he would rather have been captured by police than stop eating—was nothing but love. The region's delicious salt, spring water, and particular flora were all important elements of the stew, but it is Hye-jin's pure love for "the goblin" that stops the criminal in his tracks, makes a restaurant owner cry, and restores the senses of taste and smell of the CEO who comes to the restaurant. Indeed, the *doenjang* is so potent that it even preserves the bodies of the CEO and Hye-jin after the CEO drives his car into a ravine—in her final moments, on her way to visit the spot where she had told her lover she would wait for him, Hye-jin was carrying a large clay pot of her special *doenjang*. *The Recipe* reinvents the humble, strong-smelling *doenjang* to connect it with creativity, unconditional love, and sexual desire through the figure of Hye-jin.

While handmade food represents love and care in *The Recipe* and *Little Forest*, both films also interrupt the overplayed generational transmission tales common in food films worldwide, and in South Korean media featuring food more generally. Although Hye-won learns about food from her mother in *Little Forest*, her mother has notably only taught her these skills for Hye-won's own self-sufficiency and happiness. Her mother does not demand anything in return, although she hopes that the relationship they established through cooking and eating will help Hye-won to understand her mother's desire for self-realization away from the village. She does not mention, or even imply, that Hye-won should learn cooking for the sake of her future children, husband, or in-laws. Moreover, when Hye-won shares her food with childhood friends Jae-ha and Eun-sook, the gender dynamics are flexible—see Kwon, this volume, for an exploration of *Little Forest* as a queer narrative—and despite the understated mutual romantic interest between Hye-won and her male childhood friend Jae-ha, Yim does not allow this interpersonal dynamic to overwhelm the film at all. Hye-won and Jae-ha may or may not become a couple, and Hye-won's mother may or may not return. Ultimately, the love and care Hye-won shows for her friends through preparing food is inseparable from the love and care she develops for herself, and viewers can see Hye-won's growing satisfaction with herself in the many scenes in which she eats happily alone. Importantly, however, *Little Forest* cannot be collapsed into the Hollywood neoliberal female empowerment genre (as in the *Eat Pray Love* variety) or South Korean neoliberal "Candyrella" narratives (like TV dramas *Coffee Prince* or *My Name is Kim Sam-Soon*, among many others).[28] Hye-won discovers herself through planting, harvesting, preparing, and eating food, but "herself" is as solidly connected to the village community as it is *not* dependent on patriarchal family and romantic relationships for sustenance.

The community-mindedness and abundance of female bonding scenes in *Little Forest*—whether of Hye-won with Eun-sook or in flashbacks to moments with her mother—is completely absent in *The Recipe*. Viewers first meet Hye-jin when she wanders to a restaurant in the countryside and begins working as well as lodging there. She and the woman who owns the restaurant are friendly with each other, and Hye-jin's *doenjang jjigae* moves her to tears—however, Hye-jin does not work there long enough for true bonding to occur. When the journalist follows the clues back to the village where Hye-jin grew up, he learns that the area is famous for *meju*. An old woman in another village remembers Hye-jin's arrival there, and her beautiful connection with the young *makkeoli* maker known as "the goblin," and subsequent heartbreak when he did not return from Japan. Hamilton observes that Hye-jin "has devoted her life to serving the most delicious soup that will nurture and cure," but it is romantic love that motivates her, rather than the sense of community found in *Little Forest*. Hamilton goes on to compare *The Recipe* with Lee's earlier script for *301, 302*, which featured two women, of which "one is obsessed with cooking and eating, using it as a substitute for sex and friendship; one is repulsed by the taste and smell of food

Figure 6.3 Hye-jin (*The Recipe*) waits for the *doenjang* to ferment while she waits for her lover to return

as an unwanted intrusion into her body."²⁹ Hye-jin derives pleasure from the healing people obtain from her stew, but waits for her love to return forlornly, as everything else is subsumed by romantic love. *The Recipe* takes on mythological qualities, with the bean paste operating as a symbolic object between the mystical star-crossed couple. The *doenjang* endlessly ferments as Hye-jin waits, coming to represent a doomed love. In *Little Forest*, food sustains in the present and makes promises for the future, suggesting the possibility of love for Hye-won. However, this love is not limited to romantic love.

Another aspect of overlap between *Little Forest* and *The Recipe* is their strong dichotomy between instant/convenience foods vs. traditional/local foods. In *Little Forest*, the only time packaged foods are shown is in the flashback scenes of Hye-won's time in Seoul. Hye-won also experiences the sting of rejection when she goes to deliver a handmade boxed lunch to her boyfriend while he is working, and overhears his friends commenting on how unusual this is in this day and age. When Hye-won hears her boyfriend say that he would rather she use the time she spends cooking for him to devote to her studies—and it would be easier for him just to buy something for lunch—she turns around without delivering the lunch, vowing never to express her care for him this way again. Back in her childhood home in the countryside, packaged snacks are entirely absent—even when *anju* (dishes to accompany alcoholic drinks) are needed when Hye-won and her friends drink her homemade *makkeoli*, Hye-won makes the crackers herself. The scene in which Hye-won's acts of love via cooking are indirectly rejected by her boyfriend find a parallel in Lee Seo-gun's earlier script for *301, 302*, as one of the lead characters in that film is similarly rejected by her husband, who says he would prefer to eat Western fast food than eat his wife's elaborate meals. This drives the woman to binge eat alone, a symptom of her loneliness. In *The Recipe*, Hye-jin's food is never rejected, and "the goblin" lovingly caresses her hands, which are rough and dry from repeatedly handling the fermented beans (in order to transmit the important *sonmat*, or "taste of hands" that sets a food apart as homemade). The pungent, rustic *doenjang* becomes sensual. The contrast between convenience food and homemade food in *The Recipe* is illustrated through side characters: as the journalist goes deeper and deeper into experiences of fermented food culture in his quest to solve the *doenjang jjigae* mystery, other members of his team annoy him with their constant snacking. A detective friend "jams food into his mouth while talking on the telephone, eats from a bag of chips while working on his computer, slurps a small container of fast food during a phone call in the company cafeteria,"³⁰ and after visiting the restaurant where Hye-jin was previously employed the journalist snaps "you just ate!" at a member of the camera crew who whines that she is hungry. Unlike Hye-jin's *doenjang jjigae*, these other foods that are made carelessly or are mass produced simply cannot fill a person up properly.

Several South Korean food trends make their way into the food media landscape of which *The Recipe* and *Little Forest* are a part; "well-being,"[31] traditional revival and buy-local movements (encompassed by the slogan *shin to bul yi*, or "the body and land cannot be separated") are present in *The Recipe*, and a *meokbang* and v-log aesthetic combine with overall greater eco-awareness in *Little Forest*. Several other highly successful recent South Korean films prominently feature food—and the senses involved in preparing and eating food—most notably *Extreme Job* (dir. Lee Byeong-heon, 2019) and *Parasite* (dir. Bong Joon-ho, 2019). Ryu Seung-ryong, who plays the TV news journalist to maximum comedic slapstick effect against the tragic love story in *The Recipe*, reprises this comedic slapstick mood as an undercover cop in *Extreme Job*, the second top-grossing South Korean film of all time (as of 2021). In *Extreme Job* the ultimate fast food, Korean fried chicken, takes center stage. Undercover cops trying to bust a drug lord buy a fried chicken restaurant as their cover, but then are hampered in their mission by the restaurant's unexpected success. Here, too, unconventional recipes play a key role, as one of the cop's family recipes creates an unanticipated culinary sensation, spread far and wide by social media. In *Parasite*'s tale of social inequality another unconventional dish illustrates the widely divergent experiences and expectations of rich and poor: *jjapaguri* (translated in the English subtitles as "ram-don," and created through mixing instant noodle brands Chapagetti black bean noodles and Neoguri ramen). When wealthy Mrs. Choi (Yeon-gyo) asks her housekeeper (Park Chung-sook) to make the instant dish, she confuses Chung-sook utterly by telling her to add *hanu* (expensive Korean sirloin beef). The hybrid recipe is a slap in the face to Chung-sook, showing her the extent of the Park family's wealth and their blatant conspicuous consumption (during a scene in which her family are in hiding around the mansion, in danger of being caught in their scam when the Park family returns early from a weekend excursion). The incongruous melding of the cheap, accessible instant noodles with the expensive beef constitutes a "culinary crime," and in part this is because the cheap/instant and the expensive/local—for *hanu* is nothing if not prized as hyper-local—collide in one dish. If the fried chicken restaurant in *Extreme Job* is a setting and *jjapaguri* is a symbol in *Parasite*, *doenjang* and *doenjang jjigae* in *The Recipe*, and the various local creations in *Little Forest* connect women and food in far more substantial ways.

CONCLUSION

At the end of *Little Forest*, Hye-won returns to the countryside house in the spring. Before she left in the winter, she plucked a dried persimmon from its drying rack in front of the house, savoring its sweetness but resolving to leave to try to make it in Seoul again anyway. When she returns in spring, she does not look defeated, but rides vigorously around the village on her bicycle. A wide shot again treats viewers to the lush countryside landscape, appearing that much wider after shots of Hye-won's cramped apartment in Seoul and her view of the crowded city skyline. When she gets back to the house, she notes that the door is open and the curtains flutter in the breeze, and a smile spreads across her face. She walks in slow motion toward the door, with the expectation created that her mother is at last waiting inside. The food Hye-won has made throughout the film is visually linked to the countryside landscape, and as she approaches the house, faint sounds are heard from the kitchen. The care of the community for Hye-won, and Hye-won's care for the community, connect in a sensuous circle of tastes, smells, sounds, and textures.

At the end of *The Recipe*, Hye-jin's story is already finished, and the journalist tells the camera what was in the magical *doenjang*:

> a clay pot into which plum blossoms have fallen, salt dried by the sun and stored over time, beans cultivated by a wild boar piglet, water from deep in the mountain, malt from plum wine, the sound of crickets, sunshine, wind, and tears . . . And as for how to make it? You wait.

The journalist has visited the potter to ask about the clay pot, and has tasted the salt and water; in flashbacks viewers have seen Hye-jin's addition of malt bestowed by her beloved, and finally her tears while she waits. The natural word has also contributed, with a young boar disturbing the beans and close-up shots of crickets making music on the *meju*. In the end only the natural world is left, with all the people at the core of the story gone. Without love, there is no food. Despite the many differences between *Little Forest* and *The Recipe*, and the different paths taken by the directors, both in the end affirm connections between women, land, food, and the senses. Hye-won's and Hye-jin's *sonmat* ("taste of hands") in their cooking is not in service to tradition, but rather self-realization, community, and love. The same can be said of the hands and minds behind the cameras, as Yim and Lee have forged new paths for female filmmakers in South Korea and stretched the existing boundaries of filmmaking.

NOTES

1. Yim's 2018 film is an adaptation of the Japanese film of the same name, directed by Junichi Mori. The Japanese version was produced in two parts, with "Spring/Summer" released in 2014 and "Fall/Winter" in 2015. Mori's film was itself an adaptation of a manga by Daisuke Igarashi, serialized 2002–2005.
2. Cynthia Baron, *Appetites and Anxieties: Food, Film, and the Politics of Representation* (Detroit, MI: Wayne State University Press, 2014).

3. Jee Hee Kim and Jai Suk Bang, "Yeonghwa *Riteul Poresteu* sok kongganjeok teukseonghwa uimi e daehan gochal" [Contemplation on the Spatial Characteristics and Meaning of Hometown in the Movie *Little Forest*: Focusing on the return to rural communities], *Wonkwang Journal of Humanities* Vol. 20, no. 3 (December 2019): 299–324. Yong-hee Kim, "Yeonghwa *Riteul Poresteu* e natanan siganui uimiwa keu yeonghwa hyeongsikjeok guhyeon e daehan yeongu" [A Study on the Meaning of Time and Its Formal Embodiment in the Film *Little Forest*], *Asia Yeonghwa Yeongu* [Asian Film Research] Vol. 12, no. 1 (March 2019): 87–112.
4. Julia Mayer, "Animal Magnetism: On South Korean Director Yim Soon-Rye," *Metro Magazine* 171, 2012, 58–62.
5. Gwi-eun Han, "Yim Soon-rye yeonghwa e natanan dongsidaeseonggwa cheongnyeon kaenyeomui sesokhwa" [The Contemporaries and Profanation of Young Adult in the Films Directed by Lim Sun-Rye], *Baedalmal* Vol. 62 (June 2018): 203–30.
6. For a comparison of Mori's and Yim's adaptations, see: Eun-Kyung Chin, "Ilsangseongeuro bon nongchonyeonghwa bigyo Hangukgwa Ilbonui *Riteul Poresteu* reul jungshimeuro" [Comparison of rural films from quotodiennete focusing on *Little Forest* from Korea and Japan], *Literature and Environment* Vol. 19, no. 1 (March 2020): 101–27.
7. Yim's *Little Forest* is filmed in the rural area of Miseongri, in Gyeongbuk province. In Hye-won's voiceover toward the beginning of the film, we learn that the village is so remote that there are no convenience stores or other shops, and Hye-won must ride her bike to get to stores or the outdoor market. In contrast, Mori's adaptation follows the manga's setting of remote northern Tohoku prefecture in Japan. Tohoku often signals economic and social marginalization in Japanese literature and film, and this long-standing marginalization took on even greater poignancy after the Fukushima nuclear disaster in March 2011. Fukushima is in Tohoku, and many suspected that the Japanese government covered up the extent of the damage *because* it took place in Tohoku. The setting of Gyeongbuk in the Korean adaptation does not signal marginalization in the same way, as historically it was the southwest (Jeolla) rather than southeast (Gyeongbuk) that was marginalized from the center. In the late 2010s, there is a relatively weaker sense of regionalism in South Korea, but instead a wide divide between the Seoul metropolitan area and everywhere else.
8. Kitae Kwon, "Olcho debwijak champae, yuhakpa yeonghwa gamdok 2inui gago" [Crushing defeat of debut films at the beginning of this year, the resolve of two overseas film directors], *Donga Ilbo*, 5 March 1998, <https://www.donga.com/news/People/article/all/19980305/7326944/1> (last accessed 1 June 2021).
9. It should be noted that Lee had particular connections to the South Korean film industry via her mother, novelist-turned-businesswoman Kim Sukyoung (who founded the publishing house Yeoleumsa) and father Lee Sang-ho, doctor and head of Woolideul Hospital. Lee's parents invested in director Jang Jin's "Digital Chat" project prior to his producing *The Recipe*. As of 2021, Lee Seo-gun is listed as the representative of Yeoleumsa publishing house. <https://news.joins.com/article/2943214> (last accessed 4 June 2021).
10. Djuna, "*Doenjang* (2010)," *Djuna Yeonghwa Nakseopan*, 18 October 2010, <http://www.djuna.kr/xe/review/937588> (last accessed 3 March 2021).
11. Seongjin Hwangbo, "Dansun 'eumsik yeonghwa'ga anine" [It's not a pure 'food movie'], *The Minjok Medicine News*, 19 October 2010, <https://www.mjmedi.com/news/articleView.html?idxno=19953> (last accessed 28 May 2021).
12. In-young Nam, "Korean Women Directors," in *Korean Cinema from Origins to Renaissance*, ed. Mee Hyun Kim (KOFIC, 2007), 164.
13. Mayer, "Animal Magnetism," 60.
14. Darcy Paquet, "The (few) women breaking through in Korean cinema," *British Film Institute* (BFI.org), 3 August 2017, <https://www2.bfi.org.uk/news-opinion/sight-sound-magazine/features/women-korean-cinema> (last accessed 5 May 2021).

15. Ibid.
16. Juhyeon Lee, "Dansunhago sunsuhago kusuhan masi beeoinneun yeonghwa 'Doenjang'" [*The Recipe*, a film that supports a simple, pure and delicate taste], *Cine21*, 20 October 2010, <http://www.cine21.com/news/view/?mag_id=63187> (last accessed 15 May 2021).
17. Hajin Choi, "Doenjang (The Recipe, 2010)," *Inside Seocho*, 30 July 2019, <http://www.insideseocho.com/news/articleView.html?idxno=4570> (last accessed 17 May 2021).
18. Yumi Lee, "Yeonghwa 'Doenjang' Jang Jin kamdok sigan + kongryeok bulgu doenjangjjigae e jeongsini pallin nameoji. . ." [In the film "The Recipe," despite director Jang Jin's time and effort, it remains just a preoccupation with bean stew], *Jeonbuk Domin Ilbo*, 17 May 2019, <https://www.domin.co.kr/news/articleView.html?idxno=1243571> (last accessed 23 May 2021).
19. Changse Lee, "Lee Changseui mubi seutori: Bihaindeu mubi seutori, 'Reobeu reobeu'" [Lee Changse's Movie Story: the behind-the-scenes story of "Rub Love"], *Sport Korea*, 1 May 2019, <http://www.isportskorea.com/mstory/?mode=view&no=20190430145219777&field=&keyword> (last accessed 26 May 2021).
20. See <https://www.timeout.com/movies/rub-love> (last accessed 5 May 2021).
21. Mayer, "Animal Magnetism," 60.
22. David Sutton, "Synesthesia, Memory, and the Taste of Home," in *The Taste and Culture Reader*, ed. Carolyn Korsmeyer (New York: Berg, 2005), 312.
23. J. Zhang, "Tasting Tea and Filming Tea: The Filmmaker's Engaged Sensory Experience," *Visual Anthropology Review* Vol. 33, no. 2 (2017): 141–51.
24. Djuna, "*Doenjang* (2010)."
25. Antonetta L. Bruno and Somin Chung, "Mokbang: Pay Me and I'll Show You How Much I Can Eat For Your Pleasure," *Journal of Japanese and Korean Cinema* Vol. 9, no. 2 (2017): 155–71.
26. Jooyeon Rhee, "Gender Politics in Food Escape: Korean Masculinity in TV Cooking Shows in South Korea," *Journal of Popular Film and Television* Vol. 47, no. 1 (2019): 56–64.
27. Grace Jung, "Aspirational Paternity and the Female Gaze on Korean Reality-Variety TV," *Media, Culture and Society* Vol. 42, no. 2 (2019): 191–206. Myoung-Sun Song, "Cooking Love in Asia: Food, Belonging and the Making of a Multicultural Family on Korean Film and Television," *International Journal of Media and Cultural Politics* Vol. 15, no. 2 (2019): 197–211.
28. Bonnie Tilland, "Baker Kings, Rice Liquor Princesses, and the Coffee Elite: Food Nationalism and Youth Creativity in the Construction of Korean 'Taste' in Late 2000s and Early 2010s Television Dramas," *Acta Koreana* Vol. 24, no. 1: 1–22.
29. Dotty Hamilton, "Appetite and Aroma: Visual Imagery and the Perception of Taste and Smell in Contemporary Korean Film," in *Food on Film: Bringing Something New to the Table*, ed. Tom Hertweck (Lanham, MD: Rowman and Littlefield, 2015), 284.
30. Hamilton, "Appetite and Aroma," 274.
31. Jesook Song, *South Koreans in the Debt Crisis: The Creation of a Neoliberal Welfare Society* (Durham, NC: Duke University Press, 2009).

CHAPTER 7

"I Want to Live a Life that I Choose": Romanticized Queer Family and Nature in *Little Forest* (2018)

Kwon Jungmin

Yim Soon-rye, a leading film director in South Korea (hereafter "Korea"), has consistently paid attention to the diverse and marginalized within society, and her work illustrates realistically and scathingly the absurdities that they confront in their ordinary lives.[1] Yim has gravitated toward focusing on unconventional relationships forged through solidarity against the adversities that exist within hetero-patriarchal society. The characters in her films *Three Friends* (1996), *Waikiki Brothers* (2001), and *Forever the Moment* (2008) fail to establish, survive, or sustain a "normative" family life in Korea, which would stereotypically consist of a leading father, a caring mother, and (male) offspring to continue the lineage. These sometimes nomadic, often embattled characters instead construct new interpersonal communities that grant them a sense of security, stabilization, and emotional attachment, replacing their original families. Yim's work became even more varied in this manner a decade after her feature-film debut, once she assumed a representative position within the Korea Animal Rights Advocates organization (KARA) in 2009. Already known for her interest in animal rights, after 2009 Yim started to incorporate the theme into her films, and *Rolling Home with a Bull* (2010) and *Sorry, Thank You* (2011) both attest to the director's advocacy for a harmonious coexistence with animals and nature. Her exploration of unconventional forms of communal solidarity, as well as her interest in animal rights and rural life, therefore make Yim an unconventional and iconoclastic storyteller.

Yim's most recent film, *Little Forest* (2018), is consistent with these approaches. The director's search for new kinds of community and her passion for nature could be said to culminate here, as she sheds light on alienated young people in neoliberal Korea, their queer relationships and camaraderie, and their new lifestyles in pastoral locales. Like her previous films, *Little Forest* reflects upon contemporary Korean social issues, such as the employment struggles of young people, the emergence of post-heterosexual families, animal rights, food culture, and a romanticized concern for nature. Here, the director envisions a space wherein feminism, environmentalism, and queerness combine to surmount the hetero-patriarchy that permeates Korean society. As such, Yim, a once-acerbic critic of Korean society, now offers that to "go back to (Mother) nature" is the simple answer to the convoluted issues of age, class, gender, sexuality, and environmentalism. This is a choice that perhaps demonstrates Yim's authorial transition from provocative dissident to relaxed storyteller.

This chapter examines the rendering of family and space in *Little Forest*, dynamics through which Yim's feminist, queer, and ecological approaches are interwoven. It discusses how Yim fleshes out a new model of kinship, which I would call a queer family, as it does not require the heterosexual man emblematic of a conventional family unit. Then it moves on to examine the diegetic space of the film in relation to the idea of queer family to see how nature operates in the narrative to characterize the protagonists and their relationships. I endeavor to offer a critical analysis of Yim's romanticizing and dichotomizing perspectives about gender, queerness, and space, and ultimately argue for wider cinematic explorations of the diversity of queer communities that embody a fluidity beyond the traditional modernist binaries.

QUEER FAMILIES AND QUEER ECOLOGY

Based on pervasive ideas of the consanguineous and hetero-normative nature of the population, the nuclear family remains the rudimentary unit of Korean society. But the modern definition of family, as Duc Dau and Shale Preston have put it, is increasingly "open to change."[2] Many nations have witnessed such change, and Korea is no exception. Responding to a variety of social transformations, including industrialization, urbanization, transnationalization, and the rise of female political and financial standing since the 1990s, individuals have sought and tested many new kinds of family arrangements. These new formations often deviate from the norms of patriarchy, legal establishment, blood relations, or hetero-marital relationships. This is related to changing attitudes toward the family.[3] For example, the number of Koreans who believe marriage is mandatory has dwindled from 36.7 percent in 1996 to 19.7 percent in 2019,[4] as two out of ten Koreans abandon marriage as a life necessity. Important here is the gender difference, as women are more liberal about marriage, divorce, and having children, suggesting that they are more likely than men to embrace new family forms.[5] This phenomenon has led to a declining number of marriages and a surge in one-person households. Per comparative research conducted between 2001 and 2017,[6] the 2017 youth cohort was inclined to be "more resistant to conventional familial ideology and negative [about marriage and a family] based on paternal kinship."[7] In short, younger generations are likely to be more open-minded about non-traditional family structures.

This chapter investigates the atypical notions of family explored in *Little Forest* that are on the rise and contravene traditional ideas in Korea. In doing so, it calls these atypical families queer families. The concept of 'queerness' here draws upon scholars who consider the term as "not limited to the domain of sexual orientation or gender subversion."[8] Citing Michel Foucault who considered homosexuality as "a way of life," Jack Halberstam, for instance, "detach[es] queerness from sexual identity" and conceptualizes it "as an outcome of strange temporalities, imaginative life schedules, and eccentric economic practices."[9] Another prominent queer scholar, José Esteban Muñoz, regards queerness as constructively performative and "essentially about the rejection of a here and now and an insistence on [the] potentiality or concrete possibility for another world."[10] Queerness is, therefore, not only an identity category but also representative of the manifestations of quotidian practices that challenge extant systems and envision new norms. Accordingly, the term is understood as a "broad critique of multiple social antagonisms, including race, gender, class, nationality, and religion, in addition to sexuality," relative to the discipline of queer studies.[11] Transferring these ideas wholesale to Korea, a place in which queerness is not yet sufficiently condoned or discussed, is undeniably questionable.[12] Nonetheless, because Western approaches to queerness recognize a variety of identities and pursue transcendent political notions of solidarity in diversity, they proffer useful frameworks for approaching Korean queerness that might help to disturb the country's discriminatory heteropatriarchal culture.

Although Halberstam repudiates the compatibility of queerness and family, much scholarly attention has been paid to unearthing divergent types of queer families that challenge the validity of "the privatized heterosexualnuclear family" in modern society.[13] As Anne M. Harris and Stacy Holman Jones argue, the family is a space wherein the performance of queering practices will "disturb, disrupt, and disorient normative social, cultural and political practices."[14] Inspired by "queer, feminist, intersectional, and life course perspectives," Samuel H. Allen and Shawn N. Mendez argue that family is "constructed through social interaction rather than solely by legal or consanguineous relationships."[15] This suggests that "*any* two or more people who feel emotionally committed to each other [emphasis added]" can form a family, regardless of whether they have a legal or blood relationship.[16] Despite this comprehensive concept, queer families that have enjoyed public recognition have largely remained those that emerged from same-sex marriage and adoption, a limitation common to many scholarly projects about queer families.[17] Put another way, academic discourse about queer families has entertained a restricted array of topics, such as marriage, parenting, and youth, indicating that queerness is still debated primarily as it pertains to identity categorization, not as a practice of disrupting dominant values.

When it comes to what constitutes a queer family, the discussion in this chapter aspires to inclusivity and not to identity discussions focused on gender and sexuality. Here, "queer" is used to describe many kinds of families, whether they involve "queer" members or not (in individual identarian terms). In other words, all families that deviate from male-led, cohabitational, licit, reproductive relationships and carve out new ways of building familial communities and lifestyles. Predicated upon contemporary understandings of queerness, this viewpoint is applied equally to relationships and community units. In short, if a relationship or community of people involves a non-conforming way of life or queer practice that unsettles existing norms it is categorized as queer.

Queerness is adopted to describe not only the relationships between human beings but also between people and nature. Queerness has been positioned as the antithesis to "nature," which is compulsorily equated to motherhood and procreation.[18] In other words, the assumption was that unruly queers do not obey the natural order, which can be considered as coterminous with reproduction. According to Greta Gaard, emergent ecofeminists in the 1990s and queer theorists refuted this essentialism, pointing out that this version of nature was a constructed discourse anchored in Western dualism. Gaard posits that heterosexual male culture and domination are associated with environmental destruction and the oppression of the "Other," in terms of nature, women, and queer people. The tyranny of "urban hetero-patriarchy" provoked not only ecofeminist movements but also the idea of queer ecology instituted in the early 2000s.[19] Before, the general assumption was that queerness was "a product of the urban." However, scholars noticed "the growing visibility of these [queer] communities" in rural areas, which took forms dissimilar to their urban counterparts.[20] This queer rurality encouraged academic attempts to connect queerness and nature. Catriona Sandilands defines queer ecology as "a form of cultural, political, and social analysis centrally focused on interrogating the relations between the social organization of sexuality and ecology, akin to [the] environmental justice scholarship on race and ecofeminist thinking about gender."[21] It is not limited to the discussions about ecological LGBTQ issues but is also "about drawing insight from queer cultures to form alternative, even transformative, cultures of nature."[22] In short, queer ecology is precisely the kind of exploration into establishing rebellious relations between queer people and nature that *Little Forest* demonstrates.

FAMILY AND NATURE IN THE WORK OF YIM SOON-RYE

Yim first explored the notion of family in relation to alienated members of Korean society in her feature debut, *Three Friends* (1996). In the film, Yim follows three young men, who have just graduated high school and do not feel a sense of belonging anywhere, particularly as their own families are violent, oppressive, and negligent. As the "characters move further and further from mainstream society [they suffer] marginalization, despair, sorrow and grief,"[23] and ultimately the only family that remains, albeit less conspicuously, is their small circle of friends. Yim's second feature, *Waikiki Brothers* (2001), focuses on the story of a struggling small-time band. Seong-u, the central character and band leader, seems passionless, but always continues to make music. A family bond is rarely suggested because most of the characters are financially and emotionally unable to maintain a traditional type of household. Instead, Seong-u's band functions as a family for people to freely join and leave. Characters at different stages of their life join the band following their own dreams, struggle with the band's problems, and then often leave, as they have no obligation to commit to the band, or its loosely related, shifting family. According to Gwi-eun Han (2018), although Yim's films do not go as far as to offer promising endings for her seemingly hopeless characters, her narratives suggest that her protagonists will survive through "solidarity and friendship," and that these are the virtues most needed in the neoliberal era.[24] Arguably, this notion of survival through friendship is the dominant vision that permeates Yim's oeuvre. *Forever the Moment* (2008), Yim's most commercially successful film, offers an even more optimistic vision of a new familial community. In this respect, the female handball players in the film all have troubled family backgrounds. Mi-sook's husband is hounded by creditors, taking her family to the verge of collapse, Hye-kyeong is divorced, and Jeong-ran has difficulties with becoming pregnant. These players find sanctuary in the team's quest to win an Olympic gold medal, as it provides an alternative form of community that offers them a means of escape from their malfunctioning hetero-normative family lives.[25] Although they fail to triumph, Yim does not portray the team piteously. Rather, she privileges the actions and activities of solidarity and mutual compassion that define their time together.

These three films demonstrate that the traditional Korean hetero-patriarchal family can be both oppressive and limiting for individuals. Instead, new forms of family are acknowledged to free the characters from the bonds of hetero-normativity and familial labor that regulate individual lives in the late capitalist era.[26] *South Bound* (2013) shows how such examples of individual liberation can happen within an existing family. An atypical paternal figure, Hae-gab, refuses to conform to any social institutions that restrain his freedom. And while his hetero-oriented family cannot completely deviate from Korean social norms, his eccentric practices hint at how a seemingly hetero-normative father and family can be considered as queer in a particular context. The significance of *South Bound* is that here Yim embraces the non-conventional possibility of a father figure. In contrast, depictions of fathers in Yim's previous films mostly represent them as a force of hetero-patriarchy that fetters other family members. With *South Bound*, Yim seems to accept the possibility that fathers, and indeed all men, can "free themselves from patriarchal masculinity."[27]

Yim's films since the 2010s propose progressive family types that incorporate animals, as she became more involved with animal rights activism. *Rolling Home with a Bull* (2010) and *Sorry, Thank You* (2011) illustrate how animals can constitute key components of the family and help family members (not least patriarchal figures) mature. While the narrative of human growth through animal contact is unoriginal, and the ways in which the director incorporates animals into her plots are not unique, what is notable is that her interest in animal rights and nature is not a one-off narrative device. In this respect, Yim's work has increasingly highlighted the significance of the environment and "green" lifestyles, and sought to depict alternative lifestyles combining queer families with an eco-friendly vision, as for instance in her latest film, *Little Forest*.

QUEER FAMILIES AND ROMANTICIZED NATURE IN *LITTLE FOREST*

Little Forest tells the story of Hye-won, a twenty-something woman living in Seoul. Having grown up in a rural town, her teenage wish was to live in a glamorous city. The reality of Seoul, however, is harsh. While preparing for the teacher certification exam, she works at a convenience store to earn a living. Unfortunately, while she fails the test, her boyfriend passes it, which registers mixed feelings in Hye-won's mind. Her frustration takes her back to Uiseong-ri, her hometown which she had largely forgotten since leaving for college. Here, Hye-won rejoins her relatives and childhood friends Eun-sook and Jae-ha, and mulls over her future. After a year, she determines to settle there. The narrative entails many flashbacks depicting the important relationships that Hye-won has made over her life, with her mother, friends, and boyfriend. This reminiscing helps her to appreciate the people in her life and remember what is important.

Among Hye-won's past relationships, the one she recalls most frequently is that with her mother, who remains unnamed. When Hye-won was four, her family moved from a city to Uiseong-ri so that her sick father could convalesce in his hometown. After his death, her mother decided to stay in the village. The family became a single-parent household without a hetero-patriarch, and the mother and daughter relied deeply on each other. The mother was knowledgeable about nature, farming, and cooking. She prepared numerous foods for her daughter and recounted stories relating to the sustenance of life and nature, stories that the young Hye-won often could not understand. In the flashbacks it is shown that the mother loved Hye-won yet often enjoyed playfully mocking her. Then, surprisingly, the mother suddenly left Hye-won after Hye-won finished her college entrance exams. A goodbye letter indicated that she wanted her own life and therefore had to abandon parenting.

Over the years the two had remained out of contact, as Hye-won never tried to find her mother. But upon her relocation to Uiseong-ri from Seoul, Hye-won received another letter from her mother, the first contact after their separation. The letter included only a recipe for potato bread that Hye-won had kept requesting while they lived together. Upon hearing of this, Hye-won's aunt on her father's side called the mother "crazy enough to leave an ungraduated high-schooler behind." In this respect, while the mother had sacrificed her own desires to raise Hye-won securely in a small town, she could also be considered selfish, as most Korean parents support their offspring until marriage. Such non-traditional personality traits render not only the mother but also the relationship between her and Hye-won queer, not least in the sense that their family lacks a father—a hetero-patriarchal center who has women servile to the gender hierarchy. If her husband were alive or Hye-won were male, it would be unlikely that the mother would leave to follow her dreams, since women are strongly pressured to support male family members in Korea.[28] In the last scene of the film, Hye-won returns home from a bike ride and finds someone, most likely her mother, at home, and the film ends with Hye-won walking in to the house with a smile. After years of separation, the mother comes back to her daughter and is ready to welcome her. Interestingly, the director chooses not to depict the reunion and instead only hints that the two women will now live a peaceful life together as before. Such a narrative climax is uncommon in Korean family dramas, as perhaps it would be in reality. In this regard Soon-Mi Lee has asserted that "institutionalized familyism takes for granted that individual survival is guaranteed only through the family [which] accordingly functions as a 'repression' that hinders solidarity among individuals ... The urgent task is to dismantle the gender segregation ... normativity of a (nuclear) family."[29] In the case of *Little Forest*, the absence of father/patriarch involuntarily liberated the mother and daughter from coercive institutionalized familialism and caused them to challenge the normativity of the Korean family, something which renders the family queer.

Another important relationship in the film is formed between Hye-won and her childhood friends, Eun-sook and Jae-ha, who all grew up together in the town. After both Hye-won and Jae-ha left for college, the three didn't interact closely. Eun-sook went to a local community college and has been working at a local bank. She is dissatisfied with small-town life and desires to "escape" to Seoul. Jae-ha landed a white-collar job in a city but became disillusioned with urban life and its "fraud and petty tricks." Realizing that his "heart would burst out" with dissatisfaction, he returns to Uiseong-ri and lives a contented life as a farmer. Each of three lacks, has left, or resists a patriarchal hetero-patriarchal relationship: Hye-won grew up fatherless and left her boyfriend; Jae-ha departed the masculine hierarchical structure of his company after being publicly shamed by his male boss; and Eun-sook strikes her incompetent and harassing sexist male boss and steals her father's precious ginseng liquor.

Despite their lapse in contact, the three do not seem distant and Jae-ha and Eun-sook welcome Hye-won back. They spend substantial time together, cooking, eating, farming, and engaging in outdoor activities, and are intimate enough to come and go without hesitation. In respect of contemporary Korean reality, the increase in single-person households among younger generations often encourages such intimate communities of friends to ease isolation and cultivate a sense of belonging.[30] Consequently, friends have increasingly replaced the traditional importance of family for many younger people. In a survey about Koreans' changing values over the last two decades,[31] people who chose friends for providing a sense of belonging were on the rise, from 18 percent in 2008 to 21.4 percent in 2016, while those who pointed to their families decreased from 49.9 percent to 43.2 percent. Among younger generations, this tendency is more conspicuous: 71.3 percent of twenty-something interviewees shared their concerns with friends in 2016, while only 19.2 percent did the same with family. In 2006, the ratio was 51.5 percent with friends and 33 percent with family, implying a big transition for the younger generation in terms of where they gain such intimate support. Additionally, due to the changes in lifestyles over the last few decades, such as heightened mobility, the significance of cohabitation as a means to establish an independent household is vanishing. Indeed, some queer theorists do not consider living together with someone to be a critical factor in determining what constitutes a family,[32] and in this respect, a group of friends can increasingly be termed a family. These new familial constellations challenge the patriarchal dominion of the traditional "nuclear" unit, and such queer family groupings are at the vanguard of these new trends in Korean family formation.

What makes the idea of familyhood based on friendship in *Little Forest* even queerer is the ambiguous nature of the relationships depicted. At the beginning of the film, Eun-sook proclaims to Hye-won her love for Jae-ha, but contra to her straightforward personality, Eun-sook doesn't confess her affections to Jae-ha, and seems to care more about maintaining the friendship. Whether Jae-ha is aware of Eun-sook's feelings is initially unclear, as he seems to miss his ex-girlfriend from the city. Hye-won is also still technically in a relationship with her boyfriend in Seoul and does not consider Jae-ha as a potential romantic partner. That both Jae-ha and Hye-won are not in the mood for another romance is underlined when Eun-sook asks Hye-won about her feelings for Jae-ha and she sighs, "I am not interested in romance at all. [I am sick of] romance in the city and here." Hye-won's disillusionment with the city could therefore be said to extend to matters of the heart, and when all three are together, or even paired off, they behave like old friends.

Whether Jae-ha has feelings for either Eun-sook or Hye-won is not unearthed until the end of the film. There are merely several nebulous allusions. For example, Jae-ha tells Hye-won about why he broke up with his girlfriend and explains that he found the long-distance romance difficult. When Hye-won asks how his girlfriend responded, Jae-ha says she asked whether he had another girl in his hometown. Then the long shot frames Eun-sook running toward the two friends, potentially foreshadowing Jae-ha's feelings, as she takes a seat next to him. In another scene, Jae-ha is (romantically) paired with Hye-won. After a massive typhoon, Hye-won visits Jae-ha's orchard. Jae-ha picks out a ripe red apple for Hye-won and says "I have kept my eyes on it to give it to you even before the typhoon. Unlike you, it endured the typhoon." This symbolic line connotes two desires: one to give a pretty apple to Hye-won and another to advise his wandering friend who has given up city life. Lastly, when Jae-ha's ex-girlfriend visits Uiseong-ri, he notifies her that he likes someone else. Later, however, Jae-ha confesses to Hye-won and Eun-sook that he didn't really have anyone in mind, but just wanted to deter his ex-girlfriend. Until this final moment, the audience is unable to conclude exactly where Jae-ha's romantic affections lie.

But those questions are not the core of the film, rather *Little Forest* orbits around the platonic familial relationships that the three forge after leaving their hetero-patriarchal worlds, not only between Jae-ha and each of the two women but also between Hye-won and Eun-sook. These are all in a sense queer relationships. The two women spend a lot of time together, worry each other, cook together, form a (vague) rivalry over Jae-ha, and argue and reconcile like a couple. While experiencing this, they mature together and come to understand each other better. The precise nature of these relationships among the three friends is left undefined, straddling friendship, romance, and familiality. After having a very enjoyable time with Eun-sook and Jae-ha, Hye-won is finally ready to call her abandoned boyfriend in Seoul whom she hesitated to contact before. She delivers a message congratulating him on the exam and telling him she wants to break up. The close-up of her face indicates she feels unburdened, and we know that her queer family of friends has both healed and helped her to move beyond her heterosexual relationship. Whether any of them has or had a heteroromantic partner or falls in love does not negate their queer familial bond with each other. Their desires for romance, either hetero or homosexual, are not strong (as evidenced in Hye-won's speech that she is sick of romance) and instead only the queer intimacy between them remains as important. This is indicative of the mentality of young Koreans who laugh at themselves for being of the *sampo* generation (giving up three things, that is, courtship, marriage, and childbirth due to their financial hardship), and instead of pursuing hetero relationships that may require money to maintain, they choose forms of interpersonal intimacy based on friendship through which they can form a different kind of family.

The last layer of queer relationality is among the townsfolk of Uiseong-ri, who know one another well and look after each other. Seemingly blunt and forthright, Hye-won's aunt looks out for her with great care. Also, out of the blue, an old village uncle comes by Hye-won's house and leaves a hen, whose eggs she enjoys daily. One remarkable point about the villagers in the film is the paucity of men of any age. While in reality the gender ratio in agricultural areas is only minimally balanced toward women,[33] *Little Forest* represents women far more than men. Female characters speaking more than a single line include: Hye-won, Eun-sook, the mother, Hye-won's aunt, and three neighborhood women; whereas the only substantive men are Jae-ha and a postal carrier, with the fathers of Jae-ha and Eun-sook remaining unseen. When Hye-won assists her aunt and Jae-ha with farming, her uncle and Jae-ha's father are never present. Even the uncle who gives her a hen occupies only a few seconds of screen time. The women of Uiseong-ri could therefore be said to perform the double occupation of farming and housework while also forming a community of care that does not require a hetero-patriarchal man to function. *Little Forest*'s connection between farm labor and women-centered community is redolent of the 1970s US lesbian separatist movements that built up experimental, self-sustaining communities in isolated farming areas and explored ways to make alternative ecological relationships, against the hetero-patriarchal exploitation of women and nature.[34] In an article about the lesbian separatist communities and queer ecology, Sandilands claims that these women took "feminism into the landscape and, in turn, [drew] new ideas about gender."[35] While women in Uiseong-ri also seek non-conventional gender roles alongside their interactions with nature, this female-oriented community does not ostracize men; Jae-ha is well-embraced, for example. But the way Uiseong-ri operates as a community is queer in that it disrupts the normative rural hetero-patriarchy.

These queer relationships are strongly mediated by nature. Uiseong-ri is an isolated place surrounded by mountains, and lacks even a grocery shop. Here, the people move with seasonal changes, not modern temporality, and Hye-won's queer relationships also transition with nature. Her friends spend a whole year farming together, following the agricultural processes that correspond to each season. Their endless chats always accompany seasonal dishes, the ingredients of which Hye-won grows. While cooking, Hye-won recalls what her mother told her about food materials concerning nature and life. At the time, Hye-won couldn't figure out what she meant, but finally, she slowly comes to understand the mother she thought had abandoned her. Cooking and nature play an indispensable role in helping Hye-won maintain queer relationships with others and heal herself. Thus, the greatest living presence in *Little Forest* is undeniably nature, as Hye-won's aunt exclaims. In one scene, the aunt and Hye-won are devastated when the rice harvest is ravaged by a typhoon. Their frustration is even greater because the aunt reserved farm machinery for its cultivation the following day. To Hye-won, who is upset, the aunt resignedly states, "We can't fight against what nature does." They spend a day fixing the ruined field, and Hye-won learns more about the laws of nature. In *Little Forest*, nature is presented as "an active and unpredictable entity and not just a stand-in for abstract principles or desires."[36] In short, nature enables the queer characters and relationships to exist.

ROMANTICIZED DICHOTOMY

In its exploration of queer relationships, *Little Forest* constantly accentuates the idea of Uiseong-ri as a utopia. The letter that the mother left before her departure reads, "I wished you [had] taken root here. Whenever you experience a hard time, I believe you will be able to overcome if you remember the smell of dirt, the wind, and the sun in this place." In this regard it is revealed that the mother chose to remain in Uiseong-ri because she wanted to give her daughter a sanctuary, and indeed, Hye-won ultimately returned to the shelter of its community. Throughout the film, the city is illustrated as a space where characters have difficulties. The idea is that competitive capitalism impedes humane life, while the countryside is romanticized as a place where otherwise hopeless individuals can find meaningful answers. This kind of binary depiction is not original, yet it does play innovatively into the aspirations of younger generations in contemporary Korea. According to Ki eun Kim, Korean youth are unable to rest or achieve fulfillment because of their "excessive working hours and unstable employment."[37] Such difficulties have led to several new trends among young people as they struggle to find small indulgences to offset their merciless daily lives. These include: *so-hwag-haeng* (small but certain happiness), *wo-la-bel* (work-life balance), organic food, cooking culture, *meok-bang* (food porn), and the back-to-earth campaign. *Little Forest* embodies all of these fads and, accordingly, younger moviegoers found the narrative very relatable.[38]

In depicting the city and nature, *Little Forest* employs several dualistic ideas intertwined with the dichotomy of urbanity and rurality. Urbanity is associated with men, hetero-normativity, capitalism, and individualism; rurality with women, queerness, a self-sustaining economy, and communalism. If we look at male urbanity and female rurality in the context of *Little Forest*, Jae-ha secured a full-time job in a city, but voluntarily left after struggling with its capitalist hierarchical culture. Likewise, it was only Hye-won's boyfriend who passed the certification exam. Unlike her male counterpart, Hye-won's city life was unsuccessful in terms of both finance and career. According to Jesook Song, young people globally experience a "high rate of youth unemployment and a rapid rise in the cost of public goods and services. [And this unemployment is] seamlessly connected to the situation of basic subsistence, including housing."[39] However, this economic difficulty is not ungendered, as "women occupy the majority of part-time jobs and men take up the reduced portion of full-time jobs."[40] Put simply, women can't afford a city life to the degree that their male counterparts can. On the flip side, Eun-sook's life in the countryside is not easy either. Although she has a secure full-time job, as a bank teller her labor is markedly gendered. She always has to smile, wear a tight skirt, serve coffee to customers, and humor her middle-aged male boss. She is in a predicament because she chose an office job over farming, which *Little Forest* depicts as the natural career choice for women. The lives of female farmers, including the mother, Hye-won's aunt, and villager aunts are depicted as less challenging, and their engagement with nature is romanticized.

Little Forest takes urban heterosexuality versus rural queerness, a second gender dichotomy, and rebuts the common associations on either side.[41] We have seen that Uiseong-ri supports multiple queer communities. In contrast, the city is where Hye-won's and Jae-ha's previous heterosexual relationships took place. No heterosexual couple is visually involved in *Little Forest*; the three friends form a queer triad, the mother is widowed, and the female villagers' husbands are absent. As a third dichotomy, the film explores urban capitalism versus a rural self-sustaining economy. In the city, Jae-ha had to struggle while waiting for his payday and could not "live a life" based on his own decisions. Similarly, Hye-won was literally "hungry" and had to tolerate customers' constant rants. While capital and infrastructure apparently abound in the city, they are depicted as inaccessible. In opposition to the glamorous hardship of Seoul, Uiseong-ri is inconvenient yet welcoming. While the local market is remote, and the bank is the only air-conditioned place, the townspeople are kindhearted enough to help with the farming and share their food and resources. Finally, urban individualism contrasts with rural communalism. Hye-won was always forlorn, eating and working alone in Seoul. In Uiseong-ri, she always eats and works with her friends or other community members. And even when she is alone, she looks happy because she has delicious homemade food and beautiful nature around her. Hye-won's feeling of devastation in the city is therefore remedied through her relationships with friends, villagers, animals, and food in Uiseong-ri, and she winds up shielding herself in this restful place.

Little Forest's dichotomies critique urbanity, men, heterosexuality, capitalism, and individualism and lionize rurality, women, queerness, self-sustaining economy, and communalism. The dualistic thinking raises several issues. First, urban life is warped through this representation. Hye-won's single life is depicted as busy, hungry, and desolate, which is not always true in reality. For instance, Shuang Li surveyed young, single households in Korea and concluded that they are "more likely to participate in social activities than others from a multiperson family, make thick relationships with friends, romantic partners, and pets," and "spend considerable leisure time with close acquaintances."[42] In short, young urbanites revel in the single life, revealing the false binary between urban isolation and rural communalism. Second, the illustration of idyllic agricultural life is superficial. Today, the farming economy is capitalized and community life encounters various conflicts through the influx of external money and migrant working populations.[43] While Hye-won is free from media technology and overwork, hers is an ostrich-like depiction of rural living. In reality farming populations suffer from a lack of labor, lack of infrastructure, and poverty, meaning that rural youth also confront numerous hardships just like their urban counterparts.[44] Thus, urban young people's aspiration for a greater quality of life is unlikely to be fulfilled in a rural community such as that presented in *Little Forest*. Lastly, the equation of men with urbanity and women with rurality replicates existing stereotypes around gender roles. Although the rural women in Uiseong-ri are depicted as active leaders and disrupters of the gender hierarchy, the dichotomy of urbane males versus women as mother figures in charge of housework and parenting remains. Many more men than women occupy Jae-ha's city office space, and Jae-ha himself "chose" between rurality and urbanity, an option which wasn't extended to Hye-won. Thus, the only main male character's involvements with rurality and his relationship with nature feature less inevitability than those of Hye-won and other women. Perhaps most frustrating is the depiction of rural men in Uiseong-ri, as they do not take on any traditional female roles at all, although the rural women also do the "men's" job in the "masculine" work of farming. None of the male characters, including Jae-ha, are shown doing any "feminine" work such as cooking or parenting. This implies that the women naturally do twice as much work as the men, just as their urban counterparts must struggle to balance their careers, parenting, and housework.[45] Simply understanding nature as feminine, as Sandilands points out, "is not at all subversive."[46] And this critique is transferable to *Little Forest*, which fails to challenge the dichotomy between men/culture and women/nature by not allowing its male characters to have a relationship with nature or to undertake conventional female tasks. As Christine Bauhardt argues, "we cannot develop an emancipatory concept of our relationship to the environment and to nature without deconstructing the age-old intertwining of nature and femininity discourses and thematizing the analogy between the productiveness of both nature and the female body."[47] In that sense, *Little Forest*'s minimal attempts to destroy this intertwining arguably merely legitimize the existing gender order.

Little Forest is defiant in its advance of queerness in friendship, familiality, and communalism. But it espouses a patriarchal dualism of gender division and maintains conformist perspectives when it comes to gender issues, which arguably renders the film anti-queer, not least as Angela Jones claims that "queerness is a refusal: it is a dismissal of binaries, categorical, and essentialist modalities of thought and living."[48] Were *Little Forest* to challenge such modalities, its effects would be more progressive. In this respect a combination of possible alternative narrative components easily comes to mind, from the inclusion of male house-husbands, female white-collar bosses, and urban queer people, to a realistically commercialized rural life. The insufficiency of its endeavor to subvert this hierarchical dualism therefore dilutes the queer quality of *Little Forest*.

LITTLE FOREST: UTOPIA? OR HETEROTOPIA?

Michel Foucault conceptualized the term *heterotopia*, as a counter-site where varied deviant behaviors might take place.[49] Heterotopia stands in opposition to utopia, as a heterotopia can exist in reality in numerous contexts, whereas utopias are always "unreal."[50] With characters making unconventional and heterogenous relationships that reflect the changing forms of family in contemporary Korea, *Little Forest* embodies a heterotopia. Yet it simultaneously illustrates a utopia, as the conditions for supporting such queer individuals are romanticized through their unrealistic rural lifestyles. While a film does not need to directly depict reality, it is arguably politically irresponsible to evade and distort reality in a way that consolidates the existing order of society. Not least as such descriptions of utopia can daunt people with queerness who seek and/or practice "an insistence on potentiality or [the] concrete possibility for another world."[51] In this sense, Yim's auteurship has retreated from that of being a realist, focused on critically depicting heterotopias, to that of a utopian optimist.

Nonetheless, this chapter ultimately must reiterate the importance of Yim's explorations of new relationships between humanity and nature in *Little Forest*. Despite being unable to surmount many of the ingrained hierarchies and dichotomies of Korean society, Yim does demonstrate many new types of family—not quasi-families but queer ones—that challenge the hegemony of the normative hetero-patriarchal family. As mentioned, such explorations are common to Yim's previous films, for instance, in the relationship among the three protagonists of *Three Friends* (1996), the teammates in *Forever the Moment*

(2008), and people and animals in *Rolling Home with a Bull* (2010). These precursors all prove that Yim has long pursued the cinematic envisioning of a diversity of queer families in her work. Bernstein and Reimann emphasize the importance of illuminating the potential existence of all such queer families, writing that this "variety of family structures must be visible so that we can choose family forms that will suit our diverse interests and needs."[52] In this respect, Yim and *Little Forest* deserve attention for showcasing a variety of new potential Korean family structures situated in between utopia and heterotopia.

NOTES

1. Gwi-eun Han, "The Contemporaries and Profanation of Young Adults in the Films Directed by Lim Sun-Rye," *Korean Language* 62 (2018): 202–30; Min Guk Jin, "The Reality Reappearance System Research of the Director, Soon-Rye Lim-<Three Friends>, <Waikiki Brothers>, <Forever the Moment>" (Master's thesis, Seoul, Dongguk University, 2008); Jae-Jin Koo, "A Study on Time and Memory in Film Text," *Korean Literature Education Research*, no. 34 (2011): 243–69; Yoo-ran Lee, *Lim Soon-Rye* (Seoul: Seoul Selection, 2008).
2. Duc Dau and Shale Preston, eds., *Queer Victorian Families: Curious Relations in Literature*, 15 (New York/ London: Routledge, 2015), 2.
3. Gallup, "Survey of Koreans' Consciousness and Values" (Sejong: Ministry of Culture, Sports and Tourism, 18 December 2019), 20, <https://www.korea.kr/archive/expDocView.do?docId=38759> (last accessed 15 May 2021).
4. Gallup, 18; WinGKorea Consulting, "A Study on the Trends and Prospects of Koreans' Perceptions and Values of 20 Years" (Sejong: Ministry of Culture and Tourism, 22 December 2017), 39, <http://www.prism.go.kr/homepage/origin/retrieveOriginDetail.do;jsessionid=748C0F68F158DD3EB2D6E7ACA03DF3BC.node02?cond_research_name=&cond_research_start_date=&cond_research_end_date=&cond_organ_id=1371000&research_id=1371000-201700066&pageIndex=3&leftMenuLevel=120> (last accessed 15 May 2021).
5. Gyeong-hye Han, "Korean Social Trends 2016" (Daejeon: Statistics Korea, 2016).
6. Gye-sook Yoo, Min-ji Kang, and Ji-Eun Yoon, "Young Adults' Family Concepts and Values among Never-Married in their 20s: A Comparison of Two Cohorts in 2001 and 2017," *Family and Culture* Vol. 30, no. 3 (2018): 42–69.
7. Ibid., 59.
8. Angela Jones, *A Critical Inquiry into Queer Utopias* (New York: Palgrave MacMillan, 2013), 12.
9. Judith Halberstam, *In a Queer Time and Place: Transgender Bodies, Subcultural Lives*, Sexual Cultures (New York: New York University Press, 2005), 1.
10. José Esteban Muñoz, *Cruising Utopia: The Then and There of Queer Futurity*, Sexual Cultures (New York: New York University Press, 2009), 1.
11. David L. Eng, Judith Halberstam, and José Esteban Muñoz, "What's Queer About Queer Studies Now?," *Social Text* Vol. 23, no. 3–4 (2005): 1.
12. Todd A. Henry, ed., *Queer Korea*, Perverse Modernities (Durham, NC: Duke University Press, 2020).

13. Robert Goss and Amy Adams Squire Strongheart, eds., *Our Families, Our Values: Snapshots of Queer Kinship* (New York: Harrington Park Press, 1997); Valerie Lehr, *Queer Family Values: Debunking the Myth of the Nuclear Family*, Queer Politics, Queer Theories (Philadelphia: Temple University Press, 1999); Mary Bernstein and Renate Reimann, eds., *Queer Families, Queer Politics: Challenging Culture and the State* (New York: Columbia University Press, 2001), 1; Samuel H. Allen and Shawn N. Mendez, "Hegemonic Heteronormativity: Toward a New Era of Queer Family Theory: Hegemonic Heteronormativity," *Journal of Family Theory & Review* Vol. 10, no. 1 (March 2018): 70–86; Anne M. Harris et al., *Queering Families, Schooling Publics: Keywords*, Routledge Critical Studies in Gender and Sexuality in Education 8 (New York: Routledge, 2018).
14. Anne M. Harris and Stacy Holman Jones, "What Have We Learned? Keywords," in *Queering Families, Schooling Publics: Keywords*, ed. Anne M. Harris et al. (New York: Routledge, 2018), 5.
15. Allen and Mendez, "Hegemonic Heteronormativity," 70–1.
16. Bernstein and Reimann, *Queer Families, Queer Politics*, 2.
17. Goss and Strongheart, *Our Families, Our Values*; Lehr, *Queer Family Values*; Bernstein and Reimann, *Queer Families, Queer Politics*; Dau and Preston, *Queer Victorian Families*; Allen and Mendez, "Hegemonic Heteronormativity"; Harris et al., *Queering Families, Schooling Publics*.
18. Greta Gaard, "Toward a Queer Ecofeminism," *Hypatia* Vol. 12, no. 1 (1997): 114–37; Catriona Mortimer-Sandilands, "Unnatural Passions?: Notes Toward a Queer Ecology," *Invisible Culture: An Electronic Journal for Visual Culture*, no. 9 (Fall 2005).
19. Catriona Sandilands, "Lesbian Separatist Communities and the Experience of Nature: Toward a Queer Ecology," *Organization & Environment* Vol. 15, no. 2 (2002): 138.
20. Mortimer-Sandilands, "Unnatural Passions?," 13–14.
21. Sandilands, "Lesbian Separatist Communities," 133.
22. Ibid., 135.
23. Lee, *Lim Soon-Rye*, 18.
24. Han, "Contemporaries and Profanation," 204.
25. Jin, "Reality Reappearance."
26. Han, "Contemporaries and Profanation," 216.
27. Jin, "Reality Reappearance," 85.
28. Youna Kim, *Women, Television and Everyday Life in Korea: Journeys of Hope* (London; New York: Routledge, 2005), 6.
29. Soon-Mi Lee, "Transformed Familism and Gender Difference in Family Attitudes among Unmarried Youth," *Locality and Globality: Korean Journal of Social Sciences* Vol. 40, no. 3 (2016): 25.
30. Shuang Li, "The Life and Family Values of One-Person Households as a New Family Form: Focusing on Young Adults in South Korea and China" (Master's thesis, Seoul, Chung-Ang University, 2019).
31. WinGKorea Consulting, "A Study on the Trends and Prospects," 34, 36.
32. Mary Bernstein and Renate Reimann in their anthology titled *Queer Families and the Politics of Visibility* define a family as follows: "The term "family" refers to groups of individuals who define each other as family and share a strong emotional and/or financial commitment to each other, *whether or not they cohabit*, are related by blood, law, or adoption, have children, or are recognized by the law [emphasis added]" (3).
33. Korean Statistical Information Service reported that 49.2 percent of the farming population were male and the rest were female in 2016.
34. Sandilands, "Lesbian Separatist Communities."
35. Ibid., 148.

36. Ibid., 147.
37. Ki eun Kim, "Signifying 'Small but Certain Happiness': Structured Consumption of Millennial Women" (Master's thesis, Seoul, Yonsei University, 2019), 31.
38. Seon-hee Yoo, "The Success of a Movie Depends on Word of Mouth, not Production Cost," *Hangyere Sinmun*, 6 December 2018, <http://www.hani.co.kr/arti/873316.html> (last accessed 15 May 2021).
39. Jesook Song, *Living On Your Own: Single Women, Rental Housing, and Post-Revolutionary Affect in Contemporary South Korea* (Albany: State University of New York Press, 2014), 2.
40. Ibid., 7.
41. Scott Herring, *Another Country: Queer Anti-Urbanism* (New York: New York University Press, 2010).
42. Li, "The Life and Family Values of One-Person Households," 70–6.
43. Si-hyun Park and Yong-woog Choi, "Factors for City People's Return to Rural Areas and Its Impacts on Korean Rural Society and Economy" (Seoul: Korea Rural Economic Institute, 2014).
44. Jinyoung Eom, Kwangseon Kim, and Jieun Lim, "The Changes in Rural Labor Market and Policy Tasks" (Naju: Korea Rural Economic Institute, 2016).
45. Sooyeon Huh and Hansung Kim, "Time Use and Division of Housework in Dual-Earner Households in Korea," *Korean Journal of Family Welfare* Vol. 6, no. 64 (2019): 5–29.
46. Sandilands, "Lesbian Separatist Communities," 146.
47. Christine Bauhardt, "Rethinking Gender and Nature from a Material(Ist) Perspective: Feminist Economics, Queer Ecologies and Resource Politics," *European Journal of Women's Studies* Vol. 20, no. 4 (November 2013): 363.
48. Jones, *A Critical Inquiry into Queer Utopias*, 12.
49. Michel Foucault, "Of Other Spaces: Heterotopias," *Architecture/Mouvement/Continuité*, no. 5 (1984): 46–9.
50. Ibid., 11–12.
51. Muñoz, *Cruising Utopia*, 1.
52. Bernstein and Reimann, *Queer Families, Queer Politics*, 11.

CHAPTER 8

Korean Cinema and Me: An Interview with Yim Soon-rye

Molly Kim

M.K: This is the very first book in English on a Korean woman filmmaker. Firstly, congratulations! I think that the reason why we have not previously had a volume wholly dedicated to a Korean female filmmaker (either in Korean or in English) is that they don't have enough films to support a full-length book. However, you have directed the highest number of films among Korean women filmmakers and most of them were commercially and critically successful. So, finally, here we are, doing this interview for your and our first volume in English on a Korean woman director. Since this book covers most of your features and some short films, what I would like to ask you about first is how those films were created and what the Korean film industry was like when each one was made? So, with that in mind, let's talk about your films one by one.

You studied film in Paris for your MA and came back to Korea to become a director. You started your film career as a scripter for *Out to the World* (1994) directed by Yeo Kyun-dong who was one of the most celebrated young filmmakers of the 1990s. How did you engage with the project?

Y.S.R: When I came back home, I was thirty-three years old. I had only "studied" film, you know, theory and that kind of thing, so I needed to gain professional experience to become a director. Though I knew very little of him, I went to see Im Kwon-taek asking if I could participate as a staff member, maybe as a scripter for his new project, but Mr. Im was in the middle of his *The Son of General III*. Then I looked for other projects, but it was hard to get a position since I was considered too old to work as a staff member. It was then I got an offer from Yeo Gyun-dong asking if I would like to work on his film. I had known Yeo personally and he wanted to give me a chance, I guess.

M.K: With that experience, you were able to make your very first short film?

Y.S.R: Yes. Fortunately, I got to know the top talents in the Korean film industry through *Out to the World*, including the director Yeo Kyun-dong, the director of photography Yu Young-gil, the sound director Lee Myung-hwa, and all other leading talents of Korean film. It became a great introduction for me as a starter and it helped me immensely when recruiting staff members for my own movie later. Otherwise, it would have been difficult or impossible to have such talented members in my crew since I didn't go to film school in Korea. Although I had an education in France, it didn't help me much in getting started in the film industry because I didn't have any work experience and didn't know much about technology. You know, it was the era of [35 mm and 70 mm] film cameras, but I didn't have skills to handle film cameras. In short, I learned all those practical skills on the set of *Out to the World*.

M.K: Your first short film, *Promenade in the Rain*, brought you great critical acclaim. You won the highest honor at the 1st Seoul Short Film Awards founded by Samsung. People must have been surprised because it was your first film.

Y.S.R: I made this film to test myself and see if I had any real talent as a filmmaker. I got lucky enough to achieve the highest honor at the award ceremony and was then recognized by film critics and especially by producers. Based on the success of my short film, I got an offer from Kim Eun-young, a woman producer at Samsung Youngsang Biz[1] to make my own feature film. The script I wrote for my first feature was not big budget. The budget was about 15 million Korean won [about 50,000 US dollars], which was a very, very low budget at that time. I think Samsung was willing to provide funding for it because they wanted me to have a good start since I was their first awardee of the film award they'd just launched.

M.K: I can't help noticing that the movie theater in *Promenade* was playing *Getaway* starring Kim Basinger and Alec Baldwin. Was it your favorite film back then? (Laughs.) The film was shown in many scenes in your film. I love *Getaway* by the way. It is on my favorite weekend movie list.

Y.S.R: (Laughs) I didn't remember that *Getaway* (Roger Donaldson, 1994) played within the film. The theater in the film was not a movie set, it was an actual theater, a rundown cinema called Hwa Yang Theater located in the red-light district in Seoul. I was able to use the site right before it shut down. Maybe that theater was playing the film at that time.

M.K: So eventually your short provided you with the opportunity to move onto a formal debut with *Three Friends*, your first feature film. This film granted you global recognition especially through winning the NETPAC Prize at the very first Busan International Film Festival [BIFF] in 1996.

Y.S.R: As soon as I completed shooting *Three Friends*, the Busan International Film Festival was launched. *Three Friends* was an arthouse film featuring non-professional actors as the main characters. It had more chance at film festivals than in commercial movie theaters. I thought that it was great timing because I could submit *Three Friends* to the BIFF. Also, Korean cinema was at a turning point because it was a time when new young directors such as Hong Sang-su and Kim Ki-duk were coming out and their first films also became recognized globally through the BIFF. *Three Friends* along with *The Pig Fell into the Well* (*Doejiga umul-e ppajin nal*, 1996) by Hong and *Crocodile* (*Ag-eo*, 1996) by Kim received a NETPAC Prize, and New Currents, respectively, at the first year of the BIFF.

M.K: Overall, how would you describe your impression of the Korean film industry, a.k.a "Chungmuro." Up until this point of your career, you experienced quite a lot of professional success after your return from France including on film productions, at the film festival circuit, etc. Was it something you had been dreaming about?

Y.S.R: It was 1993 when I started my career by taking the scripter position for Dir. Yeo. From the perspective of the film industry, there was a huge transition within the industry. The director-oriented, old studio system was collapsing, and we were finally witnessing a producer system run by young, talented producers including Shim Jae-myung, Shin Cheol, and others who designed films for younger audiences. By the time I started shooting *Three Friends*, the industry was led by this new generation of producers and creators. I also was one of those "young people" trying to do something new. For *Three Friends*, I worked both as a director and producer, and so I was able to try out many new things and experiments. For instance, I recruited young staff members instead of the trained professionals who had worked in the industry for decades because I really wanted to keep the budget low and experiment with things. I even recruited an Australian D.P. (director of photography), which was unprecedented in Korea until then. I also used the digital, AVID editing system which operated not using celluloid film. Not many people could handle it in Korea at that time [but because] AVID were seeking out a market in Korea, they were willing to lease their equipment and an operator to me. So basically, myself and the operator from the AVID did the editing together and it became the first digital editing that ever happened in Korea (laughs). I remember that other Korean film editors used to visit our editing room to learn how to do digital editing. As such, *Three Friends* was an innovative project which introduced new people, technology, and processes into Korean filmmaking.

M.K: Many newspaper and magazine articles termed *Three Friends* "problematic," and "provocative," particularly because of the depiction of the main characters. Why do you think this film was viewed that way?

Y.S.R: I think because the characters in my films never succeed (laughs). And some of them are gay. The three boys in *Three Friends*, the band members in *Waikiki Brothers*, the athletes in *Forever the Moment*, none of them succeed. I made my protagonists fail at the end of each movie, whether it is a coming-of-age drama, a music film, or a sports film. By doing so I guess I broke the most sacred, generic rule (laughs) of these three genres where success is the most important thing narratively. This also goes against the tradition of Korean commercial cinema and what most audiences expect to see, you know, the triumphant moment that celebrates the hero's victory. However, I don't think these failures are the end of anything. I always wanted to say to Koreans, especially young people, that it is completely ok to not succeed. Even if you fail at something, you can always try again and even if that doesn't work either, it is ok to give up.

M.K: Let's move on to your second feature, *Waikiki Brothers* (2001), which is one of the most beloved films in your filmography. It took five years to release *Waikiki Brothers* [hereafter *Waikiki*] following *Three Friends*. This is quite a long time given your busy history of regular productions. What did you do for those years and how was your second film conceived?

Y.S.R: *Three Friends* brought me great fame especially from a critical standpoint, but it didn't do well commercially. I was a bit confused about what to do next. You know, *Three Friends* was never anything like a commercial film or a movie following predictable genre conventions, which I betrayed in every possible way. In fact, maybe it is fair to say that the film was not a crowd-pleaser, which made me want to have a break for myself. Besides, taking multiple roles as a director and producer for *Three Friends* had tired me out and I wanted to slow things down a bit.

M.K: And you collaborated with Shim Jae-myung's Myung Film[2] for the first time in making *Waikiki Brothers*?

Y.S.R: Actually, Shim did not like *Waikiki* at first. It was her partner, the director Lee Eun who loved the film. Shim didn't think this film had any commercial potential, and it was maybe too depressing. However, after she came back from the Cannes Film Festival where she was invited due to her mega-hit film, *Joint Security Area, JSA* (Park Chan-wook, 2000), she finally decided to do *Waikiki*. I think she thought it would be ok even if *Waikiki* didn't do well at the box office because they had a big hit with *JSA*. So, I was able to produce it with Lee.

M.K: There are so many interesting aspects to the film, but most of all, I think it is unique because it is a musical drama about a band that struggles to make a living and never becomes successful. Yet, despite the continuous disappointment suffered by the band members throughout the film, audiences tend not to feel sad because the film features such an engaging collection of songs, many of which were beloved 1970s and 80s pop songs in Korea. As such, music plays a pivotal role in this film.

Y.S.R: Yes. The songs featured in the film are all favorites of mine. We even made an OST (original soundtrack) album for this film and there were thirty-five songs (Korean and foreign combined) used, which was quite a lot.

M.K: How did you clear the copyright for the music? It must have cost you a fortune.

Y.S.R: We hired someone who was supposed to manage that issue. And he was very certain about clearing copyright. Later I found out that he didn't clear the copyright for the foreign songs so we were not able to show this film outside of Korea as much as we'd like to.

M.K: One of the remarkable things about this film that many people don't know is that through it you introduced many new talents to Korean cinema, such as the young, stage actors who later became huge stars including Park Hae-il (ex. *Memoirs of Murderer*) and Hwang Jung-min (ex. *Narco Saints, Veteran*). How did you discover them?

Y.S.R: I never wanted "familiar" faces back then. I avoided casting professional actors, instead I would send my assistant director to take pictures of young people on the street who would fit into the character that I needed. For *Waikiki*, I didn't go for that much of an unconventional approach for casting (and I couldn't since I was working with a major production company), but still I didn't want to use popular actors. So, l turned my attention to Dae Hak Ro [the theater district in Seoul] to search for talented but less well-known actors, and found Lee Eol, the main character of the film. As for the others, I cast Hwang Jung-min through the special audition that took place at Dae Hak Ro for stage actors. Hwang was one of them that auditioned and I immediately thought that he had something special. Although he was in his early twenties, Park Hae-il was already famous for his strong performances within the theatrical community. I heard about him and went to see his play, and I was completely overwhelmed. He was colossal, in terms of his energy on the stage and performance. So, I fully realized how good the actors were, but I didn't know they would become the superstars they are now. Also, I cannot take full credit for discovering these actors because they were already making their reputation in the theater and it was only a matter of time before they would be picked up [for film or television].

M.K: Let's talk about *Forever the Moment* [henceforth *Forever*] – your first commercial hit and the highest-grossing film among your productions, being ranked at the top of the box office for three weeks.[3] This is a film that must have brought many positive changes to you in your life as a filmmaker. And certainly here you demonstrated your potential as a commercial filmmaker.

Y.S.R: Ha ha. Yes, I must admit that. I had made films that generated positive reviews from critics, such as *Waikiki*, but I wanted to make something more audience-friendly, you know, cheery and easy to understand. Simply speaking, I wanted wider audiences to see my films. Maybe I was a bit worried that my films were being viewed by just a small share of audiences who were purely cinephiles. So *Forever the Moment* is the film that reflects my desire to reach out to a wider audience. Then, when I saw people laughing and crying at the premiere of *Forever*, I thought, "oh this is not bad." I think here I realized that it is also important to make a film that touches many hearts. Before *Waikiki*, I had this rigid, and naive notion of "what cinema should be"; you know, I didn't want to compromise my idea of cinema/art under any circumstance. But definitely, I expanded my professional horizon through *Forever*, and not just because of its commercial success but also through the overall filmmaking process [involved].

M.K: Obviously you are an established filmmaker in Korea, but people also recognize you as an activist. You became the leader of KARA, Korea Animal Rights Advocates, in 2009. How does your activism echo in your cinematic work?

Y.S.R: As much as I am engaged with animal rights, I am also very much interested in Buddhism. I am not sure which started first, but my love for animals and Buddhism is kind of the same thing to me, in terms of the measure of respect given toward the lives of animals. *Rolling Home with a Bull* (2010) reflected my personal fascination with Buddhism. The film is based on a novel of the same title written by Kim Do-yeon. Also, *Sorry, Thank You* (*Mianhae,Gomawo*, 2011) was another film which I directed and produced to support animal rights.

M.K: Your film, *South Bound* (2013) is a filmic adaptation of the popular Japanese novel *Sausubaundo* (サウスバウンド) written by Okuda Hideo, one of the leading writers in Japan. How did this project come about?

Y.S.R: As you can see from my filmography, I stopped writing my own scripts after *Forever*. *Forever* was the first feature film that I was hired to (only) direct by a major film company. And it did well. After that point, I received many directing offers, mostly popular, genre films. I found out that I didn't have any talent for writing a genre film especially targeted at the commercial market. And this was fine with me because I was getting enough (directing) work to take on anyway. *South Bound*, *The Whistleblower*, *Little Forest*, and *The Point Men* which is being released now, are some of the film projects that a producer or colleague has brought to my attention.

M.K: Most of your films tend to feature male protagonists, except *Little Forest*. In contrast, the majority of films directed by women center around a female character. This is particularly so in the case of the films produced by female directors in Korea.

Y.S.R: I don't have a set of rules or dogma for the gender of a main character. It really depends on what kind of story I want to tell. I was always interested in the issue of violence in Korea, particularly when I was in France. When you are outside of your own country, you get to see it more objectively, and you become more critical. That's when I realized how much violence takes place in the military, in the home and in the workplaces of Korea which is heavily male-centered and patriarchal. So, I became engaged with the subject of masculinity through stories that were usually narrated by male characters.

M.K: What does *South Bound* mean to you? The film marks exactly the midpoint of your filmography.

Y.S.R: The filmmaking process was hellish. I had chosen to do it because I really liked the anarchical nature of the protagonist, who was completely opposed to any kind of authority. But as you know the reality (of making the film) was the opposite.[4] It is ironic, but I don't feel like it is my film, although it is listed as one.

M.K: Shortly after leaving *South Bound*, you took on directing *The Whistleblower*. And you completed it in two years. It was a film about the Hwang Woo-suk scandal.[5]

Y.S.R: There was a book, a sort of reportage that detailed the scandal and we wanted to use the book as the basis for the film. However, it was very difficult to acquire the rights for the book for filming since the author wasn't particularly willing. However, Shin, the producer (and my work partner since *The Whistleblower*), relentlessly talked to the author and finally achieved the rights to film the book. Then, when I read the first draft of the script I wasn't really attracted to it. I considered it was simply a bad script so I gave up. However, I changed my mind when I read the original book, and I thought that I shouldn't let it go that easily as it was too important a story to pass on. I gave them the OK, but still there were a number of issues that we had to consider and be careful about. For one thing, since Hwang Woo-suk was still alive and a very powerful man, we could not attack him in the film. Besides, we didn't make the film to accuse this one person; instead we wanted to portray this event as a phenomenon, in terms of a phenomenon that's accumulated through multiple layers of social corruption.

M.K: Tell me about the casting. Did you have all the actors you wanted from the outset?

Y.S.R: Mostly yes. I was lucky to have Park Hae-il again for this film. I hadn't met him since *Waikiki Brothers* but he was very interested in this project and we finally united again. It was hard to cast the right actor for *The Whistleblower*, because given the title of the film Jae Bo Ja [The Attestant], the role of the attestant or whistleblower was actually a small one and the film centered around the role of the alleged transgressor. Then Yoo Yeon-seok came along. He was a childhood fan of Park Hae-il, and he was so excited to act with his role model.

M.K: After this film, you participated in supporting the debut film of Choi Jung-ryul, *Glory Day* (One Way Trip, 2015), as a producer. This film helped to create many new stars including Ryu Joon-ryul who also appears in *Little Forest*.

Y.S.R: I am credited as a producer for three films: *One Way Trip* (*Geullolidei*, 2016) is one of them. I got to know this young director, Choi Jeong-ryul, when he was in the production team for one of my early films. He came to me with his possible debut project saying he didn't have anywhere to go with the film. I knew his talent and I had my own production company, so I took him in. I just lent my name to him (laughs).

M.K: It seemed that you had a break between *The Whistleblower* and *Little Forest* of around three years.

Y.S.R: Actually, I got an offer to direct from a Chinese film company. It would have been a remake of a Hollywood film, a movie based on food. We spent quite some time working on it but it didn't happen eventually. Then I moved on to *Little Forest*.

M.K: How did your Korean version of *Little Forest* come along? Did you see something special in the [two] original (Japanese) films?[6]

Y.S.R: (Laughs.) I don't know, I did not particularly love or dislike the originals. But aside from my personal preferences, I wanted to do the remake because I am someone interested in nature. I liked the fact that this story was about nature, and the relationship that humans have with nature. These were small independent films that only gathered an audience of around 10,000 people in Japan, and I had to think how I could develop this story into something with more commercial potential. Luckily, in a leading role we were able to attract the actress Kim Tae-ri who had just become a big star after the success of *The Handmaid* (*A-ga-ssi*, Park Chan-wook, 2017), but she alone could not carry the whole project. There had to be something else, such as the inclusion of elements that would attract Korean audiences. The first thing we did was to combine the two-movies of the Japanese franchise into one film. As you know, the Japanese original *Little Forest* consisted of two films. The first installment was set in the winter and spring, and the second part in the summer and fall, ending back with winter. I decided to combine [this narrative of] four seasons into one feature film. Because this movie wasn't going to be a blockbuster, I strongly felt that it should not be a series. In my mind, as a person who has made arthouse films that would normally end up with audiences of ten or twenty thousand people (not that they are not important), I wanted to make a film that could attract as many people as possible.

M.K: One of the biggest transformations that I liked was the fact that the role of mother, or motherhood became significant in your version. In the original, the relationship between the heroine and her mother is vaguely mentioned but not necessarily detailed or explored. In your version, it instead becomes crucial, especially to the lead character Hae-won. The feelings that she has toward her mother, of love and hate, plus multiple other elements such as nostalgia, tenderness, etc., become a form of guidance that she seeks out when her life gets tough.

Y.S.R: I had to think how I was going to "localize" the narrative. In the Japanese original, the heroine maintains a very secluded life, she doesn't go out or meet people but finds comfort in nature and food. But human relationships, especially those with one's family or mother, are very important in Korean culture. Koreans are very relationship-oriented people, (laughs) you know? So I wanted to incorporate this into the story.

M.K: We have finally reached your latest film, *The Point Men*. This is the biggest film in your career, in terms of the scale of production and budget. How did this project come to you?

Y.S.R: Again, my work partner, Shin, told me about this project when we were finishing *The Whistleblower*. I guess he thinks that I am a countable person when it comes to "controversial issues" (laughs). *The Whistleblower* deals with one of the most talked about and controversial issues of the time, but I tried to be as objective as possible. I know films can be inclined in some direction, but even if the person or case we portray deserves to be criticized, I don't want my film to be "the attack" relative to the subject we deal with. Shin thinks I am very skilled at [maintaining this objective balance], and that's how and why he sent me this *The Point Men* script. It is a story about missionaries being captured by the Taliban. Again, it is a sensitive issue where a diplomat is involved, but it was not my intention to make this film as a complete accusation of the behavior of the Taliban. I think the most important thing when you portray a real-life event is to find balance.

M.K: The budget for this film came to around 150 billion Korean won (approx. 13 million US dollars) and this does not include P&A (promotion and advertisement) costs. This is one of the most "expensive" films you ever produced. Are you a bit intimated? (Laughs).

Y.S.R: I would be a liar if I said I was not scared about the money that went into the project. But when you think about it, just as I choose my actors because I have faith in them that they can do the work, the investors and the production company must have had the same faith in me. Confidence is important and it is a driving force that can move this kind of mega-project forward. And, while I have my own fears, I try to stay positive and believe in myself. I let my confidence overpower the fear.

M.K: And this also marks you out as the only female director who has created this kind of big budget, blockbuster film which was completely the preserve of male directors until you came in.

Y.S.R: That is true. However, I did not decide to do this film to satisfy my sense of justice or responsibility. It is true that I was the only woman director working in the commercial sector during the 1990s after Lee Mi-rye left.[7] Since then, there have been numerous talented young women directors that have come into the industry, even though the gender ratio is still disproportionately favoring male directors. For the last two to three years, we witnessed a variety of genre movies and commercial films that have been directed by female filmmakers. I feel (although, as I said, I didn't start this film out of responsibility) that if I do this right, many more female filmmakers will be assigned to big projects and finally break the binary notion that divides women/independent/small budget vs. men/mainstream/big budget.

M.K: You are right. It is common that male independent filmmakers move up to making commercial films after their first or second recognizable success, but it rarely happens with female independent filmmakers, no matter how successful their independent films were. That is why the gender disproportion (of directors) is so big in commercial films compared to independent films. I hope your film *The Point Men* sets a good example, letting investors know about more the female talent in the industry. As I mentioned at the beginning of this book, you have many "first" labels, for instance you are the first female director to win Best Director at the Korean Film Critics' Awards, and the first (and only) female director to shoot more than ten films. How do you feel about having so many "first ever" titles?

Y.S.R: I have earned those titles not because I was particularly good or talented but because of the working environment of the Korean film industry. I would be lying if I said I didn't enjoy such honors, but I can't simply celebrate that I have garnered so many "first (and only)" titles. What bothers me is that I am still the "first and only" for many of these titles. I really want my records to be broken by new (female) talents. For example, there has not been another single female filmmaker who has produced more than ten theatrical releases. There has been no woman filmmaker who produced a film budgeted over 10 billion won (8.31 million dollars). This means that there has been no transition from my generation to the next.

M.K: I don't want to generalize but, I think there is a tendency that it takes longer for women directors (in Korea) to make their next film (if there is a next film) than male directors.

Y.S.R: This seems true. We have quite a lot of women filmmakers who left their career after one or two films, just like Park Nam-ok and Hong Eun-won did. And even if they are lucky enough to go on, there is a very long break in between their productions. I think it takes longer for female directors than male directors [to work on new projects], because once they (male directors) are proven commercially and/or critically it is easy to see how they move onto the next project, but with women filmmakers, even if their success is visible, it is just hard for them to move on. Investors tend to hesitate when it comes to female directors.

M.K: Nevertheless, there has been a dramatic increase of women in the Korean film industry since you came in in the late 1990s, especially at a staff level.

Y.S.R: Yes. When I started my film career in 1996, only a few positions could be taken by women. The movie industry was heavily gendered. Scripters were all women and make-up people were mostly women but even props and costumes which are now considered as a woman's job used to be taken only by men. I would say women were about 10 percent of the entire film crew, although of course this could be different depending on which film set you were on. However, these days, if I take the example of the set of my own film, *The Point Men*, the gender ratio was about 50/50, or slightly more women than men, which is ideal. But of course this [ratio] is different at the level of director.

M.K: I have a final question for you. You have worked in the industry long enough to witness many changes and developments. And many changes within the film industry have taken place and are still taking place since the outbreak of COVID-19. What kind of critical changes have been there for you and how do you think these will affect the Korean film industry in the long term?

Y.S.R: To begin with, we have one of the largest and most dynamic film industries in the world. The global recognition for *Parasite* (*Gi-saeng-chung*, Bong Joon-ho, 2019) and *Squid Game* (*Ojingeo game*, Hwang Dong-hyuk, 2021) has elevated the status of Korean cinema and Korean culture altogether. However, COVID-19 critically affected the Korean film industry. Movie theaters are near bankruptcy and Korean movies are postponing their releases. I hear there are more than 200 films waiting to be released, my own *The Point*

Men included. As a result, it will be hard for big movies to be made for a while. We won't be able to see many blockbusters for some time. Instead, more and more filmmakers are moving to OTT streaming platforms which are supplying an incredible amount of money to creators. This could be good and bad. It is bad that there will be a sharp decrease in film productions and even if they are made, the kinds of movies to be made will be somewhat simplified. On the other hand, it is good that there has been a large demand for Korean drama productions (by Netflix and other streaming companies) and this is creating a lot of jobs for film people here, but, clearly, there has been a noticeable gender discrepancy in the workplace relative to these new platforms too.

M.K: I have noticed that also. Take the example of Netflix, they are producing a lot of original dramas here in Korea (there has been a soaring demand since *Squid Game*) but we only had one drama directed by a woman filmmaker so far, Lee Kyung-mi's *The School Nurse Files* (*Bogeongyosa aneunyeong*, 2020). All the other dramas for Netflix and other streaming services currently in production are being directed by male directors. I think that the gender discrepancy is much more extreme in the OTT industry, maybe because of the industry's clear inclination to certain genres such as action and horror which not many women filmmakers are specialized in.

Y.R.S: I agree with you. We can't simply wait for the industry to change. I think the kinds of films that [Korean] women filmmakers tend to produce should be more diversified. We see a predominant number of issue-oriented social dramas directed by women about rape, labor, and other women's issues. I mean, this is great. I do think these films are important and tremendously valuable. But, at the same time, we need more women in commercial films and OTT dramas too. I would like to see action films, thrillers, horror, and sci-fi films fused with women's issues and themes delivered by women. This will be our homework for the next few years: as a [female] filmmaker it's about how will we survive in the film industry and how we will get our voices out there and make ourselves visible in the even more male-dominated OTT industry. I know there is a lot of female talent within the industry, and in particular a surge of female producers recently. I think if we think more strategically about the ways that we, as female creators, cater to the larger public, we will soon have some very successful years, whether it is through traditional cinematic releases or streaming platforms.

NOTES

1. Samsung Youngsang Biz was the forerunner of the current CJ Entertainment.
2. Myung Film is a major production/distribution company founded in 1995 by Shim Jae-myung, a producer, and her partner and producer, Lee Eun.

3. *Forever the Moment* achieved audiences of 4,044,582 during its theatrical release over three weeks. Box-office records provided by KOFIC (Korean Film Council) <https://www.kobis.or.kr/kobis/business/stat/boxs/findDailyBoxOfficeList.do> (last accessed 13 October 2021).
4. There was a collision between the main actor Kim Yoon-seok and Yim Soon-rye. It is credited as Yim's film but the director was replaced at the end of production.
5. For a detailed description of this scandal, please read David B. Resnik, Adil Shamoo, and Sheldon Krimsky's online article, "Fraudulent Human Embryonic Stem Cell Research in South Korea: Lessons Learned," in *Policies and Quality Assurance* Vol. 13, no. 1 (2006).
6. The Japanese original film(s) are based on the same titled manga by Iragashi Daisuke: The films are divided into two parts: *Little Forest: Summer/Autumn* (2014) and *Little Forest: Winter/Spring* (2015), both directed by Mori Junichi.
7. Lee Mi-rye is a woman filmmaker active in the 1980s. She worked in the film industry prior to Yim Soon-rye's emergence.

Index

301, 302, 97–9, 107

A Woman Judge, 1–2, 13
art cinema, 31, 33
AVID system, 39, 45, 132

BIFF (Busan International Film Festival), 4, 131–2

Choi, Eun-hee, 2
Chungmuro, 5, 15, 99–100, 132
CJ Entertainment, 38–9, 101, 141

ecofeminism, 9, 47–9, 60–2
Extreme Job, 97, 109

feminism, 46–7, 49, 60–1, 64–5, 79, 114, 122
Fly, Penguin, 31, 47, 54, 60
Forever the Moment, 28, 36–7, 47, 54, 98–100, 102, 113, 117, 126–7, 133–5, 142
Foucault, Michel, 44, 51, 62, 71, 115, 126, 129
French New Wave, 34, 44

gaze, 62, 64–8, 70–9, 98, 112
Glory Day, 137

Handmaiden, The, 67
high concept films, 12
Hong, Eun-won, 13, 140
Hwang, Hye-mi, 2, 13
Hwang, Woo-suk, 73–4, 80, 89, 95, 136

If You Were Me, 47, 60, 64, 66, 79, 84
Im, Kwon-taek, 40, 130
IMF (International Monetary Fund), 5, 48, 51, 65, 101

Jang, Sun-woo, 3, 6, 40
Jeong, Jae-eun, 29, 47, 79
Joint Security Area, 3, 133

KARA (Korea Animal Rights Advocates), 49, 57, 113, 135
  Sorry, Thank you, 47, 53, 57, 60, 113, 118, 135
KOFIC (Korean Film Council), 111, 142
Korean New Wave, 1, 3–7, 11, 40, 45, 98
Korean War, The, 1, 13, 40

Lee, Kyung-mi, 141
Lee, Mi-rye, 2, 5, 13, 28, 139
Lee, Seo-gun, 2, 10, 96–8, 101–2, 105, 108, 111
Lee, Su-yeon, 7
Little Forest, 9–10, 46–7, 49, 53–4, 57, 58–61, 64, 96, 98, 99–100, 102–5, 108–11, 113–16, 118, 120–4, 126–7, 137

Marriage Story, 12
masculinity, 12, 14, 18–21, 25–7, 29, 92, 112, 136
Meokbang, 105, 109
Myung Film, 133, 141

neoliberalism, 48
NETPAC, 4, 131–2
New Korean Cinema, 3, 11, 44, 84, 93–4

Okuda, Hideo, 84, 135
Out to the World, 3, 13, 99, 130–1

Parasite, 45, 97, 101, 109, 140
Park, Chan-wook, 3, 48, 60, 67–8, 79, 133, 137
Park, Chul-soo, 97–9
Park, Hae-il, 74, 133, 137
Park, Nam-ok, 1, 12–13, 28, 140
Point Men, The, 7, 135, 138, 140
Promenade in the Rain, 3, 4, 8, 13, 28, 30–3, 35–6, 39–40, 62, 99, 131

queerness, 10, 114–16, 124–6

Recipe, The, 10, 96–9, 101–2, 104–12
Rolling Home with a Bull, 5, 9, 12, 14, 23–5, 27, 29, 31, 46–7, 49–50, 53, 59–60, 100, 102–3, 113, 118, 127, 135
Rub Love, 2, 97, 99, 101–2, 112

Samsung (Youngsang Biz), 11, 15, 28, 38–9, 45, 131, 141
Seoul Olympics, 83
Seoul Short Film Awards, 4, 11, 15, 131
Shiri, 38
South Bound, 47, 53–4, 57, 81–2, 84, 86–8, 92–3, 117–18, 135–6
Squid Game, 140–1

Take Care of My Cats, 47
Three Friends, 6–7, 11, 12–15, 17–18, 23, 25, 27, 31, 39, 44, 47, 54, 60, 84, 99–100, 102, 113, 117, 125, 127, 131–3

Waikiki Brothers, 5, 8, 11–12, 14, 22–5, 27, 29, 30, 35–6, 39–41, 47, 54, 60, 64, 84, 99, 102, 113, 117, 127, 133, 137
Weight of Her, The, 9, 31, 64–6, 68–9, 72–5, 78
Whistleblower, The, 9, 14, 47, 53–4, 64–6, 72–6, 78, 81–2, 89, 91–3, 137–8
Widow, The, 1–2, 13, 28

Yeo, Kyun-dong, 1, 99, 113, 130–1

EU representative:
Easy Access System Europe
Mustamäe tee 50, 10621 Tallinn, Estonia
Gpsr.requests@easproject.com

www.ingramcontent.com/pod-product-compliance
Lightning Source LLC
Chambersburg PA
CBHW051129160426
43195CB00014B/2408